Sexual Identities and the Media

"This book provides just the kind of introduction to the topic we have long needed. It gives the reader the historical context and conceptual tools needed to critically engage with the complex issues that arise when the politics of sexual identity intersect with media representations. And it does so in a thoroughly accessible manner and through an impressive range of examples."

—Ron Becker, Miami University, *author of Gay TV and Straight America*

"Resisting a clean or tidy narrative of LGBTQ visibility and progress, *Sexual Identities and the Media* weaves a rich and complicated intervention into how sexualities are named, historicized, produced, commodified, contained, and resisted on the mainstream cultural screen. The book anticipates and fosters a broad range of engagement points for students. Both contemporary and durable, the text balances current examples with a complex web of theoretical tools from humor studies, media studies, critical/cultural studies, gay and lesbian studies, and queer theory, offering a complicated examination of the mediating of sexual identities."

—Dustin Goltz, DePaul University

Sexual Identities and the Media encourages students to examine media as a site of negotiation for how people make sense of their own and others' sexual identities. Taking a critical/cultural approach, Wendy Hilton-Morrow and Kathleen Battles weave together theory, synthesis of existing research, and original analysis of contemporary media examples in order to explore key areas of debate, including:

▶ an historical context for contemporary GLBTQ representations;

▶ the advantages and limitations of media visibility, including a discussion of the strengths and limitations of stereotype research and the quest for "positive" representations;

- ▶ the role of consumer culture in constructing GLBTQ identities;

- ▶ strategies of mainstream media resistance by GLBTQ community members, including oppositional/queer reading strategies and the production of media products by and for the GLBTQ community;

- ▶ the closet as a structuring metaphor in both GLBTQ identities and engagement with media;

- ▶ the complexities of comedy as a popular narrative device in GLBTQ portrayals;

- ▶ media representations of GLBTQ bodies as sites of non-normative desires and gender identities.

Featuring an enormous range of discussion questions and case studies—from celebrity coming-out narratives, transgender models, and slash fiction writers to *Glee* and *Modern Family*—this textbook offers a timely, informative, and demystifying introduction to this vital intersection in contemporary culture.

Wendy Hilton-Morrow is Associate Professor of Communication Studies and Associate Dean of the College at Augustana College. She is co-editor of *War of the Worlds to Social Media: Mediated Communication in Times of Crisis* (Peter Lang, 2013).

Kathleen Battles is Associate Professor in the Department of Communication and Journalism at Oakland University. She is the author of *Calling All Cars: Radio Dragnets and the Technology of Policing* (University of Minnesota Press, 2010) and co-editor of *War of the Worlds to Social Media: Mediated Communication in Times of Crisis* (Peter Lang, 2013).

Sexual Identities and the Media

An Introduction

Wendy Hilton-Morrow and Kathleen Battles

Routledge
Taylor & Francis Group

NEW YORK AND LONDON

First published 2015

by Routledge
711 Third Avenue, New York, NY 10017

and by Routledge
2 Park Square, Milton Park, Abingdon, Oxon OX14 4RN

Routledge is an imprint of the Taylor & Francis Group, an informa business

Library of Congress Cataloging-in-Publication Data

Hilton-Morrow, Wendy.
    Sexual identities and the media : an introduction / Wendy Hilton-Morrow, Kathleen Battles.
        pages cm.
        Includes bibliographical references and index.
    1. Sexual minorities in mass media.   I. Battles, Kathleen.   II. Title.
    P96.S58H55   2015
    306.76—dc23
    2014036441

ISBN: 978-0-415-53296-9 (hbk)
ISBN: 978-0-415-53297-6 (pbk)
ISBN: 978-0-203-11451-3 (ebk)

Typeset in Warnock Pro
by Apex CoVantage, LLC

Editor: Erica Wetter
Editorial Assistant: Simon Jacobs
Production Editor: Emily How
Copyeditor: Sue Cope
Proofreader: Nikky Twyman
Cover Designer: Gareth Toye

Printed and bound in the United States of America by
Edwards Brothers Malloy on sustainably sourced paper

For Stan Anderberg and Jim Cobin—Wendy
For Rachel Andrews—Kathy

Brief Contents

Contents

Preface

▶ ABOUT THE BOOK

Sexual Identities and the Media: An Introduction grew out of our frustration with a lack of an accessibly written book capable of introducing the topic to undergraduates, providing them the foundation they need to move on to more challenging primary source materials. While there are many books providing overviews of the issues and debates related to *gender* and the media, there is no corollary for *sexual identities* and the media. Most of the work in this area is either in the form of article- or book-length case studies, with very few aimed specifically at undergraduate students. This book grows out of our own experiences as educators who often feel that case studies do not provide sufficient context and perspective for helping students make sense of this complex terrain.

This book is written with the student in mind. We have worked to make the writing clear and accessible, avoiding unnecessary jargon. We weave together theory, syntheses of existing research, and original analysis of contemporary media examples, all with an eye to boiling complicated ideas down to a comprehensible level. This has sometimes required us glossing over some finer points of theoretical and methodological distinction in an effort to get to the "meat of the matter." At the same time, we believe this approach does not mean we have sacrificed introducing students to the complexities of the relationship between sexual identities and the media or the variety of methodological and theoretical approaches. Though we ourselves are grounded in critical cultural theories and methodologies, we believe the book is useful in a wide variety of classroom settings as we consider the breadth of approaches to the topic.

In putting together this project we made two choices that we think will work for students and instructors. First, we decided not to organize the book in either a traditional media studies (by medium or by industry/text/audience) or identity studies (one identity group per chapter) based format. The first three chapters represent the heart of the book. Chapter 1 introduces students to the study of sexual identities. While students in women and gender studies programs will no doubt find some of this material familiar, students in media studies and communication might not. At the same time we introduce some of the key features of the field of media studies that students in that field might find familiar, but others might not. Chapter 2 provides necessary historical context that current college students likely have little awareness of, but whose debates and media practices continue to resonate today. Chapter 3 introduces students to the concept of visibility. A key part of this chapter is moving students beyond a superficial equation of visibility to social and political progress for minority groups. In this chapter, we introduce what we call a "yes, but" approach, in which we encourage students to recognize the ways media both enable and constrain how we understand sexual identities.

The rest of the book follows from there by exploring the themes set up in the first three chapters across five sites: commercial culture and GLBTQ identity; resistance to dominant media practices by GLBTQ producers and audiences; the closet as a central metaphor for organizing GLBTQ experience and media practices; comedy, considering the way both jokes and genre formats shape representations of and by GLBTQ communities; and, finally, bodies, in which we consider representations of same-sex intimacy and transgender bodies as key sites of lingering cultural anxieties about non-normative sexual and gender identities. We believe this structure allows the book to challenge the assumptions about both sexual identities and the media with which students will come to class. While we have worked to provide examples from across a range of media, this book does reflect our own grounding in the study of television. However, the issues raised in each chapter cut across a range of media. In addition, each chapter considers how the same issue can be approached in more than one way, and thus evaluated in more than one way.

The second key feature of the book is the inclusion of activity-driven "textboxes". Each chapter contains textboxes that offer activities and questions that can be used for in-class activities, but also adapted as on-line activities, paper assignments, or even as video assignments. These are designed, of course, to help instructors, but they also are designed to provide students with questions that synthesize, expand upon, or apply concepts learned in each chapter. Textboxes often include suggested media examples, many of which are easily available through streaming services such as YouTube, Netflix, Hulu, and Amazon. Alternatively, we encourage students to use their knowledge of popular culture to consider additional texts, sites, or practices for further exploration.

▶ ABOUT THE AUTHORS

We have taught about issues of sexuality and the media for more than a decade and a half in a variety of settings, including liberal arts colleges, flagship state universities, and regional universities. We also have been writing and publishing together for over a decade. We both are white and middle-aged, but we diverge from there: one of us identifies as lesbian, one as straight; one of us has three children, the other none; one of us lives near where she grew up, the other one has lived everywhere. We have made generous use of airplanes, Skype, FaceTime, email, and the plain, old telephone in order to complete this project.

Acknowledgments

Who we would like to thank!

Together we would like to thank the team at Routledge. Erica Wetter has been all one could ask for in an editor. Gently encouraging, always optimistic, and never wavering in her enthusiasm for the project. Thank you also to Simon Jacobs, whose fast responses to our endless flurry of emails were matched only by his professionalism and unwavering support. We'd also like to thank all of our reviewers, Lynn Comella, Bill Eadie, Melanie Kohnen, Esther Rothblum, Katherine Sender, and an anonymous reviewer. We especially would like to acknowledge Ron Becker. From the proposal stage, his input has been incredibly insightful and supportive. From taking time to talk with us to fast turnaround of materials, he has been a stellar reviewer. Thank you also to Alfred Martin and Melanie S. Kohnen for sharing their work with us before publication. Thank you also to our intrepid research assistant, Ashleigh Curp. From following vague directions to finding images, securing permissions, and dealing with citations, she has really made the final stages of this project manageable.

▶ WENDY

In the final months of this project, I've cracked open fortune cookies with the following messages: "Now is a good time to finish up old business." "Learn Chinese: Bùjiŭ (boo-jee-oo) Soon." "The difference between a dream and a goal is a deadline." Whether it was a sign of the imminent completion of this book or that I'd eaten too much take-out food by the end of it, I'd like to thank the many people that helped move this project from a dream to its ultimate deadline.

The first is my co-author, Kathy, whom I refer to as my "creative soulmate." I consider myself blessed to have such a dear friend who shares the same passion for teaching about media, gender, and sexuality that I do. Regardless of author order, this project has been an equal partnership every step of the way. Kathy's insights, experiences, and obsession with screens have made this book the rich text that it is. I also thank her wife, Rachel Andrews, for sharing her with me and putting up with the both of us.

I also would like to thank the many people at Augustana who have seen me through this endeavor. Sharon Varallo wrote an enthusiastic letter of support for my sabbatical release based on only a brief description of the project and her unwavering faith in my abilities. David Snowball has kept my inbox filled with every related article, book review, and blog post he comes across. I am a better teacher and person because of him. Not only did Dave and Sharon help pick up my slack in the department, so, too, did Ellen Hay, Steve Klien, and Jared Schroeder. I've long known that Augustana has some of the best librarians there are, but this project made me intimately aware of how wonderful and incredibly speedy our interlibrary loan workers are, particularly Sherrie Herbst. Emilee Goad and Katie Scharnagle offered me organizational help and plenty of smiles. Kate Butler's emails have made me laugh out loud more times than not, and I'm so delighted she agreed to be featured in Chapter 5. Vickie Phipps reminded me not to take myself or work too seriously and generously shared her time to "play" with cover design ideas. Pareena Lawrence has had great patience with me as the final revision stages of the book overlapped with my transition into a new position.

Thank you also to my friends and family who have put up with my MIA status for longer than they would like. Jennifer Klocke is always there when I come up for "a breath," and pedi dates with Joy Hayes have been incredibly therapeutic. In their ever-supportive way, my parents, Bona and Mark Hilton, became full-time grandparents for part of a summer. I also can't imagine a better daycare provider than Diann Gano, who has enriched my children's lives and my own and is responsible for the Crate and Barrel catalog example in Chapter 4. To my husband, Jay Morrow, I owe the greatest debt of gratitude. For the final two months of this project, he was a single father, chauffeur, cook, housekeeper, launderer, and massage therapist. He may never fully understand what drives me, but without him I'd get nowhere. He and our three beautiful boys were my greatest incentive to finish.

Finally, I dedicate this book to my uncles, Stan Anderberg and Jim Cobin. Thank you for loving me, my family, and each other.

▶ KATHY

The first person I'd like to thank is my co-author. Working together on a project this overwhelming and long-lasting would not even have been possible without Wendy. We often joke that we each have one half of a brain. Fortunately for us we don't have two of the same halves. We've known each other for almost 15 years now—Wendy has been friend, confidante, professional advisor, hair consultant, life coach, and most importantly someone who I know will get all my dumb jokes.

Of course there are a lot of other people to thank for their support for what my friend Rob Sidelinger refers to as my "coloring book." First, I would like to thank my department and colleagues at Oakland University. The "media ladies," Rebekah Farrugia and Erin Meyers, who assigned preview chapters in their classes, answered odd questions about media, and in general are just great people to work with. Other colleagues who have especially lent their moral support include Kellie Hay and Valerie Palmer-Mehta.

Special thanks go to Rebekah and Kellie for sharing their research on the Detroit hip-hop scene. I have been lucky to have an extraordinarily supportive department chair in Jenn Heisler. Thank you to all my students in my various gender, sexuality, and media courses over the years. They never cease to challenge, frustrate, delight, and amaze me. Thank you also to the Morrow "boys," Jay, Matthew, Joshua, and Joseph, for letting me camp out in their house and take up way too many hours of Wendy's time.

Finally, I'd like to thank all the friends who have supported me, even when I've been cranky and neglectful: Rob Sidelinger, Naomi Andre, Safiya Andre, Joy Hayes, Lisa King, Robin Allen, Andrea Knutson, Kevin Laam, Tim Anderson, Mary Garrett, Lana (Brown) Kosnik Joe Rowley, and last, but never least, Lori Weatherwax. Special thanks to my mom for her patience in missing out on summer fun. But, most important of all, my humblest gratitude goes to Rachel Andrews. She has been book widow, sounding board, complaint department, food deliverer, cheerleader, confidante, good company, and always my number one fan. Somewhere in this crazy process we *finally* were able to get legally married after 21 years (though our marriage was only legal in the state of Michigan for 12 hours)! I can't imagine where I would be without her, even though I often wonder how she puts up with me. I dedicate my work here to her.

Introduction

Three days before President Barack Obama announced his support of same-sex marriage in May 2012, Vice President Joe Biden appeared on NBC's morning news program *Meet the Press* and publicly declared his own support for marriage equality. Until that point, the Obama administration had offered only muted support. During Biden's appearance, he credited the program *Will & Grace* (1998–2006) for shifting attitudes:

> When things really begin to change, is when the social climate changes.
> I think *Will & Grace* probably did more to educate the American public than almost anything anybody's ever done so far. And I think people fear that which is different. Now they are beginning to understand.
> (Harmon, 2012)

Whether or not Biden spoke out of sync with the administration, there can be no doubt this one appearance set off a chain of events that led to the administration's public support of marriage equality.

FIGURE 1.1 *Will & Grace* opening credits
Source: **Season 3, National Broadcasting Company.**

When *Will & Grace* (1998–2006) first aired on NBC, it helped launch a wave of mainstream television programs and films that featured gay and lesbian characters. It was a time in media history some now refer to as the "gay 90s." Across an array of media, people continue to encounter an astonishing number of gay, lesbian, bisexual, transgender, and queer (GLBTQ) images. They can be found on popular fictional programs like *Modern Family* (2009–), *Pretty Little Liars* (2010–), and *Orange is the New Black* (2013–), on reality programs ranging from *Cake Boss* (2009–) and *Top Chef Masters* (2009–) to *Transamerican Love Story* (2008–) and *RuPaul's Drag Race* (2009–), in movies like *Brokeback Mountain* (2005), *Capote* (2005), and *Milk* (2008), and even in the *Harry Potter* book and film series, after J.K. Rowling's announcement that the beloved Hogwarts headmaster, Dumbledore, was gay. Meanwhile, gay celebrities like Ellen DeGeneres, Rosie O'Donnell, Ian McKellen, Chris Colfer, Ricky Martin, and Neil Patrick Harris enjoy mainstream popularity while being open about their sexuality. More recently, transgenderism also has become more visible, with trans actresses like Laverne Cox and Harmony Santana securing key roles in film and television, trans model Lea T gaining international success in the fashion world, and trans celebrity Chaz Bono dancing in front of a television audience of more than 20 million people as a contestant on *Dancing with the Stars* (Seidman, 2011).

At the same time that GLBTQ images have proliferated in the media, major changes also have been happening in the social, legal, and political spheres. By 2014, 19 states and the District of Columbia recognized some form of same-sex union rights, and one year earlier the Supreme Court overturned the Defense of Marriage Act (DOMA), which had denied federal recognition of same-sex marriages. In another indication of the shifting political tide, in 2011, the U.S. military repealed its nearly two-decades-old policy of Don't Ask, Don't Tell (DADT). Additionally, public opinion polls find young people leading the way toward growing public acceptance of homosexuality, and gay-straight alliance groups are commonplace in colleges, high schools, and even junior highs around the country.

Yet, all of this apparent progress for and acceptance of gay, lesbian, bisexual and transgender people is just one side of a complex cultural landscape related to sexual identities. For, as much as things are changing, we live in a moment rife with contradictions. For example, in the same month, September 2010, that major cities like Atlanta, Dallas, Minneapolis, and Richmond all hosted gay pride events, media shared the stories of 11 teenagers from around the country who, subjected to GLBTQ harassment, reached such a point of desperation that they took their own lives. In 2011, the Supreme Court ruled that it is within the First Amendment rights of Westboro Baptist Church members to protest outside military funerals while holding signs with inflammatory anti-gay rhetoric like "Fag troops" and "You're going to hell." Meanwhile, 2012 Republican presidential candidate Mitt Romney attempted to clarify his stance on gay rights to a gay Vietnam War veteran by saying, "I oppose same-sex marriage. . . At the same time, I would advance the efforts not to discriminate against people who are gay" (Friedman, 2011). There is little doubt that, a decade and a half into the 21st Century, America finds itself in a contradictory and confusing time when it comes to the social and political status of GLBTQ people.

The 21st Century also has been a time in which media forms and content continue to proliferate and play an increasingly significant role in our lives, particularly for young people. Children between 8 and 18 report spending seven-and-a-half hours a day using smartphones, computers, television, and other electronic media (Kaiser Family Foundation, 2010). The same report estimates that, thanks to multi-tasking, young people actually cram nearly 11 hours of media content into that seven-and-a-half-hour window. Such statistics also point to changes in the way that people are consuming media. Young people (ages 12–24) now spend more time on the Internet than with any other form of media (Edison Research, 2010), and almost three quarters of teens and young adults use social media sites (Pew Research Center, 2010).

Given the important role that media play in our lives as we attempt to gain information, stay connected, or just be entertained, we must ask what role they play in our attempts to make sense of the competing cultural meanings about our own and others' sexual identities. The purpose of this book is to help you think about that very question by introducing you to some of the key areas of academic research and debate on sexual identities and the media. A note here about the way this book uses the term "sexual identities" is necessary. While transgender people claim an array of sexual identities, transgender primarily describes a non-normative *gender* identity. Nonetheless, there are strong historical links between transgender and gay and lesbian communities. For this reason, we have included transgender identities in the scope of this book. However, for the sake of brevity, we use the term "sexual identities" as an umbrella term for GLBTQ identities when not speaking exclusively about transgender identities.

In helping you to consider the complex issues associated with sexual identities and the media, this book will cover the following material: Chapter 2 will introduce you to the significant social and political eras and events in GLBTQ social and cultural history. Chapter 3 will consider some of the central tensions present in discussions about GLBTQ visibility. Chapter 4 will explore the multifaceted relationship between sexual identities and consumer culture. Chapter 5 will discuss appropriation and production as strategies used to resist dominant messages about sexuality in mainstream media. Chapter 6 will consider media's role in shaping our understandings of sexuality through the logic of the closet. Chapter 7 will explore the complicated qualities of comedy and camp in media representations of GLBTQ characters. Chapter 8 will contemplate how the visual imagery of GLBTQ bodies in the media may spectacularize non-normative sexualities. Finally, Chapter 9 will reflect upon current conversations about sexuality and what they may mean for future directions of thinking about sexual identities and the media.

Before we dive into those conversations, though, this chapter will lay an important groundwork for the remaining chapters. The first part of the chapter will tease out some of the language used to think about and talk about sexuality and sexual identities and then consider some key areas of conversation and contestation about sexuality and the best way to achieve sexual equality. It also will consider how conversations toward that end can risk erasing other important identity differences. The second part of the chapter will introduce different approaches for thinking about the relationship between media and identity. The first is a social scientific approach, which generally studies representations of different groups at the individual level, considering how media representations may influence our perception of identity. The second, a critical/cultural approach, engages broader questions about the role that media play in constructing social identities. Finally, the chapter will consider how the digital age has complicated further any discussions about media and identity.

▶ STUDYING SEXUAL IDENTITIES

Many people use the language of sexuality in their everyday conversations without stopping to contemplate the meanings of the words they use. Comparatively, those whose job it is to think about sexuality issues (e.g., activists and academics) may spend an inordinate amount of time considering the meanings of the words they use, but they may ultimately use them in different ways. This is because a single definition rarely is able to fully encapsulate both the broad scope and subtle nuances of the language of sexuality. What follows is our attempt to sort out for you some of this language and to relate these terms to differences in the ways people think about issues of sexuality. Understanding these differences is important because they inform academic discussions about sexual identities and the media. It also is important to recognize, however, that our understandings of sexuality and the language we use to think and talk about it is rooted in culture and history. This book considers sexuality from a 21st Century Western perspective so the ideas and language reflect a 21st Century Western way of thinking about sexuality. Not only does the language we use reflect historical and cultural understandings of sexuality, it also has the possibility of limiting our imaginations of other ways to comprehend this topic. At the same time, the language used is continually in flux as cultural meanings are continually negotiated. Be mindful of these perspectives as you consider the definitions and descriptions offered below. (Textbox 1.1 asks you to imagine alternative frameworks for thinking about sexuality.)

BOX 1.1   Alternative Sexuality Models

As will be elaborated on in Chapter 2, when sexologists began to categorize people by their sexual behaviors and attraction, sexual orientation became key to thinking about sexuality. This sorting out of people's sexuality based upon the sex-gender of the person to whom they are attracted took hold and has been a central organizing principle to most understandings of sexuality. Although some sex researchers, like Alfred Kinsey, have attempted to complicate this binary system by introducing a continuum concept of sexual orientation or expanding the factors considered in determining a person's sexual orientation (e.g., the degree of attraction to different sexes), the model generally has held.

As Stein (1999) points out, traditional categories of sexuality (i.e., heterosexuality and homosexuality) leave little room for people who are transgender or intersexed

(Continued)

or attracted to transgender or intersexed people. Likewise, why do we not consider the sexual orientation of the person to whom someone is attracted? Our current notion of sexual orientation presumes that it would be the same as the individual who is attracted to the person. However, as Stein (1999) points out, there are lesbians who desire and act upon sexual desires toward gay men. There also are gay men who only desire sex with straight men. This is really only the tip of the iceberg. The sex and sexuality of people that a person is "oriented" toward is only one part of a sexuality equation that might include sexual desires that include objects, acts, venues, frequencies, etc. Our culture does have terms for some desires/behaviors (e.g., "object fetishism," "nymphomaniac," "exhibitionist," "sadomasochist"), but these labels, which generally carry pejorative meanings, typically are secondary to a person's narrowly defined sexual orientation.

Consider for a moment how our worldviews might be different if sexual orientation was not limited to a two- or three-category system or if the sex-gender of sexual partners were not the defining principle. Develop an alternative framework for thinking about sexual identities. Instead of using sex-gender as the basis for determining sexual orientation, develop a completely new organizing principle. You might begin by using some of the desires and/or behaviors mentioned above, but then see how creative you can be. Once you have your new system, develop new identity labels to replace our current GLBTQ "alphabet soup." Think about how your new system would change social and political arenas.

Sexuality, Sexual Orientation, Sexual Identity—What Does It All Mean?

The term "sexuality" typically is used as an umbrella term to describe "the quality of being sexual" (Weeks, 2011, p. 198). This use of the word emerged in the early 19th Century and was furthered by sexologists at the end of that century. Although this definition is fairly straightforward, it fails to capture the complexity of all that people may associate with "being sexual." The Sexuality Information and Education Council of the United States (SIECUS) attempts to identify those broad associations:

> Human sexuality encompasses the sexual knowledge, beliefs, attitudes, values, and behaviors of individuals. Its various dimensions involve the anatomy, physiology, and biochemistry of the sexual response system; identity, orientation, roles, and personality; and thoughts, feelings, and relationships. Sexuality is influenced by ethical, spiritual, cultural and moral concerns.
>
> (quoted in Plante, 2006, p. xvii)

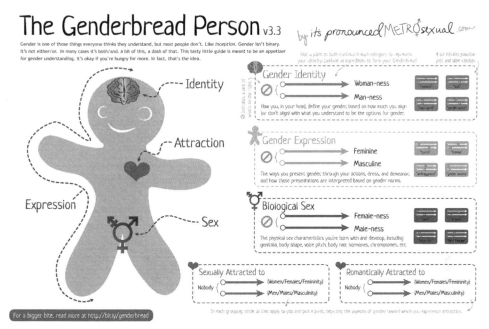

FIGURE 1.2 The Genderbread Person illustrates one way to think about the diversity of sexual identities
Source: **itspronouncedmetrosexual.com by Sam Killermann. Reprinted with permission.**

Given the extensive scope of all that sexuality might imply, the term increasingly is used in its plural form, suggesting that there are multiple, if not infinite, forms of sexuality.

One element of people's sexuality is their sexual orientation, commonly defined by the sex-gender of the person to whom they are sexually attracted. Some people think of sexual orientation as a binary—people are either heterosexual or homosexual. Sometimes the category of bisexuality is added into the mix, but people are supposed to fit neatly into one of these two or three categories. The reality, though, is that sexual orientation is much more complicated than that. To begin with, several factors may contribute to determining a person's sexual orientation. For instance, Plante (2006) notes that some definitions of sexual orientation include people's fantasies, feelings, and behaviors. However, our current way of thinking about sexual orientation leaves little room for situations in which people's fantasies, feelings, and behaviors do not necessarily align with each other or when they might change over time. The limitations of the popular binary understanding of sexual orientation also become clear when considering people who fall outside our binary understandings of sex and gender, as will be discussed later.

In American culture, another aspect of people's sexuality has played an increasingly important role: the concept of sexual identity. A person's sexual identity considers "how o people understand themselves, how do they think of themselves; do they label themselves, and do they announce or enact that identity to an audience or in a social setting?" (Plante, 2006, p. 200). This definition by Plante should not be understood as suggesting that sexual identity is determined solely at an individual level. As people think about, label, announce, or enact their own sexual identities, they are creating linkages between themselves and others with similar sexual identities. As Weeks (2011) writes, "identity tells us about what we have in common with some people, and what differentiates us from others" (p. 187). While everyone has a sexual identity, sexual identities matter in a different way to those with marginalized ones. Being able to connect with other people based on those identities allows people with non-normative sexualities the opportunity for self-recognition and self-valuation, things usually taken for granted by most people. Many people also see sexual identity as the basis for being able to confront, challenge, and change a homophobic and heterosexist society. (The "Heterosexual Questionnaire" in Textbox 1.2 draws attention to how heterosexism marginalizes sexual minorities.)

BOX 1.2   The Heterosexual Questionnaire (M. Rochlin)

Purpose: The purpose of this exercise is to examine the manner in which the use of heterosexual norms may bias the study of gay men's and lesbian's lives.

Instructions: Heterosexism is a form of bias in which heterosexual norms are used in studies of homosexual relationships. Gay men and lesbians are seen as deviating from a heterosexual norm, and this often leads to the marginalization and pathologizing of their behavior. Read the questionnaire below with this definition in mind and respond to the questions.

1. What do you think caused your heterosexuality?
2. When and how did you first decide you were a heterosexual?
3. Is it possible that your heterosexuality stems from a neurotic fear of others of the same sex?
4. Is it possible that your heterosexuality is just a phase you may grow out of?
5. If you've never slept with a person of the same sex, is it possible that all you need is a good gay lover?

6. Do your parents know that you are straight? Do your friends and/or roommate(s) know? How did they react?
7. Why do you insist on flaunting your heterosexuality? Can't you just be who you are and keep it quiet?
8. Why do heterosexuals place so much emphasis on sex?
9. Why do heterosexuals feel compelled to seduce others into their lifestyle?
10. A disproportionate majority of child molesters are heterosexuals. Do you consider it safe to expose your children to heterosexual teachers?
11. Just what do men and women *do* in bed together? How can they truly know how to please each other, being so anatomically different?
12. With all the societal support marriage receives, the divorce rate is spiraling. Why are there so few stable relationships among heterosexuals?
13. Statistics show that lesbians have the lowest incidence of sexually transmitted diseases. Is it really safe for a woman to maintain a heterosexual lifestyle and run the risk of disease and pregnancy?
14. How can you become a whole person if you limit yourself to compulsive, exclusive heterosexuality?
15. Considering the menace of overpopulation, how could the human race survive if everyone were heterosexual?
16. Could you trust a heterosexual therapist to be objective? Don't you feel s/he might be inclined to influence you in the direction of her/his own leanings?
17. There seem to be very few happy heterosexuals. Techniques have been developed with which you might be able to change if you really want to. Have you considered trying aversion therapy?
18. Would you want your child to be heterosexual, knowing the problems that s/he would face?
19. What were your first reactions upon reading this questionnaire?

(M. Rochlin. Printed in the *Peace Newsletter*, 1982, Issue #488, p. 14. Reprinted with permission.)

The Alphabet Soup of Sexual Identities

People often refer to the "alphabet soup" of sexual identities, an ever-growing list of terms inclusive of historically marginalized sexual and gender identity categories. The basic list includes L(esbian), G(ay), B(isexual), and T(ransgender). In recent years, Q(ueer) has been added, and sometimes a whole mouthful of other letters like a second

Q(uestioning), A(lly), I(ntersex), H(IV-affected), and even W(hatever). Like all identity labels, those applied to sexuality carry with them certain histories and are tied to particular ways of thinking about the meaning of sexuality as an identity marker. Below, we consider some of the most common labels attached to sexual identity categories. In addition to including a definition of each term, the descriptions also place many of them in an historical context.

▶ *Heterosexual*: This term today refers to a sexual identity in which people find themselves sexually attracted to people of the opposite sex. Before the 20th Century, heterosexuality used to refer to someone pathologically concerned with the opposite sex. In general, however, heterosexuality has mostly gone unnoticed or unmarked in discussions of sexuality. Because it is the perceived norm, scholars, scientists, activists, and everyday people have not spent a lot of time thinking about it. Yet, over the past 20 years, the term increasingly has come under question, with a number of theorists pointing to the fact that heterosexuality, like other sexual labels, is a cultural construction. Also, sexuality scholars are drawing attention to the fact that within heterosexuality, not all sex is treated equally and certain types of sex (e.g., prostitution, sadomasochism) and the people who engage in them are marked as deviant. Gayle Rubin's concept of the "charmed circle" (see Textbox 1.3) illustrates this point.

▶ *Homosexual*: Most commonly, this term refers to a sexual identity in which people find themselves sexually attracted to people of the same sex. In that sense, it often is understood as the binary opposite of heterosexuality. Originally identified with behaviors, over the course of the 20th Century the term was used to label people who either engaged in same-sex sexual activities or expressed desires for people of the same sex as pathological. Based on this history, many members of the GLBTQ community do not like the use of this term as a noun.

▶ *Gay*: This term sometimes is used as a more accepted and positive alternative to "homosexual" and is used to describe people who identify themselves as sexually attracted to someone of the same sex. Unlike the term "homosexual," which grew from the medical discourses of sexology, "gay" was a term of self-determination. Adopted by U.S. activists as early as the 1950s, it gained widespread acceptance and use by the 1970s when activist groups like the Gay Liberation Front adopted the term in their struggle for social recognition and acceptance. Today, the term is recognized globally. In the GLBTQ community, the term more specifically refers to men who identify themselves as sexually attracted to other men.

▶ *Lesbian*: Lesbian is used more specifically to refer to women who identify themselves through their attraction to other women. In reality, the term has a complicated and contested history. The term originates from its association with the Greek poet, Sappho, who lived on the island of Lesbos and wrote about love between women. By the late 19th Century the term took on more negative connotations and for the first half of the 20th Century was used to describe women who seemed more masculine than feminine. With the emergence of the second-wave feminist movement in the late 1960s, lesbianism began to be associated more positively with both women's and gay liberation. Still, the connection between lesbianism and masculinity in women remains, as well as between lesbianism and more radical strains of second-wave feminism. Therefore, some young female activists reject the term.

▶ *Bisexual*: This term refers to people who identify themselves by their attraction to people of both the same and the opposite sex. A far more recent term than the ones listed above, bisexuality first was used as a term somewhat synonymous with heterosexuality. In many ways, bisexuality as a self-defined identity challenges the biological basis upon which some people make claims of being gay or lesbian. Until very recently, the term did not register as a valid or even unique identity, and gender differences can inform how it is applied. For example, Adrienne Rich's (1980) concept of the "lesbian continuum" provides an example of how women's sexuality often is understood in more fluid terms, making it more likely to fall outside of absolute classification. However, the strong connection between hegemonic masculinity and homophobia may make self-identified male bisexuality less common. (See Kimmel, 2011, for a discussion of the dominant role homophobia plays in men's relationships, thus limiting the potential of physical and emotional intimacy between men.) In addition to the potential of facing hostility from heterosexuals, bisexuals also sometimes face hostility from those who identify as gay and lesbian and view bisexuality as a phase or as a form of internalized homophobia and, thus, a refusal of the gay or lesbian identity.

▶ *Pansexual*: Sometimes referred to as omnisexual, pansexual describes an attraction to a person regardless of sex or gender. People who use this label may describe themselves as "gender blind" or as being attracted to a person's personality rather than his or her sex. The term also acknowledges a space for intersexed and transgendered people in an otherwise binary understanding of sexuality and gender.

▶ *Asexual*: This term increasingly has been adopted by people who do not experience sexual attraction to anyone. Unlike the term "celibacy," which describes someone's *behavior*, asexuality describes the lack of sexual *desire*. Only recently has asexuality begun to be studied, as it becomes more visible with the existence of asexual communities and organizations made possible by digital media.

▶ *Straight*: "Straight" has become a colloquial term for "heterosexual." The term first was used in the phrase "to go straight," which in the 1940s referred to someone who had previously engaged in homosexual behaviors but had stopped doing so. "Straight" was a reference to the "straight and narrow."

▶ *Transgender*: Transgender refers to people who experience a disconnect between their biological sex and their gender identity. When the term first gained currency in the 1970s, transgender was used as a term of self-identification by those who rejected gender norms but did not identify with transsexuals or transvestites. Today, transgender typically serves as an umbrella term for a range of identities that refuse the link between biological sex and a set of socially acceptable gender norms. Therefore, it generally is seen as destabilizing common assumptions about the "natural" link between sex and identity. While transgender refers to a person's gender identity, only in the past 50 years have homosexuality and gender variance been clearly distinguished from each other.

▶ *Tran(s)exual*: Unlike the term "transgender," which largely was created by a community of people seeking self-definition, "transsexual" began as a medical term. It was coined by Dr. Harry Benjamin, a German endocrinologist involved in clinical work with transsexuals beginning in the 1950s. The term still is used today to categorize individuals expressing strong desires to transition into a life lived as a member of the opposite sex. Some choose to do this by altering their cosmetic appearance, others seek to alter their bodies through the use of hormone treatments, and some individuals choose to undergo sex-reassignment surgery. Trans activists use a singular "s" to differentiate between their intentionally chosen sexual identity as opposed to a medically imposed one.

▶ *Transvestite*: Originating in the early years of the 20th Century, transvestite refers to a person who cross-dresses. Originally, many presumed a strong correspondence between transvestism and homosexuality. Today, it is more commonly understood that there is little link between cross-dressing behaviors and sexual orientation. The label transvestite historically has carried negative connotations and has fallen out of use by the GLBTQ community, where the descriptive term "cross-dresser" generally is preferred.

▶ *Trans**: Some writers have begun to use this term (with the asterisk) to acknowledge the gender variance that exists within the trans community. The use of the asterisk stems from computing in which the symbol represents a wildcard, or any possible characters attached to the original search term. "Trans*" includes transgender men and women, along with a range of other identities like gender-fluid, non-binary, gender queer, third gender, or agender.

▶ *Ze* and *hir*: These are gender neutral pronouns generally accepted in the transgender community. "Ze" is the neutral stand in for the terms "he" or "she", while "hir" is the alternative to "his" or "her."

▶ *Cisgender*: This term was developed by those in the transgender community to refer to individuals whose biological sex aligns with their gender expression. The Latin-derived prefix "cis" means "on the same side" and serves as an antonym to "trans."

▶ *Queer*: The term "queer" typically is used to signify an attitude toward sexuality and gender that rejects gay rights politics rooted in identity categories. However, the term has had a complex history, and its meaning continues to be contested. At the turn of the 20th Century, gay men used this label themselves before it took on a pejorative meaning and became an epithet used against gay people. The term has since been reclaimed by the GLBTQ community. "Queer" sometimes is used as an umbrella term for all non-normative sexual and gender identities. It also has been adopted by radical activists who resist what they see as the assimilationist nature of those involved in the struggle for civil rights for gays and lesbians. The term often is favored by younger activists as a specific rejection of the narrower identity categories of heterosexual, gay, lesbian, woman, and man. Instead, these activists see their identities tied less to the sex-gender of the person to whom they are attracted and more tied to a radical rethinking of gender and sex relations. In academia, the term most frequently is associated with queer theory, which will be discussed below. Given all of the possible connotations of this word, it is best to always consider the context in which it is being used to determine the user's intended meaning.

▶ *Genderqueer*: This term refers to gendered identities that fall outside the normative binary of masculine and feminine and might include, for example, people who refuse all gender labels and people who identify as both masculine and feminine. The practice of intentionally disrupting traditional gender categories by sending confusing or contradictory messages about one's sex is called *genderfuck*.

▶ *Intersex*: This term describes a number of biological variations in which people's physical sex characteristics do not align with a traditional two-sex model of male and female. An intersex condition may be discovered at birth, at the onset of puberty, or sometimes not until a person dies and an autopsy is performed. In recent decades, the medical community has drastically changed its treatment of intersex people to encourage a "wait and see" approach with children until they are old enough to have input in any medical decisions. While most intersex people choose to live their lives according to traditional norms associated with one gender or the other, an increasing number of intersexed people are rejecting a binary system of sex-gender and embracing their unique gender variations. Intersex and transgender activists sometimes work together to fight what they view as an oppressive binary sex-gender system.

BOX 1.3   The Limits of Social Acceptance

Social discourses about sexuality since the 1970s primarily have focused on sexual orientation; however, it is important to remember that same-sex desire is just one type of sexual practice for which people have been judged to be sexual deviants and, therefore, social outcasts. Gayle Rubin (1999), a cultural anthropologist and influential writer on gender and sexuality, suggests that American culture is based on a sex hierarchy, in which "marital, reproductive heterosexuals are alone at the top erotic pyramid" (p. 158). She argues that our sexual value system consists of a charmed circle of "good, normal, natural, and blessed sexuality" and the "outer limits" of "bad, abnormal, unnatural, and damned sexuality" (p. 153). While homosexuality falls to the outer limits of this sexual value system, so, too, does fetishism, pornography, sadomasochism, masturbation, prostitution, pedophilia, and polygamy. Similarly, just as homosexuality has been subject to religious, legal, psychiatric, and popular derision, so, too, have these other sexual behaviors.

Rubin (1999) argues that cultures draw lines to determine what type of sexual behaviors fall on the side of "good sex" and which do not. These lines are not historically static. Instead, they are contested terrain, as people debate over the acceptability of sexual practices that fall outside the charmed circle. However, the more elements of the charmed circle to which a person's sexuality adheres, then the more likely it is that it will move closer toward the line of "good sex." For example, monogamous gay couples who engage in private vanilla sex come closer to the line of acceptability than transsexuals who engage in S/M sex for pay.

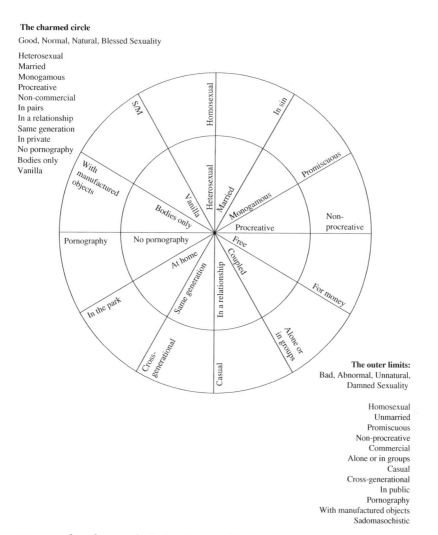

The charmed circle
Good, Normal, Natural, Blessed Sexuality

Heterosexual
Married
Monogamous
Procreative
Non-commercial
In pairs
In a relationship
Same generation
In private
No pornography
Bodies only
Vanilla

Homosexual
In sin
S/M
With manufactured objects
Vanilla
Heterosexual
Married
Monogamous
Procreative
Promiscuous
Non-procreative
Bodies only
No pornography
Pornography
Free
Coupled
At home
For money
In the park
Same generation
In a relationship
Alone or in groups
Cross-generational
Casual

The outer limits:
Bad, Abnormal, Unnatural,
Damned Sexuality

Homosexual
Unmarried
Promiscuous
Non-procreative
Commercial
Alone or in groups
Casual
Cross-generational
In public
Pornography
With manufactured objects
Sadomasochistic

FIGURE 1.3 The charmed circle of sexual behaviors
Source: **Gayle Rubin, 1993, p. 13. Reprinted with permission.**

People who fight to hold fast existing lines of acceptability often presume what Rubin calls a "domino theory of sexual peril." Rubin writes, "The line appears to stand between sexual order and chaos. It expresses the fear that if anything is permitted to cross this erotic DMZ, the barrier against scary sex will crumble and something unspeakable will skitter across" (p. 161).

(Continued)

What role do media play in enforcing the charmed circle? Brainstorm films and television portrayals of people whose sexuality falls outside of the charmed circle (e.g., fetishists, sadomasochists, prostitutes, or those engaging in cross-generational sex) and consider the following:

1. In what genres do they appear?
2. How are they portrayed?
3. How far outside the charmed circle do their behaviors put them?
4. How do their actions impact them and/or others?
5. Do their portrayals reinforce a domino theory that these behaviors lay at the brink of sexual chaos?

Essentialist and Social Constructionist Perspectives

Even if people share a common vocabulary for the way they talk about issues of sexuality, some of their underlying assumptions may result in them "talking past" each other. One example is whether someone adheres to an essentialist or social constructionist perspective of sexuality. In its popular usage, "essentialism" refers to a person's belief that an individual's sexual orientation is inherent and unchangeable. Gay or lesbian people who adhere to this perspective might express that they "always knew" they were attracted to people of the same sex or use language that reflects "discovering" or "uncovering" their "true sexual identities," which presumes that identity was always a part of them, even if they had not yet recognized it. The very term "sexual orientation" reflects an assumption that people naturally are oriented to be homosexual or heterosexual, and essentialists often look to biology as the root of what they see as predetermined identities.

In comparison to the popular usage of the term "essentialism," its use by sexuality scholars generally refers to broader understandings of sexuality. In its academic usage, essentialism refers to the assumption that sex exists a priori, or prior to, culture. As Gayle Rubin (1999) explains, essentialism is "the idea that sex is a natural force that exists prior to social life and shapes institutions. Sexual essentialism is embedded in the folk wisdoms of Western societies, which consider sex to be eternally unchanging, asocial, and transhistorical" (p. 156). From this perspective, sex is thought about at the level of the individual and is rooted in hormones and bodily desires. As a result, an essentialist approach to sexuality considers sex to be unchanged over time and across cultures. For example, a woman who has sexual desires for other women in the early 21st Century would make sense of those sexual feelings in the same way as a woman in the early 20th Century, even if the label of "lesbian" did not yet exist to describe those desires and/or behaviors. The same would hold true for people who experience gender dysphoria, or feelings that their biological sex does not align with their psychological feelings of gender. Essentialist assumptions rarely are labeled explicitly as such by people who make them, but these underlying assumptions can be found in the arguments being made. For example, arguments against same-sex marriage that rely on biblical prohibitions against homosexuality often are drawn from the perspective that homosexuality largely is unchanged in more than 3000 years.

By the late 1970s, some scholars began critiquing essentialist views of sexuality and began theorizing sexuality from a social constructionist approach. Social constructionism conceives of identity as being culturally and historically situated. People occupy sexual identities that are available to them in their time and place, and those identities help them to frame and make sense of their experiences. The divide between essentialist and social constructionist perspectives should not be understood to represent a nature versus nurture debate, both of which assume pre-existing categories for people to either be born into or to be socialized into. A social constructionist perspective does not deny that biology and hormones contribute to sexual desire, but takes up questions about the role of culture in our understandings of sexuality. Rubin (1999) writes, "The body, the brain, the genitalia, and the capacity of language are necessary for human sexuality. But they do not determine its content, its experiences, or its institutional forms" (p. 157).

We can return to our example of biblical prohibitions against same-sex sexual practices to illustrate how a social constructionist approach might raise questions about how sex and sexual practices have changed in the past 3000 years. A social constructionist might point out that biblical prohibitions against men having sex with other men are situated within a particular historical-cultural moment in which modern-day understandings of homosexuality did not yet even exist. They might contextualize ancient same-sex sexual practices within a rigid gender hierarchy in which women were the property of their fathers or husbands, sex and procreation were understood as being synonymous, ancient science conceived of male semen as containing the full essence of human life (with women's bodies serving as little more than incubators), and man-on-man rape was used as a form of domination. In recognizing how cultural conditions have changed over the past 3000 years, a social constructionist perspective suggests that our modern-day conception of homosexuality does not align with ancient same-sex practices. The next chapter will elaborate on how sexuality began to be conceived of in terms of identities rather than behaviors, but the titles of the following books illustrate an academic turn to a social constructionist perspective of sexuality: Hannah Blank's (2012) *Straight: The Surprisingly Short History of Heterosexuality*, David Greenberg's (1990) *The Construction of Homosexuality*, Jonathon Ned Katz's (2007) *The Invention of Heterosexuality* (2007), and Stephen Seidman's (2003) *The Social Construction of Sexuality*. Understanding essentialism and social constructionism will help you recognize how these perspectives have informed attention to GLBTQ issues inside and outside of academia, which is discussed below.

From Gay Politics/Theory to Queer Politics/Theory

The development of gay and lesbian studies as a legitimate discipline in colleges and universities has been intertwined with political activism. As a result, academic theory must be contextualized within the historical trajectory of the gay rights movement. As noted in the definitions above, and as will be elaborated upon in the next chapter, the idea of people's sexuality serving as a marker of their identity came into full force in the 1970s. As those with non-normative sexualities began developing communities and fighting against discrimination, they began to recognize themselves as sexual minorities. In the process, they took up an ethnic model of fighting for civil rights, sometimes referred to as identity politics. Drawing on essentialist arguments, gay and lesbian activists fought for the same visibility and rights as their straight counterparts. In short, they fought for gay people's assimilation into American culture. This line of argument has been and remains a key strategy for achieving legal and political gains. For example, in the Massachusetts Supreme Judicial Court case *Goodridge* v. *Department of Public Health* (2003), the first state court decision to legalize gay marriage, the court found that denying same-sex couples the right to marry denies them equal protection under the law, a right guaranteed by the 14th Amendment. Even those strongly opposed to gay rights recognize the powerful force of identity politics. A publication from the conservative American Family Association's publication *Homosexuality in America: Exposing the Myths* states:

> casting the debate along the lines of *one's identity as being a homosexual* rather than *one's actions as engaging in homosexual activity* . . . makes it . . . more difficult for those who oppose homosexual activities in the public area to argue their case.
>
> (Howe, 1994, p. 3, italics in original)

In academia, research on sexual identity has not been as beholden to essentialist assumptions as in gay rights political activism. During the late 1970s to the early 1980s, as gay and lesbian studies began getting a foothold in higher education, academics rejected transhistorical understandings of sexuality. Instead, they explored the role of culture and society in framing people's understandings of sexual identities. That is, they embraced a social constructionist model of sexuality. However, they did so while still adhering to a general framework of identity politics (Seidman, 1995). Although identity politics remain at the forefront of political debates about sexual equality, beginning in the mid-1980s academics began questioning the limits of this approach. They feared that the existing strain of identity politics threatened to homogenize other important differences between gay people and continued to alienate those people whose sexualities lay too far outside the bounds of acceptability. Drawing on the work of French post-structuralists, these academics suggested a radical new approach to thinking about sexual inequalities—queer theory.

Queer theory is dedicated to drawing attention to sexuality and gender as social constructions in order to deconstruct the very idea of identity categories and their attendant power relations. French philosopher and social theorist Michel Foucault's three-volume work *The History of Sexuality* (1978/1990; 1985/1990; 1986/1990) has been foundational to such queer theory projects. In it, he traces the way that medical and religious discourses contribute to the idea that people's sexualities somehow reveal an essential truth about them. A discourse is a set of meanings and practices that circulate around a particular bounded area of social experience, such as sexuality and gender. Discourses produce particular knowledge claims as the "truth" about some part of our world. Foucault (1978/1990) was concerned with the way that discourses crystallized same-sex practices into an essential homosexual identity. Referencing the term commonly used at the time to describe men who engage in anal sex with other men, he aptly states, "the sodomite had been a temporary aberration; the homosexual was now a species" (p. 43). Foucault also contended that once the category of "homosexual" was constructed, people to whom that label was applied could be identified as deviant and disciplined by the broader society.

As homosexuality became understood as a category around which to organize and give meaning to a set of sexual practices, the category of heterosexual emerged as its binary opposite. Similar to homosexuality, heterosexuality did not exist until the late 1800s, when medical discourses bound together "one historically specific way of organizing the sexes and their pleasures" into a cohesive sexual identity (Katz, 2007, p. 34). The result is today's heterosexual-homosexual identity binary. Binary systems sustain hierarchies of power as one category becomes the universalizing experience, which is defined against the devalued "Other." This is the case for familiar gender and sexuality binaries like male/female; masculine/feminine; heterosexual/homosexual; and cisgender/transgender. Queer theory attempts to destabilize seemingly natural binary identity categories by drawing attention to their artificiality and arbitrariness. For example, queer theorist Judith Butler (1990) focuses on gender categories, suggesting that gender does not exist outside of people's "performance" of it. That is, there is no such thing as "woman" or "man" without the everyday gender performances that construct them as categories to occupy. In effect, gender is a masquerade given meaning through its enactment. In challenging the naturalness of gender, Butler also disrupts any ostensibly natural associations between sex, gender, and sexuality.

Queer theorists also are concerned with the way that the heterosexual/homosexual binary has shaped broader cultural categories, creating a heteronormative cultural arrangement. Heteronormativity is an important concept in queer theory; it describes the way in which heterosexual privilege is woven into the fabric of society. Such a world privileges coupling, sex as a sign of intimate connection, and reproduction. Berlant and Warner (1998) suggest that social belonging necessitates adherence to these heterosexual norms, and heteronormative logics occupy even those areas of society far removed from matters of sex, such as "paying taxes, being disgusted, philandering, bequeathing, celebrating a holiday, investing for the future, teaching, disposing of a corpse, carrying wallet photos, buying economy size, being nepotistic, running for president, divorcing, or owning anything 'His' and 'Hers'" (p. 555). Heterosexuality, thus, serves as a central organizing principle in politics, law, religion, medicine, education, commerce, and, of course, media.

While queer theory developed as a critique of identity politics, many academics who apply queer theory to the study of sexuality still recognize the effectiveness of utilizing an ethnic assimilationist model to achieve social rights for GLBTQ people. However, they also critique the limitations of identity models in which the charmed circle of acceptance grows wider only for those GLBTQ people who still subscribe to hetero/homo, cis/transgender binaries and their heteronormative logics (Rubin, 1999).

Complicating Sexual Identity

As mentioned earlier, another critique of the identity politics model of fighting for equality for GLBTQ people is that it overlooks other aspects of people's identity like race, class, and gender. Once the GLBTQ community became increasingly visible following World War II and began organizing toward the political ends of achieving gay rights, sexuality became their defining identity category. When a group of people become identified by a single aspect of their shared identity, that group's identity becomes homogenized and people are viewed as being the same regardless of other areas of difference. Johnson (2005) addresses this problem in GLBTQ studies:

> [Gloria Anzuldúa] warns that "queer is used as a false umbrella which
> all 'queers' of all races, ethnicities and classes are shored under." While
> acknowledging that "at times we need this umbrella to solidify our ranks

against outsiders," Anzuldúa nevertheless urges that "even when we seek shelter under it ['queer'], we must not forget that it homogenizes, erases our differences."

(p. 127)

In people's daily realities, these differences matter. For example, imagine how the experiences of a homeless Latina transgender woman may differ vastly from those of a white transgender male college professor. The latter likely would have more access to financial resources and health care needed for a physical transition (e.g., wardrobe, voice coaching, hormones, or surgery), while the former would be more at risk of being the victim of violence (National Coalition of Anti-Violence Programs, 2013). Although these two individuals may share similar hopes for transgender legal protections and social acceptance, it would be problematic to believe there are no differences in the way they think about their own identities or in the way others view them.

Another critique of identity politics is that visibility is limited to those members of the GLBTQ community most palatable to the broader culture. This approach is a strategic one; in order to encourage those in power to consent to rights for a minority group, it can be beneficial if they view people who are part of that group as being "like" themselves. In the case of gay rights, this means that middle-class, white gay men generally serve as the cause's "poster children." Bérubé (2011) points to examples of this happening in debates in the early 1990s over whether gays should be allowed to serve in the military. One of the primary organizations working with the White House and some sympathetic members of Congress to craft a "gay response" to the controversy was "The Campaign for Military Service." The group was made up of "well-to-do, well-connected, professional [white] men," whom Bérubé (2011) describes in the following way:

Wearing the protective coloring of this predominantly white gay world, these professionals entered the similarly white and male but heterosexual world of the U.S. Senate, where their shared whiteness became a common ground on which the battle to lift the military's ban on homosexuals was fought.

(p. 207–208)

Because of the group's membership, the white witnesses they used to testify about their experiences as gay military members, and the "race analogy" arguments they made that treated discrimination based on sexual orientation as similar to race-based discrimination, the stories and experiences of non-white, gay military members, were made invisible to politicians and the broader public. In Chapters 3 and 4, we will relate these concerns about identity politics to the media and consider how GLBTQ media visibility tends to erase differences and privilege the most palatable images of gayness and, increasingly, transgender identity.

At the same time that identity politics has been critiqued for privileging one identity category over others, academics who study socially marginalized groups similarly have been critiqued for failing to recognize the complexity of identity and its relationship to social oppression. In response, some GLBTQ scholars have turned to women's studies and related fields and the concept of "intersectionality" to better theorize how the various aspects of a person's identity should be understood not as isolated categories, but as influencing each other (Crenshaw, 1989; 1991). For example, if you are an able-bodied white man, the experiences you have had as a man cannot be understood outside of the other aspects of your identity, like being white and able-bodied. Similarly, other people interact with you based on the intersections of those identities. The concept of intersectionality goes beyond the individual level, however. It also suggests that social oppression does not operate along individual identity categories. If we apply this perspective to sexual inequalities, then intersectionality requires us to consider heterosexism in the context of other social inequalities like sexism, racism, and classism, which both shape and are shaped by sexual oppression.

Some queer theorists, though, are uncomfortable with the use of the term "intersectionality," because it is theoretically rooted in identity categories, and queer theory emerged as a critique of identity politics. Johnson (2005) suggests a field of "quare studies" as a way to bridge queer studies and black studies in a way that does not privilege or erase sexual or racial identity. Writing from a performance studies background, Johnson (2005) proposes "theories in the flesh" that "emphasize the diversity within and among gays, bisexuals, lesbians, and transgendered people of color while simultaneously accounting for how racism and classicism affect how we experience and theorize the world" (p. 127). He points to examples of folklore and literature that challenge assumed hierarchies by considering how within oppressed groups, some people still are culturally privileged. For example, straight African-Americans are culturally privileged over gay African-Americans.

Until fairly recently, much of the research on sexual identities and the media has not taken up questions of race, class, and/or gender. GLBTQ media representations have been disproportionately white, male, and upper class. Demonstrating how privilege operates, these unmarked categories largely have gone by without attention. This is changing, though, with scholars drawing attention to these privileged categories. For example, Kohnen (2014) positions GLBTQ representations in American film and television within the context of whiteness. Also, as GLBTQ media representations become more diverse, an increasing number of scholars are taking up questions of race, class, gender, and even age (see, for example, Goltz, 2010). We will raise questions of race and gender throughout this book, but we also recognize these topics deserve more attention than the space of this book allows. Additionally, this book focuses exclusively on Western media and operates from Western understandings of sexuality. (Text-box 1.4 provides suggestions of documentaries that address sexuality in non-Western contexts.)

BOX 1.4   Gender and Sexuality in a Cultural Context

FIGURE 1.4 Husband and wife during their traditional wedding ceremony
Source: **Antony Thomas, 2005, *Middle Sexes: Redefining He and She.***

As this chapter discusses, our understandings of gender and sexuality are cultur-ally and historically situated. In Western cultures, our gender-sex system is rooted in a Judeo-Christian tradition that emphasizes binary thinking (e.g., Adam and Eve) and privileges heterosexual procreation (e.g. "Be fruitful and multiply"). This Western way of thinking about gender and sexuality has informed many areas of social life, including familial arrangements, civil and criminal laws, and even med-ical practices. If you have lived your entire life in Western culture, then you may never have stopped to imagine alternative understandings of gender and sexu-ality. The documentaries below introduce viewers to alternative understandings of sexuality and gender found in different cultures, including non-Western ones.

(Continued)

In addition to thinking about how these films' content demonstrates the cultural specificity of gender and sexuality, also consider who produces and narrates the films. Are films' creators from inside or outside of the culture they describe? Consider how the cultural perspective of the documentary makers may shape the stories that they tell.

Be Like Others: Transsexual in Iran (2008). A look at young Iranians who undergo sex reassignment surgery.

City of Borders (2009). A conversation with the owners and patrons of a Jerusalem gay bar.

God Loves Uganda (2013). An account of how American Evangelicals spread conservative beliefs, including homophobic views, in Uganda.

The Hijras: India's Third Gender (2002). An introduction to a religious community of men in India who challenge categories of male and female.

Jerusalem is Proud to Present (2008). An account of the obstacles faced by members of Jerusalem's LGBT community center as they plan an international World Pride event.

Ke Kulana He Mahu: Remembering a Sense of Place (2001). An introduction to the gay scene in Hawaii and a look at how attitudes about sexuality have shifted over time.

Kuma Hina: A Hawaiian Model for Gender Diversity (2014). The story of a transgender Native Hawaiian teacher as she attempts to encourage love, honor, and respect for gender diversity.

Middle Sexes: Redefining He and She (2005). An examination of sexual and gender variance around the globe that includes perspectives from modern science and people's life experiences.

Paper Dolls (2006). The story of five Filipino transsexuals who emigrated to Israel, working as healthcare providers for elderly Orthodox Jewish men by day and performing as drag queens at night.

Two Spirits (2009). The story of a "two-spirit" Navajo youth killed because of his non-normative gender/sexuality.

World's Worst Place to Be Gay (2011). An investigation into the institutionalized homophobia found in Uganda.

▶ THE RELATIONSHIP BETWEEN MEDIA AND IDENTITY

Academics concerned with issues of sexual identity oftentimes turn to media to consider the role they play in circulating particular understandings about sexuality. Just as

GLBTQ studies include a range of approaches with varying assumptions and theoretical perspectives, so, too, does media research. Media scholars seek to gain a comprehensive understanding of popular media forms, particularly print (newspapers, magazines), radio, television, film, the Internet, and gaming. Their breadth of research spans contemporary and historical aspects of the media industry, regulation of the media industry, the commercialization of mass media, representations in various media (film, television shows, advertisements, websites, popular music, video games), media technologies, the impact of media on individuals and society, the ways that people make sense of media messages, and more recently the growing role of everyday individuals in creating media content. Media researchers might study the work of individuals in a newsroom or the broader role of the commercially based media system in determining the kinds of content available. They might study a single television program to see how it relates to broader cultural concerns or study a broad range of images to examine broader patterns of representation. When it come to audiences, media researchers might use a laboratory setting to gauge the short-term impact of specific media messages, survey research to gauge longer-term impacts, or use ethnographic methods to study how people use and make sense of the media in their everyday lives. They might consider how particular technologies, such as the television or Internet, impact the relationships between individuals, politics, business, etc. No matter the particular question or method used, most media scholars agree that grasping the cultural and social impacts of media requires a multifaceted approach.

The study of media draws from two primary camps of research, a mass communication tradition and a media studies tradition. Mass communication research emerged with the introduction of new technologies that allowed for mass dissemination of messages (e.g., radio and television) and draws primarily from the social sciences, particularly sociology and psychology. Mass communication theorists initially were concerned with the effects of media at both the individual and societal levels. However, as a subset of media researchers and theorists began drawing more from the fields of political science, literary studies, and anthropology, the label of media studies increasingly was applied to a body of work that concerned itself with increased attention to the cultural implications of media. The development of new media technologies allowing for narrowcasting and two-way communication also have led some researchers to prefer the term "media" over "mass communication" to describe their field of study.

A key area of inquiry for media scholars in both camps is the relationship between media and identity, and how they conceive of the relationship between media and identity likely depends on whether they come from a social scientific mass communication tradition or a cultural studies approach found in media studies. The first way of thinking about media and identity is viewing identity as prior to media, that is to say that identity categories are treated as generally stable, identifiable, and self-evident. This relationship is explored most commonly within the social scientific approach to the study of media. The second way of conceiving of the relationship between media and identity involves thinking of media as part of the process of constructing identity. Identity is conceived of as less fixed than in the social scientific approach. These are not always two discrete approaches, and slippages between the approaches can occur; however, recognizing some of the underlying assumptions about identity that inform these approaches will better help you understand the research on sexual identities and the media that you will encounter.

The Social Scientific Approach: Identity Prior to Media

The social scientific approach, as mentioned above, often is associated with the field of mass communication and derives primarily from the fields of sociology and psychology. McQuail (2010) describes this approach as

> offer[ing] general statements about the nature, working and effects of mass communication, based on systematic and objective observation of media and other relevant sources, which can in turn be put to the test and validated or rejected by similar methods.
>
> (p. 13)

In striving to be scientific, the field of mass communication operates as part of a broader scientific approach to the study of many forms of communication that presume reality exists outside of our perception of it. The goal of this approach is to strive for objectivity and the production of clear, empirically based data. Scholars and activists using this approach employ a variety of methods and are far more likely to use quantitative forms of analysis and experiment-based studies than are those working within the critical/cultural paradigm. Both academics and activists complete this kind of work, and activists often turn to social scientific approaches for their clear, data-oriented results, which are more easily conveyed to the general public than the work completed in a critical/cultural approach.

A social scientific approach rarely theorizes the relationship between media and identity, but is informed by an assumption that identity formation happens prior to culture, broadly, and media, specifically. It treats identity categories, such as race, gender, and sexuality, as self-evident, stable categories. While not all people who embrace a social scientific perspective to the study of communication embrace an essentialist view of identity, they nonetheless see the relationship between media and identity as one that can be harmful if distorted and "negative" images of social groups circulate, but one that can be beneficial with the circulation of "positive" images. For example,

Calzo and Ward (2009) surveyed college students to determine whether correlations exist between their media use and their attitudes about homosexuality. Saucier and Caron (2008) conducted a quantitative content analysis of the content and advertisements in gay men's magazines to study their objectification of men's bodies. As in the case of these studies, a social scientific approach considers how media shape social and individual attitudes and perceptions of already existing, identifiable, and understandable social groups. That is, they do not question the identity categories that they study or theorize broader relationships between media and identity as social categories.

In addition to being concerned with the creation of positive and negative representations of social groups, sometimes scholars are interested in questions of accuracy. That is to say that representations of various groups in some way accurately reflect some concrete reality associated with a particular group. Scholars working in this model generally try to measure the media representations of certain groups of people in order to compare them to the "real" characteristics of this group, looking for ways that messages about particular social groups are either accurate or distorted. For example, GLAAD (Gay and Lesbian Alliance Against Defamation) regularly uses quantitative content analysis to look for patterns in GLBTQ representations. The underlying assumption of a social scientific approach is that media content can shape people's views about a particular social issue or group of people and can impact an individual's psychological state.

This view of media is accompanied by a view of the audience that more often emphasizes the power of media to persuade or impact individuals. An early version of this thesis was the hypodermic needle theory, which held that media had a direct impact on individuals, injecting them with their messages. Today, very few scholars hold this view, and most think of media audiences as fairly active in negotiating meanings. However, scholars working in the social scientific tradition nonetheless hold onto the idea that distorted messages generally have a negative impact on individuals and society, as people come to act in the world based on *false* information. In this view, media have an impact on identity, but only in impacting how people feel about their own and others' identities as either male, female, gay, lesbian, or transgender. Broader issues of identity construction generally are left unasked.

Critical/Cultural Approach: Media Prior to Identity

The critical/cultural approach focuses on somewhat different sets of questions than the social scientific approach. More interpretive than scientific, this approach is marked by attention to the broader contexts within which media operate. While sometimes drawing from the social sciences, this approach also is informed from humanities-based theorizing, including cultural studies, literary theory, semiotics, linguistics, feminism, psychoanalysis, philosophy, queer theory, and film theory. The methodological approaches are more interpretive, and one is far less likely to use quantitative analysis or work toward scientific objectivity. Drawing on a range of theoretical approaches, critical/cultural scholars explore the connection between media and broader social and cultural power relationships, considering media to be a key agent in contributing to broader systems of meaning. While objectivity is valued in the social scientific approach, the critical/cultural approach is openly political. As Baran and Davis (2012) explain, critical/cultural scholars "start from the assumption that some aspects of the social world are deeply flawed and in need of transformation. Their aim is to gain knowledge of that social world so they can change it" (p. 15). They use textual analysis, ethnography, and theoretical concepts to examine both how people make media within institutions and how they make sense of media messages in their everyday lives.

While social scientists usually see identity as being formed prior to media exposure, independent of it, or somehow distorted by media, critical/cultural scholars are interested in the ways that media construct ideas about subjectivity and sexuality. Rather than seeing media as saying something about a pre-existing group, media is understood as a central site for negotiating the very meanings of identities and for making particular identity categories available in the first place. In this way, media are conceived of as a social institution, similar to families, schools, and religion.

Scholars in the critical/cultural approach work with a model of communication that considers language and practices as flexible and open to interpretation. A key model that has guided this line of inquiry is Stuart Hall's encoding/decoding model (1980). Hall's model generally understands media as a key site for the construction and circulation of dominant discourses about identity categories such as race, gender, and sexuality. Hall's approach looks at the process through which meaning is created in our media system. The encoding process includes all of the practices that go into making a mass media text, from the individual activities of a production team to the broader economic structures of the media industry. The process of making a media text is complex, with many different people coming together to produce the second node, the text. Bearing the traces of a number of competing ideas, most media texts exhibit a degree of fluidity in their meaning, what later media scholar John Fiske called polysemy (1986). The word "text" also is important here, because key to the encoding/decoding model is the understanding that meaning making does not occur until the text actually is "read" (watched, listened to, consumed, etc.) by an audience member, the decoder. In the encoding/decoding model, meaning making is understood as a shared process between the encoders and decoders.

Hall's model does not suggest, though, that decoders are free to take *any* meaning from a text. Rather, both encoders and decoders share a similar set of ground rules

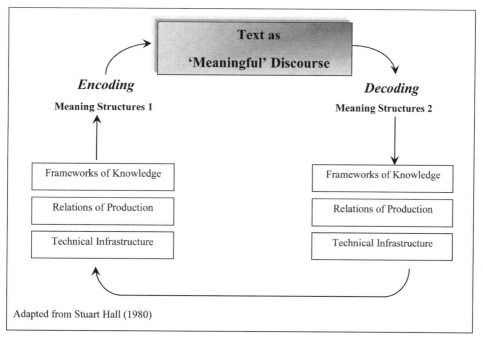

FIGURE 1.5 Encoding decoding
Source: **Adapted from Stuart Hall, 1980, p. 130. Reprinted with permission.**

that are brought together in the "codes" of the text. Codes are signs in a text, ranging from technical aspects, like camera angles, lighting, and sound to cultural signifiers, including clothing props, and dress. Audiences are able to make sense of these codes because they draw on cultural meanings. What is important for many cultural studies scholars is that the activities of audiences in making meaning feed back into the process of cultural creation, as encoders and decoders work together to produce meanings about the world. While those with the power to create media messages have more power, decoders still play a crucial role in the process. For example, Sender's (2003) focus group interviews with straight and gay audiences found a complicated relationship between advertising messages and people's varied interpretations of those messages. The relationship between media and identity in this model differs from the social scientific approach, with media not simply reflecting, accurately or not, some aspect of the real world for viewers, but instead, the media actually circulate meanings about identity categories, which in turn shape how we see ourselves and others. In this view, we do not come with our identities pre-formed, but, rather, we continually negotiate our ideas about others and ourselves in conversation with the media.

Media and Identity in the Digital Age

Our digital age has brought new challenges to thinking about the relationship between media and identity. Both of the approaches described above were developed during the era of mass communication, when television and radio were the central media of daily life. The digitization of media has led to enormous structural changes in the media industry. If both models left room for individuals to actively engage with media, in our digital media environment, the concept of media consumers as *audiences* is beginning to shift. Increasingly, scholars are understanding media consumers as *users*, who do not simply consume media, but also increasingly produce media content that can be cheaply distributed via the Internet and have increasing control over how and when they consume media content. Today, many media scholars, most prominently among them, Henry Jenkins (2012), consider the ways that the interactive nature of new media technologies is changing the relationships between audiences and industries, and even the nature of media texts. One example of media's interactive component is the "It Gets Better" campaign, a series of videos made by celebrities and everyday people, including police officers, military members, and public officials, telling young people who felt isolated and alone that their future as a gay person was a bright one. The videos became instant hits on YouTube, circulated widely through social media channels such as Facebook and Twitter, and even pop music megastar Lady Gaga adopted the language of empowerment for her "little monsters" in a widely circulated ad for Google Chrome. "It Gets Better" demonstrates how our current media landscape gives everyday people the chance to intervene in, create, dispute, and take up media in whole new ways in terms of thinking about identity. In addition, the great variety of practices in the digital media environment generally have weakened the methodological divide between scientific and interpretive approaches, so that increasingly scholars use an array of methods to grasp the complexity of new media practices. This increasingly has meant that scholars who see media as part of the process of constructing identity sometimes turn to the use of quantitative and other scientific methods.

As scholars grounded in the tradition of cultural studies, we generally embrace a constructionist perspective in considering the relationship between media and social identity, and see media as a key site for the construction, negotiation, and reinforcement of identity categories. However, it is key to realize that the scholarship produced by those who see identity as existing prior to the media yields equally important insights into the relationship between media and sexual identities. On the one hand, the distinction between these two approaches is often subtle and even irrelevant. Depending on the topic under consideration, scholars and activists working within these two traditions might come to very similar conclusions. On the other hand, sometimes the difference is of great significance, and the vast theoretical differences between these approaches might create vastly different conclusions about a particular media practice. Whether you are reading ideas in this book as they are informed from a critical/cultural perspective or encountering the wide body of research that draws from the social scientific perspective, we encourage you to think of media as a series of social practices and relationships between texts, audiences/users/consumers, institutions (corporations, production companies, governments), and technologies. The *meaning* of the relationship between sexual identity and media is not fixed in any one of these places, and the relationships between any of these sites are not one-way (though they can be unequal).

▶ CONCLUSION

This chapter has introduced you to a lot of concepts, and you likely have a lot of questions. Key to remember is that we are in a complex historical moment when it comes to GLBTQ political rights, social acceptance, and cultural visibility. We have provided you a beginning point of vocabulary to think and talk about these issues, but language, like the ideas it represents, is unstable and continually in flux. We outlined key perspectives in thinking about sexuality, including an essentialist approach, which treats sexuality as existing prior to culture, making it unchanging and transhistorical, and a social constructionist approach, which points to the role of culture and society in constituting sexual identity categories. In academia, GLBTQ studies have adhered to a social constructionist approach, but as some scholars became increasingly uncomfortable with the identity politics model informing much of the research, they developed queer theory as a way to question the very identity categories being studied. Both approaches have been criticized for homogenizing the GLBTQ community and their experiences, failing to recognize important differences like race, class, and gender. The chapter also introduced you to different ways that media research has conceptualized the relationship between media and identity, with a social scientific approach seeing identities as existing prior to media and studying how media influence the way we think about our own or others' identities and the critical/cultural approach assuming that identities are socially constructed and thus concerned with the role media play in particular identity constructions.

As you read about the relationship between media and sexual identities in the following chapters, there are some key questions to keep in mind, both about the media and about what you read about the media:

1. What central assumptions about sexual identity are made available and/or advanced by/through a particular set of media practices?

2. What role might these media practices play in our understandings of our own and others' sexualities?

3. What theoretical perspectives and central assumptions about media and sexual identities are informing the writings of the academics and popular press writers that you read? (Yes, even scholarship does not get to an essential "truth," but plays a role in the broader process of negotiating the meanings of identity.)

We certainly do not expect you to buy into every argument in this book (or made by your professor or fellow students), but we do encourage you to work in good faith to think about alternative viewpoints. When you finish this book, your opinions may or may not change, but we hope you realize that your way of looking at these issues is only one-way—and you will be making a choice about which view you take on.

▶ REFERENCES

Baran, S.J. & Davis, D.K. (2012). *Mass communication theory: Foundations, ferment and future* (6th ed.). Independence, KY: Cengage Learning.

Berlant, L. & Warner, M. (1998). Sex in public. *Critical Inquiry, 24* (2), 547–566.

Bérubé, A. (2011). How gay stays white and what kind of white it stays. In A. Berube (Ed.), *My desire for history: Essays in gay, community and labor history* (pp. 202–230). Chapel Hill, NC: University of North Carolina Press.

Blank, H. (2012). *Straight: The surprisingly short history of heterosexuality*. Boston, MA: Beacon Press.

Butler, J. (1990). *Gender trouble: Feminism and the subversion of identity*. New York, NY: Routledge.

Calzo, J. & Ward, M. (2009). Media exposure and viewers' attitudes toward homosexuality: Evidence for mainstreaming or resonance? *Journal of Broadcasting & Electronic Media, 53*, 280–299.

Crenshaw, K. (1989). Demarginalizing the intersection of race and sex: A black feminist critique of antidiscrimination doctrine, feminist theory, and antiracist politics. *University of Chicago Legal Forum*, 139–167.

Crenshaw, K. (1991). Mapping the margins: Intersectionality, identity politics, and violence against women of color. *Stanford Law Review, 43*, 1241–1279.

Edison Research (2010). *The American youth study 2010*. Somerville, NJ: Edison Research.

Fiske, J. (1986). Television polysemy and popularity. *Critical Studies in Mass Communication, 3* (4), 391–408.

Foucault, M. (1990). *The history of sexuality, volume 1: An introduction* (R. Hurley, Trans.). New York: Viking. (Original work published 1978.)

Foucault, M. (1990). *The history of sexuality, volume 2: The use of pleasure* (R. Hurley, Trans.). New York: Viking. (Original work published 1985.)

Foucault, M. (1990). *The history of sexuality, volume 3: The care of the self* (R. Hurley, Trans.). New York: Viking. (Original work published 1986.)

Friedman, E. (2011, December 12). Gay veteran steals the show at Romney endorsement event. *Abcnews*. Retrieved from http://abcnews.go.com/blogs/politics/2011/12/gay-veteran-steals-the-show-at-romneyendorsement-event.

Goltz, D. (2010). *Queer temporalities in gay male representation*. New York, NY: Routledge.

Greenberg, D. (1990). *The construction of homosexuality*. Chicago, IL: University of Chicago Press.

Hall, S. (1980). Encoding/Decoding. In S. Hall, D. Hobson, A. Lowe, & P. Willis (Eds.), *Culture, media, language* (pp. 128–138). London: Hutchinson.

Harmon, C. [Producer]. (2012, May 6). *Meet the press* [Television broadcast]. New York, NY: National Broadcasting Company.

Howe, R.G. (1994). *Homosexuality in America: Exposing the myths*. Tupelo, MS: The American Family Association.

Jenkins, H. (2008). *Convergence culture: Where old and new media collide*. New York, NY: NYU Press.

Johnson, E.P. (2005). "Quare" studies or (almost) everything I know about queer studies I learned from my grandmother. In E.P. Johnson & M.G. Henderson (Eds.), *Black queer studies* (pp. 124–157). Durham, NC: Duke University Press.

Kaiser Family Foundation (2010). *Generation M2: Media in the lives of 8- to 18- year-olds*. Menlo Park, CA: Henry J. Kaiser Family Foundation.

Katz, J.N. (2007). *The invention of heterosexuality*. Chicago, IL: University of Chicago Press.

Kimmel, M. (2011). *The gendered society* (4th ed.). New York, NY: Oxford University Press.

Kohnen, M.E.S. (2014). Queer visibility, sexuality, and race in American film and television: Screening the closet. Unpublished manuscript, Department of Media, Culture, Communication, New York University Steinhardt, New York, NY.

McQuail, D. (2010). *McQuail's mass communication theory* (6th ed.). Thousand Oaks, CA: Sage Publications.

National Coalition of Anti-Violence Programs. (2013). *Lesbian, gay, bisexual, transgender, queer and HIV-affected hate violence*. New York, NY: New York City Gay and Lesbian Anti-Violence Project, Inc.

Pew Research Center (2010). *Generations 2010*. Washington, DC: Pew Research Center.

Plante, R.F. (2006). *Sexualities in context: A social perspective*. Boulder, CO: Westview.

Rich, A.C. (1980). *Compulsory heterosexuality and lesbian existence*. London, UK: Onlywomen Press Ltd.

Rochlin, M. (1982). The heterosexual questionnaire. *Peace Newsletter, 488*, 14.

Rubin, G.S. (1993). Thinking sex: Notes for a radical theory of politics of sexuality. In H. Abelove, M. A. Barale, & D. Halperin (Eds.), *The Lesbian and gay studies reader* (p. 3–44). New York, NY: Routledge.

Rubin, G. (1999). Thinking sex: Notes for a radical theory of politics of sexuality (2nd ed.). In R. Parker, & P. Aggleton (Eds.), *Culture, society, sexuality* (pp. 150–187). New York, NY: Routledge.

Saucier, J. & Caron, S. (2008). An investigation of content and media images in gay men's magazines. *Journal of Homosexuality, 55*, 504–523.

Seidman, R. (2011, September 20). Monday broadcast final ratings: "Two and a half men," "2 broke girls," DTWS adjusted up; "Castle" adjusted down. Retrieved from http://tvbythenumbers. zap2it.com/2011/09/20/monday-broadcast-final-ratings-two-and-a-half-men-2-broke-girls-dwts-adjusted-up-castle-adjusted-down/104333.

Seidman, S. (1995). Deconstructing queer theory or the under-theorization of the social and the ethical. In L. Nicholson (Ed.), *Social postmodernism: Beyond identity politics* (pp. 116–141). Cambridge, UK: Cambridge University Press

Seidman, S. (2003). *The social construction of sexuality*. New York, NY: W.W. Norton & Company, Inc.

Sender, K. (2003). Selling subjectivities: Audiences respond to gay window advertising. In G. Dines & J. Humez (Eds.), *Gender, race and class in media* (2nd ed.) (pp. 302–313). Thousand Oaks, CA: Sage.

Stein, E. (1999). *The mismeasure of desire: The science, theory and ethics of sexual orientation*. New York, NY: Oxford University Press.

Weeks, J. (2011). *Languages of sexuality*. Abingdon, UK: Routledge.

Historical Context

The first-known use of the term "homosexual" was in 1869, when it appeared in a German pamphlet advocating the repeal of sodomy laws. A century and a half later, all branches of the government are wrestling with GLBTQ-related issues, churches are feeling growing pressure to make room in their pews for GLBTQ congregants, schools are revisiting policies in light of increasingly visible GLBTQ students, and media outlets are courting niche GLBTQ audiences. No single narrative can explain neatly how we have moved from point A to point B over the past 150 years, nor should it. After all, history is a messy business, and the writing of it always is partial and incomplete. Therefore, this chapter is not, nor could it ever be, a comprehensive history of sexuality and its representation in the media. It is just one version of events, and it is limited to developments mostly in America from the 1860s through the 1980s, focusing on three key areas: how sexual practices coalesced into sexual identities, how people with non-normative sexual identities have come together to promote social change, and how media representations of GLBTQ people have changed over time. Such historical context helps explain when and how our contemporary framework for understanding sexuality emerged and helps to situate key GLBTQ debates in which the United States currently is embroiled. Additionally, it explains the complex relationship between media and shifting cultural understandings of GLBTQ identities, which has culminated in our present era of GLBTQ visibility.

As you attempt to digest the century and a half of information boiled down in the following pages, three key themes should emerge. First, while gay, lesbian, bisexual, and transgender often are condensed into a single GLBT label, their histories have not necessarily been shared. Once sexuality and gender emerged as distinct identity labels, lesbian, gay, bisexual, and transgender advocates sometimes united together in their struggles for recognition and rights, and at other times they found themselves facing their own unique struggles. Additionally, even those united by a single label have not shared a single history, as other factors like race, class, and gender played important roles in their lived realities. A second theme in the history written here is a rejection of the popular myth of progress that social groups always are marching forward until they realize full equality. Change is not that linear. As Meem, Gibson, and Alexander (2010) remind us, "popular attitudes about sexuality evolve inconsistently based on the realities of particular moments in time" (p. 70). Factors as varied as economic climate, national security, and even biomedical anxieties and advances all have played a role in shifting levels of acceptance toward GLBTQ people over the past 150 years. Finally, just as history itself cannot be understood through a progress narrative, neither can the relationship between emerging GLBTQ identities, politics, and media representations.

As you read this history of social change, make a note of the language used to describe what today we would refer to as gay, lesbian, bisexual, and transgender people. As indicated in the previous chapter, identity labels are tied to particular ways of thinking about sexuality at particular historical moments. We have done our best to use the language most appropriate to each time period that we describe. While some academics choose to apply our current GLBT labels historically, we have chosen not to, because we believe it is important to preserve and differentiate between historically specific understandings of sexuality and gender. (Textbox 2.1 introduces Google's Ngram Viewer as a tool for tracing changes in language use over time.)

BOX 2.1   Changing Language and Shifting Identities

As this chapter illustrates, the way that people have made sense of sexuality has changed over time. In the process, new words have been introduced or existing words have taken on new meanings. Google's Ngram Viewer (https://books.google.com/ngrams) provides a way to take a "snapshot" of what topics are important at different moments over the past 500 years and to consider how language use has changed over time. An *n*-gram is a letter combination, word, or phrase, and Ngram Viewer searches for *n*-grams of the user's choosing in over five million books published between 1500 and 2008 that have been digitized by Google. Only matches found in at least 40 books are included in the database.

Using the Ngram Viewer, search for some of the terms we first introduced you to in Chapter 1: "heterosexual," "homosexual," "gay," "lesbian," "pansexual," "asexual," "straight," "transgender," "transexual" (and "transsexual"), "transvestite," "trans*", "ze" and "hir," "cisgender," "queer," "genderqueer," and "intersex." Consider the following questions:

1. When do these terms begin appearing in books?
2. When do they reach their height of popularity?
3. Do their meanings change over time? If so, when?
4. Does the use of terms correspond with the history of sexual identities in this chapter?
5. How might your results be different if the Ngram Viewer also included magazines, newspaper, or academic journals? (To find out, repeat your search in your own library's databases, like "Newspaper Source" or "American Periodical Series On-line.")

▶ EMERGING IDENTITIES: 1860S–1930S

Human beings have engaged in a wide variety of sexual behaviors for millennia; however, how we understand these behaviors has changed over time and place. As explained in the previous chapter, this is the basic assumption of a social constructionist view of sexuality. This is a good time to stop and think about what that actually means. It means that questions like, "Were there 'gay' people 2000 years ago?" are about as nonsensical as asking, "Were there 'straight' people 2000 years ago?" The answer is: not in the way we make sense of sexuality today. These are identity labels that did not exist thousands of years ago; therefore, regardless of what sexual behaviors people may have engaged in, they did not have the same frame of reference that we have today to make sense of those behaviors and to identify themselves as a distinct group because of them. While there are some who insist that these modern labels can be imposed retroactively on historical figures, many scholars caution against this, arguing that we should not use contemporary understandings of sexuality as an identity to understand how persons from the past thought of themselves (Meem et al., 2010).

For many centuries, Christianity-based law systems across the West have included laws against certain types of sexual *behavior*, but have not tied those laws to an *identity*. The English laws against buggery, the term used to describe sodomy either between two men or a man and a woman, traveled across the globe with the system of British Impe-rialism. Yet, while these laws often imposed severe consequences for sodomy between men, they focused on the sex act rather than the person. The emergence of sexuality as a marker of identity was a complicated process. Here, we will focus on two factors that, beginning in the late 19th Century in the United States and broader Western world, contributed to the construction of sexual identity: developments in medical science and changing socio-economic conditions. Together, changes in these two spheres of activity helped create the thoroughly modern idea of "homosexual" and "heterosexual" *identities* in Western culture. While these identities were not overtly named in the media at the time, they still were coded by particular mannerisms and behaviors.

Scientific Interest in Sexuality

Beginning in the mid-19th Century, it became increasingly possible for Americans to imagine organizing their identities and lives around sex outside the confines of mar-riage and procreation. This was the result of population shifts related to economic changes, which will be discussed in the next section. As popular conceptions of sex were changing, the medical community, like other social institutions, began paying increas-ing attention to people's sexual behaviors and feelings—both same-sex and mixed-sex desires. Sexuality provided a new area for medical science to focus its attention on categorizing bodies. At the same time, people began putting increased faith in medical "experts" to uncover some essential truth assumed to be contained within those bodies. The field of sexology was born, and it played a significant role in the way we think about sexuality still today.

Sexology grew out of research primarily based in Europe, as medical practitio-ners sought to understand the diversity of sexual activities. In keeping with scientific practice, sexologists sought to "classify" people based on their sexual attractions and behaviors, contributing to the idea that sexual practices somehow "define" who we are. How sexologists classified people varied. For many of them, though, sexuality and gen-der were inseparable. The term "invert" became popular for describing a person who expressed same-sex desire, used to indicate both a sexual attraction that countered the norm as well as gender appearances and behaviors that seemed more appropriate for the opposite gender. (Textbox 2.2 explores key similarities in 19th Century comparative anatomy research of race and sexuality.) In 1869, German-born Hungarian writer and sex-law reformer Karl Maria Kertbeny first used the term "homosexual" to describe same-sex erotic acts and "heterosexual" to describe erotic acts between a man and a woman (Katz, 2007). German psychiatrist Richard von Krafft-Ebing carried these terms into the medical community in his publication *Pyschopathia Sexualis*, which as the title suggests was a detailed description of sexual psychopathologies. His original edition, published in Germany in 1886, included a discussion of "homo-sexuality." "Hetero-sexuality" appeared three years later in his fourth edition (Katz, 2007). In America, the first known use of these terms was by Dr. James Kiernan, an American psychologist, who published an 1892 medical journal article on sexual perversion. Kiernan defined heterosexuality as non-procreative sexual acts between a man and a woman. Because procreation, rather than pleasure, long had served as the medical criteria of a normal sex drive, Kiernan's concept of heterosexuality was presented as sexual perversion. Comparatively, for Kiernan, homosexuality had little to do with sexual deviancy. Rather, drawing on popular assumptions about the link between biological sex, sexual attraction, and gender roles, he defined homosexuality as gender inversion. While sexologists generally conceived of homosexuality as abnormal, some also saw it as a congenital condition and, therefore, argued it should not be considered a crime. In fact, Krafft-Ebing's *Psychopathia Sexualis* (1886) often was used as a legal tool in court cases involving charges of sexual perversion. Some doctors even became social activists, working to decriminalize homosexuality and suggesting this newly defined group have full access to social rights (Meem et al., 2010).

A shift in medical thinking about sexuality in the early 1900s, particularly in the United States, led to less sympathetic understandings of homosexuals. Psychiatrists increasingly recognized the role of pleasure in people's sex drives, and male-female desire (rather than procreative potential) served as the norm in this new conception of sexuality. Same-sex desire (regardless of how pleasurable) was relegated to the realm of abnormal pathology. Whereas European sexologists had drawn on physiology to consider whether homosexuality and non-normative gender expressions could result from variations in nature, American psychiatrists increasingly drew on psychoanalysis and treated homosexuality and gender variance as illnesses and those who "suffered" from them as patients needing to be cured.

BOX 2.2   Scientific Research on Sexuality and Race

Nineteenth Century doctors and scientists assumed a connection between same-sex attraction and non-normative gender expression, and, when they began to search for a cause for same-sex attraction, their cultural assumptions influenced their research. Sexologists relied upon the scientific logic and methods from research on the comparative anatomy of races that was popular in the late 19th Century. Somerville (2000) examines the similarities in race-based and sexuality-based

(Continued)

research of the time in her book *Queering the Color Line: Race and the Invention of Homosexuality in American Culture.*

Just as sexuality is a social construct, so, too, is race. Let us unpack what that means. As we are learning in this chapter, how we have made sense of sexual difference has changed across time and cultures. The same thing is true of racial differences. How cultures make sense of the physical differences that reflect the geographic diversity of people's ancestors (e.g., skin pigmentation, hair type, eye shape) also is not fixed. For example, in the 1800s America, dark-skinned Italians and eastern European Jews were not considered "white" (Rubin, 2004). In fact, at that time, pre-Darwinian scientists debated over whether or not people of different races even descended from common ancestors (Somerville, 2000). These scientific debates did not exist in a social vacuum, but instead reflected social debates about slavery in the United States at the time. Scientists sought to locate the social inequalities between blacks and whites in suspected biological differences between bodies. Nineteenth-Century American paleontologist Edward Drinker Cope espoused such biological determinist beliefs: "Every peculiarity of the body has probably some corresponding significance in the mind, and the causes of the former are the remoter causes of the latter" (quoted in Somerville, 2000, p. 23).

Sexologists who sought to better understand the emerging "invert" from all points of scientific consideration assumed similar biological determinist logic. Somerville (2000) found a common theme in the writings of influential sexologists of the time. She explains,

> Although the specific sites of anatomical inspection (hymen, clitoris, labia, vagina) differed in various sexological texts, the underlying theory remained constant: women's genitalia and reproductive anatomy held a valuable and presumably visual key to ranking bodies according to norms of sexuality.
>
> (p. 27)

Just as research on black bodies had presumed white bodies to be the norm against which they were to be measured, research on inverts compared their bodies to the normalized heterosexual body.

Somerville (2000) found a key similarity in the conclusions of both sexologists and researchers of comparative anatomy of races with regard to women's sexual anatomy. Lesbians were reported to have "an abnormally prominent clitoris" (p. 27). In one medical journal article, the researcher reported that this finding was "particularly so in colored women." This finding also had appeared in an earlier article by a gynecologist studying differences between the genitalia of black and white women: "in his examinations, he had perceived a distinction between the 'free' clitoris of 'negresses' and the 'imprisonment' of the clitoris of the 'Aryan American woman' " (p. 27). As Somerville points out, these findings reflected social norms of femininity. At a time when white women were to be associated with purity and chasteness, bodies that did not adhere to this norm, because of race and/or sexual attraction, were perceived as more sexually inclined, and, hence, less feminine. Comparative anatomists sought to make visible this presumed difference in "abnormal" bodies, i.e., black and/or lesbian bodies.

It is easy to see how 19th Century science reflected cultural beliefs of the time; however, it can be more difficult to recognize cultural biases found in science in our current time. Read Michael Abrams' (2007) *Discover Magazine* article on research looking for a biological basis for sexual orientation (http://discovermagazine.com/2007/jun/born-gay). Answer the following questions:

1. How do the researchers determine the sexual orientation of their research subjects? Given what you read in Chapter 1, how might sexuality be more complicated than they allow?
2. Do any of the researchers in the article have a political agenda? How might their agenda influence their research?
3. Why is female sexuality rarely the focus of scientific research? How might this discrepancy reflect cultural assumptions?

Changing Socio-Economic Conditions

At the same time that medical discourses were categorizing and labeling people based on their sexual behaviors, socio-economic conditions for the first time allowed people to organize their lives in a way in which same-sex desire would emerge as a marker of personal identity. Prior to the mid-19th Century, the United States operated on an agrarian system in which family and reproduction were vital to survival. Families functioned as an economic unit, and the more children in that family, the more labor resources available to that unit. However, in the second half of the 1800s, the growth of capitalism in the United States changed that economic familial unit for many. For the first time, individuals—primarily men—were able to earn wages on their own by hiring out their labor. The changing economic landscape also involved shifts in population, away from small, rural communities to large urban centers, in which people might live away from their families and live among strangers. These changes allowed people to more easily separate sexuality from marriage and reproduction (D'Emilio, 1998). Additionally, the anonymity afforded by big-city living also reduced the risk that people who expressed same-sex desires would be "found out" and subjected to legal penalties. Although subcultural communities of men engaged in same-sex erotic behavior emerged in an increasingly urbanized England by the early 18th Century (McIntosh, 1968), it was not until industrialized, capitalist conditions prevailed in the United States that such subcultures developed here. For instance, Chauncey (1994) describes how New York gay subculture emerged by the 1890s, as gay spaces were carved out in rooming houses, cafeterias, and even entire neighborhood enclaves, like in Greenwich Village and Harlem.

However, this emerging urban gay subculture was not equally accessible to all. Chauncey (1994) notes that New York remained a segregated city, in which Harlem, marked by its free-spirited Bohemian sensibility, was the only place in which black men could congregate in commercial spaces. It was not until the early 20th Century that similar urban lesbian subcultures began to emerge, as women increasingly became independent wage earners, thus freeing themselves from familial constraints (Meem et al., 2010). However, some women with the privilege of whiteness and education did live in same-sex couplings known as "Boston marriages" in the mid-1800s. Such relationships were allowed at the time because of romantic notions of female friendship as enduring and asexual.

While the changing economic system leading up to the 1920s opened up spaces in which people could form communities and identities based on their sexual attractions, the cultural climate during the Great Depression worked to close off these new expressions of sexual identity. McGarry and Wasserman (1998) note,

> The Depression era saw a general quieting of urban nightlife, and a growing sense that the excesses of the twenties—cultural as well as economic—had caused the Great Depression. Homosexuality stood out as an easy target for those wanting to punish "excess." Suddenly, what was quietly tolerated in the 1920s become "immoral and illegal" by the mid-1930s.
>
> (p. 72)

Gay communities did not disappear altogether, but became more discreet, organizing around quiet male bars and high-end hotels across the country. Notably, these were spaces that were accessible only to middle- and upper-class white men at the time.

Media Images of an "Identity"

As social changes allowed more people to define themselves independent of traditional ties, and as medical science turned to making sense of difference, developing modern mass media reflected these cultural assumptions. As the common theory of inversion held, representations of "inverts" by and large relied on gender reversals to signify sexual "inversion." For example, Radclyffe Hall's famous 1928 novel, *The Well of Loneliness*, told the tale of "invert" woman Stephen Gordon, marked by her rejection of femininity. The press developed a number of devices to report on homosexuality, but primarily through reference to the reversal of gender norms. In general, the mass media tended to focus more on *behaviors* it found deviant.

For example, newspapers and magazines began to recognize the presence of cross-dressing behaviors by the latter years of the 19th Century. However, stories about such behaviors either marked it as deviant, covering crimes involving cross dressers, or as a source of humor, making fun of gender inversion. News stories about female cross dressers often diminished the sometimes political nature of such actions and almost always avoided issues of sexuality (see Textbox 2.3). Much like the masculine woman, the feminine man primarily was made sense of through his deviance, either represented for a laugh at his expense in newspaper and magazine cartoons, or as a source of social deviance in crime reports. As gay communities became more visible in large cities, such as New York City, by the 1920s and 1930s, newspapers began to report on this visibility, though not often in positive terms. For example, as drag balls became increasingly

 BOX 2.3   Framing of 19th Century Female-to-Male Cross Dressers

In 1863, San Francisco joined the growing list of cities to ban cross dressing in public. People who violated this ordinance "should be guilty of a misdemeanor, and on conviction, shall pay a fine not exceeding five hundred dollars" (quoted in Stryker, 2008, p. 32). It was not uncommon for newspapers to include coverage of people's violation of the law. These news accounts have been the focus of researchers seeking to understand how cross dressing was understood during the time period and how these news stories may have influenced people's attitudes about gender and sexuality.

One way that communication scholars consider the power of media texts is by applying the concept of framing. As Entman (1993) explains,

To frame is to *select some aspects of a perceived reality and make them more salient in a communicating text, in such a way as to promote a particular problem definition, causal interpretation, moral evaluation, and/or treatment recommendation for the item described.*

(p. 52, emphasis in original)

(Continued)

FIGURE 2.1 Milton Matson
Source: The Call, San Francisco, January 28, 1895.

When journalists make decisions about which elements of a story to include and how to tell that story (e.g., images, word choice, metaphorical language, narrative devices), they contribute unconsciously to a particular version of the telling of events—oftentimes one that matches their own worldview.

Applying the concept of framing to San Francisco newspapers of the 1800s, Sears (2006) examined newspaper coverage of three high-profile cases of women wearing men's clothing, including Milton Matson (see Figure 2.1). In analyzing news stories, she asked three key questions: "What was the social content of the stories that reporters narrated?" "What was the social message of these stories?" "What alternative stories of cross-dressing emerged in this press coverage?" (p. 3). Sears ultimately found that "In the 19th century San Francisco press, reporters characterized women's cross-dressing as ludicrous, dangerous, and fraudulent, crafting 'sensational' stories about deviant individuals rather than meaningful social debate" (p. 18). Sears suggests that such coverage reflected dominant ideologies about gender and sexuality at the time. She also points out that newspapers' framing of cross dressers potentially influenced the way people made sense of these events and issues. Duggan (1993) found that the framing of news stories about cross dressers even had an impact on scientific discourses of the time. She pointed to the example of sexologists drawing from newspaper accounts of a high-profile case in 1892 that involved a female-to-male cross-dressing murder defendant to advance emerging theories about "female sexual inverts."

Analyzing the way that issues related to sexuality are framed by the media often offers insights into cultural assumptions drawn upon by journalists as well as their potential influence if audiences adopt these same frames of reference. Pick a current GLBTQ issue and consider how it has been framed by news coverage. Look for clues by considering:

1. What images are used? What is depicted in the images? What meaning do they convey?
2. What language is used to describe the issue and/or people involved? What connotation does the language carry? Are metaphors or similes used? If so, what imagery do they invoke?
3. Who is allowed to speak in the story? Whose voices are given the most weight? Which voices are treated as experts? Are any voices treated dismissively?
4. How is the issue explained? Is anyone to blame? Is it treated as a problem? Are solutions proposed? What is the social significance of the issue?
5. What's missing from the story? How might the story have been told differently? What other voices could have been included? What other word choices could have been made? How would these things have altered the story?

pubic events in New York City by the 1930s, newspapers reported on the events as a burden to "normal passers-by" (Chauncey, 1994).

Cultural understandings of male gender inversion as a framework for comprehending homosexual desire led to the wide circulation of "the sissy" as a stock figure, particularly in vaudeville, the live variety shows popular in the 1880s through the 1920s. This character type carried over into silent and sound cinema, and even radio. The sissy was marked by his adoption of feminine norms, including body carriage, high-pitched voice, excessive vanity and attention to appearance, obsession with clothes, overemotionality, and bracing wit. Played for laughs, this characterization of the effeminate male frequently signified sexual inversion or perversion without actually sexualizing the character. The sissy suggested homosexuality rather than overtly representing it. An impending crackdown on questionable content in film would guarantee that homosexuality would only be hinted at for the following three decades.

Movies and then radio increasingly raised alarm for both Catholic and Protestant moral-reform groups around the nation, and both the film and radio industries faced public and regulatory pressure to avoid content considered either too violent or too sexual. Making over Hollywood's image as morally corrupt became a primary task for the newly founded Motion Picture Producers and Distributors of America (MPPDA). In an attempt to avoid government censorship, the MPPDA, headed by former United

States Postmaster General Will Hays, adopted a code of self-censorship in 1930. The Hays Code, which was not enforced until the mid-1930s, spelled out explicit rules regarding what moral reformers of the era considered dangerous content, especially crime and sex. The category of sex included specific rules for the portrayal of adultery and passion. For instance, the code stated, "Excessive and lustful kissing, lustful embraces, suggestive postures and gestures, are not to be shown" (Doherty, 1999, p, 363). Included in this list was a simple directive, "4. SEX PERVERSION or an inference is forbidden" (p. 363). The euphemism was clear: any reference to homosexuality was prohibited.

Unlike film, radio was regulated directly by the government through the injunction that the newly developing mass medium should serve the "public interest." Radio's direct reception into American households led to great anxiety over the kinds of content radio would air, and while there was no direct rule against representing forms of "sex" perversion, sexuality, in general, was not considered appropriate content for the radio. However, some scholars have examined the role that "swish" routines, drawing on vaudeville traditions, played in popular radio comedies (Doty, 1993). "Going swish" was a form of comic relief secured by the knowledge that the "swish" moment was a temporary inversion by a safely heterosexual man. One of the most memorable examples is Frank Nelson's depiction of the department store "floorwalker" on the popular radio comedy *The Jack Benny Program* (1950–1965). Other radio shows featured ostensibly gay male characters, such as the soap opera *Myrt and Marge* (1932–1946).

From their earliest media representations, characters that portrayed gender inversion in radio and film were marginalized and reduced to the narrowest set of conventions. For this reason, a strong negative association built between gender inversion and sexuality has left a legacy that continues to shape contemporary debates about sexual identity and visibility.

▶ AN EMERGING MOVEMENT: 1940S–1950S

As individuals, moralists, scientists, police forces, governments, etc. struggled over the meaning of homosexuality, by mid-century this newly constructed identity grew into the basis for a movement. World War II and its aftermath offered new opportunities for homosexuals to connect in a sense of shared identity, and medical advances contributed to the construction of a transsexual identity unique from homosexuality. However, as non-normative sexual and gender identities became more visible, homosexuals and transsexuals endured repeated demonization and intolerance. In this significant historical moment in which America was struggling to define freedom, democracy, and inclusion, disenfranchised groups began organizing themselves around their collective struggles. This marked the beginning of the homophile movement, a quest for recognition and tolerance for gays and lesbians.

Shared Identity and Shared Persecution

World War II ushered in a period of both increased opportunities for gay and lesbian persons, as well as increased surveillance and regulation. New employment opportunities for women that emerged in the World War II economy afforded women more financial and social independence, allowing them to define their identities beyond the primary roles of mother and/or homemaker. This new-found freedom included socializing in many female-only social situations. As McGarry and Wasserman (1998) note, the war "provided a protective covering" for lesbians, "who were already living women-centered lives" and often challenging traditional gender norms (p. 77). Similarly, men and women in the military found themselves frequently, if not exclusively, serving with members of the same sex. This made it easier for gay men and lesbians to identify others with an interest in same-sex intimacy. In particular, for lesbians, military service was attractive, as gender roles were less prescriptive than they were in the broader society.

Given the increased medical attention to sexuality and related cultural discourses surrounding homosexuality, government and military leaders were acutely aware and fearful of the potential for same-sex intimacy in military service. Beginning in the 1940s, the military began prohibiting the enlistment of gay men and lesbians in the military and issued psychiatric discharges to those suspected of being homosexual. They became known as "blue discharges" because of the color of the paper on which they were printed. Prior to this time, no formal policy prohibiting gays and lesbians serving in the U.S. military existed. From its beginning, the military ban on gays and lesbians was based on the premise that gay service members could not restrain themselves sexually and were therefore a threat to their heterosexual counterparts and ultimately a danger to military objectives.

Nonetheless, World War II provided many gays and lesbians the opportunity to connect with others who shared in common same-sex attraction. These new connections gave some gays and lesbians a sense that they were not isolated individuals and were instead part of a larger community of people with similar sexual identities. After the war, many settled in port cities with existing gay subcultures in order to continue that sense of belonging that they had discovered during the war. Some even began drawing connections between the discrimination they faced and discrimination faced by African-Americans and Jews (McGarry & Wassermann, 1998).

By the 1950s, gays and lesbians were under increasing legal persecution. Local, state, and federal legislators all passed laws restricting the legal rights of gay people. Anti-communist crusader Joseph McCarthy saw homosexuals as a potential threat to the security of a Cold War America. McCarthy argued that they were susceptible to blackmail, and a Congressional subcommittee was convened to address the "problem of homosexuals and other sex perverts" in government employment (Williams & Retter, 2003, p. 65). The language of the resulting document is steeped in moral judgments, reflecting psychiatric and cultural discourses of the time:

> Aside from the criminality and immorality involved in sex perversion such behavior is so contrary to the normal accepted standards of social behavior that persons who engage in such activity are looked upon as outcasts by society generally. . . . Those who engage in overt acts of perversion lack the emotional stability of normal persons. In addition there is an abundance of evidence to sustain the conclusion that indulgence in acts of sex perversion weakens the moral fiber of an individual to a degree that he is not suitable for a position of responsibility. . . . These perverts will frequently attempt to entice normal individuals to engage in perverted practices. . . . One homosexual can pollute a Government office.
>
> (p. 65–66)

Convinced by these arguments, President Dwight D. Eisenhower signed Executive Order 10450, which changed the criteria for determining security risks. Rather than limiting focus to a person's political connections, the new law allowed people's personal character to be considered. Homosexuality ostensibly called into question a person's entire character, making him or her unsuitable for federal employment. After Executive Order 10450 became law, gays and lesbians were fired from federal jobs at a rate eight times higher than prior to 1950 (McGarry & Wasserman, 1998). The attention to ferreting out gays and lesbians from workplaces extended beyond the federal government, as private companies sometimes followed suit in their employment practices. State and local laws drawn up in this cultural climate of prejudice banned bars and restaurants from serving gays and lesbians, and local police forces increasingly harassed gay citizens, sometimes arresting dozens in a single night.

Press coverage of homosexuality in the 1940s and 1950s reflected and perpetuated cultural fears of the time. Previously, homosexuality was almost never overtly named in newspapers and magazines. Instead, coverage was coded in language of sex crimes, indecent acts, deviance, or illness, with readers encouraged to read between the lines. This changed when the military began excluding homosexuals from service and newspapers turned to psychologists to make sense of homosexuality as a mental illness making a person unfit for military service (Alwood, 1996). Such coverage continued in the early 1950s, as major newspapers and magazines followed

McCarthy's lead, calling into question the moral character of homosexuals. Reporters and editors routinely used the derogatory label of "pervert" to describe homosexuals, even occasionally using equally offensive terms like "'deviates,' 'homos,' 'degenerates,' 'queers,' [and] 'fairies'" (Streitmatter, 2009, p. 15). It also was not uncommon for columnists to compare homosexuals to rapists and pedophiles. Such derisive news coverage mostly was reserved for gay men. Lesbians, whose sexuality was presumably less threatening to a patriarchal system, remained largely invisible in news coverage.

Homosexual Voices

In this climate of government and press persecution following World War II, some of the first groups to coalesce around gay rights began to emerge. These organizations formed the beginning of the homophile movement, which focused on the legitimation of gay people. In 1951, Harry Hay and a small group of other gay men founded the Mattachine Society, named after a French, male, medieval-Renaissance troupe that performed public dances and rituals in masks as protests against oppression (Katz, 1976). Hay, a communist, initially forwarded the idea that homosexuals were a minority group, distinct from the mainstream population. Drawing on Marxist thinking, Hay sought to move homosexuals from a "class 'in itself'" to a "class 'for itself.'" As historian John D'Emilio (1998) explains, the distinction is that the latter recognizes its common interests and is thereby able to collectively fight for its own rights. Therefore, the initial goal of the Mattachine Society was to educate homosexuals that they comprised "a social minority imprisoned within a dominant culture" (p. 65). At first, the activist group primarily operated in secrecy, using the underground networks of gay subcultures to draw attention to police harassment and legal discrimination against homosexuals. However, as the 1950s progressed, some members questioned the founders' radical approach and instead suggested homosexuals should merely "educate" heterosexuals to recognize homophiles as non-threatening people seeking societal acceptance. This meant rejecting the idea that homosexuals constituted a minority different from heterosexuals. As Marilyn Rieger argued at a Mattachine Society convention in 1952, "We know we are the same. . . no different than anyone else. Our only difference is an unimportant one to the heterosexual society *unless we make it important*" (quoted in D'Emilio, 1998, p. 43, emphasis in original). Such a critique of the minority group concept reflected a desire by some homosexuals to emphasize their ability to assimilate into existing heterosexual culture.

The Daughters of Bilitis (D.O.B.), the first lesbian rights organization in the United States, followed similar assimilationist strategies. The group was begun in San Francisco in 1955 by a small group of women who sought to bring together lesbians who might otherwise find themselves isolated from one another. The group drew its

FIGURE 2.2 Lesbian activist Barbara Gittings at the first homosexual rights
demonstration, Philadelphia, July 4, 1965
Source: Greta Schiller and Robert Rosenberg, 1984, *Before Stonewall: The
Making of a Gay and Lesbian Community*, photo © David Whitten/Photofest.

name from a 19th Century collection of erotic poems titled "Songs of Bilitis." This
name allowed for secrecy, with some members using the cover of a "poetry group."
The group's founders felt an exclusively female organization was necessary because
male-dominated homophile groups did not recognize what D'Emilio (1998) describes

as lesbians' "dual identity—as homosexuals and as women" (p. 93). Lesbians faced their own unique financial struggles related to gender inequalities in employment, and many lesbians also sought support in rearing children or in leaving heterosexual marriages. In addition to providing social support for its members, D.O.B. saw education as key to reducing the broader culture's hostility toward homosexual women and men. Groups like the Mattachine Society, Daughters of Bilitis, and other homophile organizations succeeded in creating social networks of homosexuals who sought to change society's attitudes about them in order to lessen their mistreatment.

As those active in the homophile movement sought to connect with each other and to gain public recognition, they increasingly turned to media to draw attention to issues facing gays and lesbians. However, their attempts to gain publicity largely went ignored by mainstream newspapers, radio, and television. As a result, members of emerging organizations, including the Mattachine Society and Daughters of Bilitis, took matters into their own hands. In 1953, five gay men who had grown impatient with the leveraged approach of the Mattachine Society began publishing a pamphlet-sized magazine called *ONE*. This was not the first gay-targeted print publication. Six years earlier, Lisa Ben, a self-identified lesbian, used her typewriter at her job at RKO Pictures to write nine editions of *Vice Versa*, giving it the tagline of "America's Gayest Magazine." Each limited-copy publication was a dozen or so stapled-together pages that introduced readers to books, motion pictures, plays, and songs with lesbian themes and provided a forum for other lesbians to write in about their own experiences. Like *Vice Versa*, the magazine *ONE* sought to provide a forum for gay voices, but it differed from *Vice Versa* in its more radical bent, its professional presentation, and its level of distribution. After one year in publication, *ONE* reached 16,000 national readers, mostly through mail subscriptions. In 1955, Mattachine Society followed with its own publication, *Mattachine Review*, a newsletter that linked its growing chapters around the country. Desiring a lesbian voice, Daughters of Bilitis began distributing *The Ladder* in 1956 (Gross, 2001; Streitmatter, 1995).

These early publications marked the beginning of an alternative gay press. For the first time, gays and lesbians were able to control their own messages, telling stories of their mistreatment by police, government, and private industries without having their versions of events controlled by heterosexual reporters and editors. As Streitmatter (1995) suggests, these publications'

> most important accomplishment was that the magazines did, indeed, *speak*. They created a national venue for homosexuals, forming an area in which lesbians and gay men could, for the first time, speak above a whisper about issues fundamental to their lives.
>
> (p. 18, emphasis in original)

Such publications and those that would follow became especially important for the growth of gay activism in the 1950s and beyond.

Transgender as a Distinct Identity

While the press played an important role in the cultural negotiation of homosexuality in the 1950s, newspapers and magazines also drew significant attention to transsexuality. Although some sexologists in the early 1900s had sought to differentiate between sexual attraction and gender expression, it was not until the much-publicized "genital transformation surgery" of Christine Jorgensen in 1952 that transvestitism and transsexualism became more widely understood as identity categories distinct from homosexuality. At the same time that the homophile movement was emerging, transgender support networks also began to appear. Although genital modification surgeries were illegal in the United States, the first male-to-female surgical transformations took place in Europe in the 1930s. Stories of these surgeries quickly spread to the United States, including in the 1933 English translation of *Man into Woman: An Authentic Record of a Change of Sex*, which detailed German sex-change experiments (Meyerowitz, 1998). Coverage of such medical possibilities generally was sensationalistic in its approach and limited to equally sensationalistic magazines and tabloid newspapers. Nonetheless, these stories provided people who experienced a similar disconnect between their biological sex and psychological gender a way to make sense of their own feelings. It also made them aware of others who shared their "condition," and offered the promise of surgical intervention.

While stories about surgical sex transformations may have been followed closely by transsexuals of the time, they did not grab mainstream headlines until the case of Christine Jorgensen. Jorgensen was a former American G.I. who traveled to Copenhagen, Denmark, for genital transformation surgery. Once initial reports that Jorgensen was a hermaphrodite were dispelled, her seemingly unbelievable story—that a biological man would choose to undergo such drastic measures as "hormone treatments, psychiatric examination, 'removal of sexual glands,' and plastic surgery" in order to become a female—caught the public's imagination (Meyerowitz, 1998, p. 173). As Susan Stryker (2008) notes, "in a year when hydrogen bombs were being tested in the Pacific, war was raging in Korea, England crowned a new queen, and Jonas Salk invented the polio vaccine, Jorgensen was the most written-about topic in the media" (p. 47). The attention to Jorgensen likely resulted from a variety of factors, including social tensions about gender roles and sexuality and a fascination with the seemingly boundless power of science in a Cold War era.

FIGURE 2.3 Christine Jorgensen, February 1953, arriving from Denmark
Source: **Courtesy of Photofest.**

Jorgensen's notoriety brought unprecedented attention to transsexuality as American news coverage for the first time clearly distinguished it from intersexuality (Meyerowitz, 1998). This was one goal of transgender activists who sought to redefine transvestitism as male cross dressing, separating it from identifications of hermaphroditism. Endocrinologist Harry Benjamin, a pioneer in transsexual research and treatment, went one step farther, differentiating between "transsexuals" like Jorgensen who sought surgical interventions, and "transvestites" who did not (Stryker, 2008).

As science offered transsexuals an opportunity for medical intervention, a clearer line between transsexualism and homosexuality began to emerge. Transsexuals required a psychological diagnosis and medical treatment in order to achieve full sexual transformation. At the same time, gays and lesbians were fighting to change medical and cultural understandings of homosexuality as a mental disorder. Homosexuality and transsexuality increasingly became understood as distinct identities, and related activism slowly began following different paths.

▶ FROM TOLERANCE TO LIBERATION: 1960S–1970S

By the 1960s, the homophile movement had achieved modest political reform, but had done so largely by promoting the view that homosexuals were just like heterosexuals and therefore should be tolerated by the broader society. As the cultural environment shifted in the 1960s and 1970s, gays and lesbians would mobilize around a distinctly gay identity. The initial stages of this new gay liberation movement would seek to challenge the system that oppressed it before shifting its focus to seek equality through an ethnic model of gayness. Media representations of gays and lesbians in the 1960s and 1970s demonstrated the perils and promise of increasing media visibility.

Gayness as Political Identity

The 1960s marked a distinctly different era for America than those before. The entire nation seemed poised for change. Young people staged anti-war demonstrations, feminists formed consciousness-raising groups, and civil rights proponents marched for equality. Prior generations' attitudes about sex and sexuality also were challenged as an era of "free love" and sexual revolution found more people exploring sex outside the traditional bounds of marriage. Additionally, gender norms became less prescriptive, particularly in the realm of fashion. Men's long hairstyles and men's and women's androgynous dress blurred visible boundaries between masculinity and femininity. Within this cultural landscape of liberation, GLBT people responded to discrimination and harassment with their own calls for collective action.

Certainly the most remembered example of such collective action happened spontaneously in what have come to be known as the "Stonewall Riots." Police raids of gay bars were routine by the 1960s, as they had been in the decades before. GLBT people generally left quickly under threat of arrest. Some bars paid off police or the Mafia in hopes of protecting their clientele from harassment. Patrons of the Stonewall Inn, a popular gay bar in Greenwich Village, were quite familiar with police raids and knew they could avoid arrest if they dispersed quickly and quietly. However, the Friday night of July 27, 1969 was different. When police showed up and started arresting employees and patrons, a large crowd gathered outside, and some people began to fight back. Eventually, more than 2000 people filled the streets, and police officers barricaded themselves inside the Stonewall Inn awaiting backup. The following night, thousands of people returned to the site of the riot for an even more violent clash with police. The weekend was a mixture of rebellion and celebration, with people throwing coins and taunting officers for taking payola, a group of drag queens forming a chorus line and singing their protests, and passersby climbing trees to gawk at the sight of it all (McGarry & Wasserman, 1998).

While the events at the Stonewall Inn have come to serve as the symbolic origin of the gay liberation movement, smaller displays of collective rebellion had been happening all around the country. Three years before Stonewall, Compton's Café in the Tenderloin District of San Francisco, a section of the city known for its sex trade, was the site of another violent rebellion. In the documentary *Screaming Queens* (2005), Susan Stryker documents how a variety of cultural factors prompted a group of "street queens" to collective action against police harassment at the all-night diner. Other documented incidents of resistance date back to 1959, when an incident at Cooper's Donuts in Los Angeles "started with customers throwing doughnuts at the cops and ended with fighting in the streets" (Stryker, 2008, p. 61). Not all confrontations with authority were violent, of course. Some GLBT people responded to mistreatment with sit-ins and informational pickets.

These collective displays of resistance were indicative of a larger shift in thinking about how best to go about improving the lives of GLBT people. While the homophile movement had been about gaining acceptance within the existing heterosexual-dominated system, the newly emerging gay liberation movement was about destroying this system. As Jagose (1996) explains,

> Homosexuality was represented as an identity repressed by heterosexist
> power structures which privilege gender-asymmetry, sexual reproduction,
> and the patriarchal nuclear family. Unlike the homophile movement, gay
> liberation theorized that the system would never be radically transformed
> by those who were invested in it. Dominant formulations of sex and gender
> categories (and the institutions which supported them) would be eradicated
> only by gay men and lesbians who, refusing to accept their subaltern status,
> would destroy the system through literal and symbolic acts of violence.
>
> (pp. 36–37)

The gay liberation movement rejected the label of homosexual, which was seen as a medical diagnosis and instead embraced the term "gay" to describe a new politicized sexual identity. Radical gay activist groups began to emerge. This included the Gay Liberation Front (GLF), which was formed shortly after the Stonewall uprising. The GLF's confrontational, countercultural approach is indicated by its very name, which was derived from North Vietnam's "National Liberation Front." The GLF advocated socialism, seeing capitalism as the root cause of the oppression of not just gays and lesbians, but other oppressed groups like racial minorities and exploited workers (Meem et al., 2010).

As the gay liberation movement constructed gayness as an intrinsically political identity, "coming out" constituted an act of radical activism. D'Emilio (1992) has suggested that positioning "coming out" in this way was a "tactical stroke of great genius" (p. 244).

Announcing one's gayness to the heterosexual world became a personally meaningful political act available to all gay people. Additionally, once gay people had "outed" themselves and were no longer protected by their privacy, they had all the more reason to become fully invested in the movement toward sexual liberation.

From its beginning, the gay liberation movement involved bisexuals, drag queens, transsexuals, and transvestites, but several factors contributed to a growing divide between transgender and gay communities. Beginning in the mid-1960s, new sex-change programs emerged at universities and research hospitals across America, ushering in what became known as the "'Big Science' period of transgender history" (Stryker, 2008, p. 93). These programs generally adhered to conservative attitudes about gender as they sought to help transsexuals "change" their sex to fit better within the established system of gender and sexuality. This approach was antithetical to the gay liberation mission of challenging established relationships between sex, gender, and sexuality. At the loss of this alliance with the gay community, transgender communities would become less political and more inwardly focused.

Gayness as Ethnic Identity

As the cultural climate of the 1960s shifted into a less radical one in the 1970s, so, too, did the agendas of many gay and lesbian activists. The gay liberation movement narrowed its focus, no longer driven by a desire to overthrow a capitalist, heterosexist system responsible for widespread oppression. Instead, it became a social movement focused more narrowly on gay rights. In this shift, gays and lesbians began more clearly to understand their oppression as comparable to that suffered by ethnic minorities. Therefore, like ethnic minorities, gays presumably were different, but entitled to treatment as equal citizens under the law. By the mid-1970s, the term "gay minority" emerged, reflecting this logic (Jagose, 1996).

Activist efforts coalesced around more formal organizations that worked for legal change and sought greater visibility for gays and lesbians. In 1971, some members of the GLF splintered off to form the Gay Activists Alliance (GAA) (now named the Gay and Lesbian Activists Alliance), a civil rights organization originally based in New York and now in Washington, DC. In 1973, former members of the GAA formed the National Gay Task Force (NGT) (now named the National Gay and Lesbian Task Force) in New York. In its first year, the NGT successfully lobbied the American Psychiatric Association to change its classification of homosexuality as a medical disorder. In addition to working for gay rights issues on the national level, gays and lesbians also sought political visibility in the form of openly gay elected officials. They launched concerted efforts to raise funds to support gay candidates and encouraged gays and lesbians to recognize their collective voting power.

Not everyone was comfortable with this new notion of a gay minority identity. Constructing an identity around sexuality left little room for racial or gender differences or for other non-normative sexual identities. Gay men and lesbians of color saw their racial identities treated as secondary categories to their sexuality. Yet, this did not match up with their lived experiences of oppression. Lesbians, too, often found themselves feeling "homeless." Many were troubled by what they perceived to be a male-dominated gay rights movement but were excluded by women's rights groups that feared a lesbian presence would hinder their primary pursuits.

Media Recognition

As gay and lesbian activism grew through the 1960s, leading to well-established communities and increased visibility in major American cities, media scrutiny continued. Most media references to homosexuality continued the strongly negative tone of the McCarthy era, representing homosexuality as pathologically deviant and gays and lesbians as pathetic creatures whose lives were marked by loneliness, isolation, despair, and trouble with the law. In newspapers, magazines, films, radio, and even occasionally TV, gays and lesbians were continually denigrated as social outcasts. Such framing of homosexuality would shape news and magazine coverage of the Stonewall Riots. However, in the wake of Stonewall, as gay activists increasingly turned their attention to advocating for better representations in the media, things began to change. By the 1970s, a range of media began to produce images of gays and lesbians that broke from those of the past, and gays and lesbians themselves continued to turn to producing their own media as a way to counter their overwhelmingly negative treatment in mainstream media.

News coverage of the emerging gay liberation movement also did little to counter negative attitudes about GLBT people. Most news outlets initially ignored the riots at the Stonewall Inn. This likely was the result of a combination of factors. Journalists were generally ignorant about growing GLBT communities, and, though the weekend riots involved thousands of people, their significance may have been diminished by larger-scale riots in ghettos in Los Angeles, Detroit, and Newark earlier that summer in which entire city blocks were destroyed and people were killed (Alwood, 1996). Two major newspapers, though, did find the events newsworthy. The *New York Times* and the *Washington Post* both carried stories the following day, although both were buried deep in the news sections. Following the lead of these news agenda setters, other newspapers and magazines would include coverage of the events in the following weeks and months. The coverage privileged the perspectives of police officers and likened gay people to terrorists, all while mocking protesters with headlines like "Homo Nest Raided, Queen Bees Are Stinging Mad." Even the mouthpiece of the alternative culture, the *Village Voice*, dubbed the events at the Stonewall Inn the "fag follies" (Streitmatter, 2009, p. 19).

FIGURE 2.4 Celluloid activist, Vito Russo
Source: Vito, **Jeffrey Schwartz, 2011, © HBO/Photofest.**

One of the most important and influential examinations of the history of gay and lesbian images in classic Hollywood films is Vito Russo's *The Celluloid Closet: Homosexuality in the Movies.* Originally released as a book in 1981, with a revision published in 1987, it finally was released as a documentary in 1995, five years after Russo's death due to AIDS complications. The project stands as a testament to Russo's role in the emerging gay and lesbian rights movements. From his active involvement in the post-Stonewall GAA to his contributions to many significant gay and lesbian publications and his involvement in AIDS activism, Russo spent his life advocating for the public recognition of gays and lesbians (Schiavi, 2011).

The Celluloid Closet project took shape throughout the 1970s. It began as a series of film screenings Russo hosted for the GAA, where he and his mostly gay male audiences would share their camp readings of films and examine the ways gays and lesbians were represented. The screenings quickly grew in popularity due to Russo's witty descriptions and interpretations. While working at the Museum of Modern Art, Russo began collecting clips of film to put together into a more formal presentation of gay images in film history. After achieving success presenting the now-named *The Celluloid Closet* on the college speaking circuit, he began working on his first book (Schiavi, 2011).

His books are unabashedly political in their examination of the social costs of a long history of negative representations and draw important links between the history of gay rights and the history of gay images in the movies. While Russo criticizes conservative moralists, he takes special aim at gays and lesbians in Hollywood who kept themselves closeted, all the while presenting the world with the idea that gays and lesbians did not exist. He urged his readers to demand recognition and Hollywood power players to come out and show the world who they really were (Russo, 1987).

Russo had begun working on a documentary version, but its production is really due to the effort of many of his friends, including producers Rob Epstein and Jeffrey Feldman. While the film stands as an excellent illustration of some of the dominant ways of representing sexuality in the movies throughout most of the 20th Century, it also reflects the more muted activist stance of the film's makers, who were afraid that too much anger would turn off audiences. It ends on a more hopeful tone than either of the books (Schiavi, 2011).

As you watch the film, consider the following questions to get you thinking about the history of gay and lesbian representation in Hollywood films.

1.   How did gay stereotypes change over time?
2.   How were gay and lesbian stereotypes linked to broader ideas about proper gender roles?
3.   How do you visually represent identities that cannot be explicitly stated?
4.   Do the representational strategies of the past continue to shape the way gays and lesbians are portrayed on film and in television today?
5.   Why did visibility emerge as such an important issue for the gay and lesbian activists?

However, newly empowered and increasingly organized gay activists responded to negative press coverage and anti-gay newspaper policies with targeted protests. The GLF held its first media protest in September 1969 by picketing the offices of the *Village Voice* until the newspaper's publisher agreed to meet with them. The following year, the GAA responded to a negative essay on homosexuality in *Harper's* magazine by occupying the magazine's offices, greeting staff members with a friendly "Good morning, I'm a homosexual. We're here to protest the Epstein article. Would you like some coffee and donuts?" (Gross, 2001, p. 43). The GAA also would conduct what were known as "zaps," with groups disrupting public performances or even live television programs by loudly protesting the oppression of gay people. (Textbox 2.4 describes the documentary *The Celluloid Closet*, one of the most enduring examples of media activism from the time.)

Activist organizations grew increasingly frustrated with industry-initiated change, particularly in Hollywood, which they viewed as doing little to change the intensely negative representations of the past. For example, despite the 1961 revised guidelines from the Motion Picture Association of America for handling depictions of homosexuality with "care, discretion and restraint," movies of that decade regularly depicted gay characters who came to violent ends, either by their own hands in response to the despair they felt, or as deserving victims of violence. Activists realized that it was not enough to merely respond to these negative depictions if they wanted to improve representations of gays and lesbians. They needed to have input on film and television scripts before they were produced. This initially happened with the help of "agents in place," the name for gay people working in the media industry who leaked to activists scripts involving homosexual storylines (Gross, 2001). If activists disapproved of the portrayals, they would pressure filmmakers and television networks to make changes to scripts before they were produced. By the late 1970s, television networks would consult openly with the Gay Media Task Force, set up in Los Angeles by the National Gay Task Force to advocate for positive GLBT media representations.

The effects of activist pressure could be seen as media began to portray a broader range of gay and lesbian representations. By the early 1970s, movies like *Boys in the Band* (1970) and *The Killing of Sister George* (1968), if not offering an exactly happy representation of homosexuality, nonetheless presented gay characters who did not die, and who were open and honest about their sexuality. More than that, they were films that were about gay life in gay communities, rather than isolated, pathetic characters. Nonetheless, pathological views of gayness continued to exist in film. In 1980, *Cruising* was made about a serial killer targeting gay men involved in the S/M leather scene. Gay activists, now having spent a decade protesting media depictions, attempted to disrupt filming in New York City gay bars with loud protests, but were unsuccessful in preventing the film's release. Their fears that the film might spur anti-gay violence were confirmed when, in November of 1980, a Harlem minister entered one of the bars where *Cruising* was filmed and opened fire with a submachine gun, killing two and wounding six (Gross, 2001).

In many ways, it was television that began to offer less violent and troubling representations of GLBT people. Although gayness on television often was played for laughs, programs like the PBS documentary *An American Family* (1973) offered a more sympa-thetic portrayal. Considered a key predecessor of American reality programming, this PBS series documented the life of a "typical" American family. During the seven-month filming process in 1971, the family went through several trials, including divorce, itself quite controversial for the time. Even more startling was the gradual unfolding of the family's oldest son's coming to terms with his sexuality. Not predicted by the filmmak-ers and taking place within the context of a single family's trials and tribulations, it offered a rare, sympathetic glimpse at homosexual life. Made-for-television movies like *That Certain Summer* (1972) and *A Question of Love* (1978) also presented the difficult dilemmas faced by gays and lesbians; however, in such programs homosexuality often was framed as a "problem" to be wrestled with (Gross, 2001).

During the 1970s, an increasing number of openly gay filmmakers began producing their own media to give voice to gay and lesbian communities. In the 1977 documen-tary *Word Is Out: Stories of Some of Our Lives*, 13 gay men and 13 lesbians shared parts of their life stories in their own words. The film, made by the brother and sister team of Peter and Nancy Adair, both gay, featured people from all walks of life, including Mattachine Society Founder Harry Hay. Describing the film, Gross (2001) writes, "In its implicit insistence on the underlying shared experiences of lesbian and gay people, *Word Is Out* reflected the emergence of a political stance centered on what came to be called identity politics" (p. 69). A shorter version of *Word Is Out* eventually would air on broadcast television on PBS. Gay and lesbian filmmakers also began producing fiction films, exhibiting them to a nationwide gay audience at art theaters. Such films portrayed main characters who were gay, but whose sexualities were treated matter-of-factly, rather than as a "problem" with which to be dealt. Gay and lesbian-produced documentaries and films would reach increasingly broader gay audiences over the next decade.

While, by and large, gays and lesbians still were represented in strongly negative terms, by the 1970s there was a sense that at least some things were changing. The most egregious forms of representation often were met with a strong activist response, and gays and lesbians were working to have their voices heard in both mainstream and alternative media. The start of the 1980s seemed to offer the chance that things would only keep improving, but the coming of the AIDS crisis would change this.

▶ DEFINED BY AIDS: 1980S

The recognition of the gay and lesbian rights movement was a pivotal moment, marked by conflict, internal disagreements, and important victories. By the early 1980s, the social position of many gays and lesbians had improved. Greater visibility had led to the emergence of less hostile and dismissive media images, but this would all begin to change over the coming decade. The AIDS crisis was devastating in human terms to urban gay communities across the United States, and there can be no doubt that the overwhelming homophobia that pervaded U.S. popular and political discourses shaped the response to AIDS in ways that ultimately led to more deaths than otherwise might have occurred. At the same time, however, the gay community, drawing on two decades of activist work, was reinvigorated and began making even more vocal demands for change.

A Common Enemy

In 1981, the Centers for Disease Control (CDC) reported a new illness that had been diagnosed in five gay men living in the Los Angeles area. Similar cases were identified in New York City. Because this disease initially appeared limited to the gay community, it became known in the popular press as "gay related immune deficiency (GRID)" (Meem et al., 2010). As the disease was found in other populations, particularly intravenous drug users, hemophiliacs, and recipients of blood transfusions, it was given the name Acquired Immune Deficiency Syndrome (AIDS). AIDS is the final stages of bodily deterioration caused by Human Immunodeficiency Virus (HIV), a blood-borne virus that progressively weakens the body's immune system. People suffering from AIDS are extremely susceptible to, and often die from, immune-related diseases, like pneumonia.

When AIDS first was discovered, the medical community understood very little about the disease, including how to treat it effectively. By the end of 1983, more than 40% of the 3000 Americans diagnosed with AIDS died from the disease (Centers for Disease Control, 1983). Hardest hit were urban gay communities, particularly in San Francisco and New York City, but also in Chicago, Los Angeles, and a number of other cities. According to the GLBT Historical Society, "'half the gay men in San Francisco were infected in the first wave' of AIDS, 'and most died'" (James, 2010). The AIDS epidemic was not confined to the United States. It claimed tens of thousands of victims as it spread internationally in the 1980s. Among the many notable victims of AIDS was French philosopher Michel Foucault. As noted in Chapter 1, his writings were foundational to queer intellectual theory.

Many argue the death toll from AIDS in the United States would have been lessened if the government had responded more quickly. However, the AIDS epidemic hit during a time of anti-gay backlash, which had grown with the election of Ronald Reagan and his New Right politics. Conservative religious leaders who had begun wading into the political fray helped fuel anti-gay sentiments. Most notably, Moral Majority founder and Baptist minister Jerry Falwell overtly linked the AIDS epidemic to the GLBT political agenda, declaring "AIDS is not just God's punishment for homosexuals; it is God's punishment for the society that tolerates homosexuals" (Reed, 2007). As Roberta Achtenberg of San Francisco's Lesbian Rights Project noted in 1986, people often showed open disdain for gay people through veiled concerns about contracting AIDS: "Instead of calling us queer . . . now they have something that's more legitimate-appearing to hide behind. AIDS provides a veil for basic homophobia" (McGarry &Wasserman, 1998, p. 231). That homophobia led to an increase in anti-gay violence in cities around the country.

Given this political climate, the association of AIDS with the gay community undoubtedly contributed to the Reagan administration's slow response to provide funding for AIDS research and public awareness campaigns. In the first years after the outbreak of AIDS, the administration budgeted no money for AIDS research. Throughout the 1980s, Congress repeatedly would allocate more money than requested by the president, but not nearly enough to combat the mushrooming epidemic, which was reaching a wider and wider range of the population. Surgeon General C. Everett Koop recognized that education about safe sex practices would be key to slowing the spread of AIDS. However, the administration feared that supporting an explicit informational campaign would be seen as promoting a homosexual lifestyle (McGarry & Wasserman, 1998).

Members of the gay community were outraged by the government's handling of the AIDS crisis. As one AIDS activist put it, "I may eventually die as a result of this disease, but I would consider my death an act of murder for the lack of government funding. I would consider it murder by my own government" (quoted in Rutledge, 1992, p. 262). The gay community quickly began taking matters into its own hands. With networks already in place from the gay rights advocacy of the 1970s, GLBT people turned their efforts toward fighting this new common enemy. Hundreds of new organizations emerged to meet the needs of those suffering from HIV/AIDS and to launch their own educational campaigns. Some groups, like ACT UP (AIDS Coalition To Unleash Power), deployed the same radical strategies of the gay liberation movement to draw public attention to the government's inadequate response to the AIDS crisis. The impact of AIDS activists could be seen by the late 1980s and early 1990s. Activists were appointed to government panels overseeing clinical drug trials, Congress passed a long-term funding package targeting cities hardest hit, and the newly passed Americans with Disabilities Act provided civil rights protections to people suffering from HIV/AIDS (McGarry & Wasserman, 1998).

The AIDS era would have lasting effects on gay politics and public awareness about homosexuality. Networks of gay rights activists were strengthened as more people and financial resources were drawn to a cause that had become a matter of life and death. Homosexuality also had become more personal for families of America's gay sons who would come home to die. In addition, it became more visible to the broader society, as AIDS and homosexuality became a regular topic of front-page news stories as well as dining-room table conversations. As McGarry and Wasserman (1998) point out, the gay liberation movement of the 1970s may have been grounded in a new politics of visibility, but it was the 1980s that brought gay people into the bright spotlight of visibility. Media played a key role in this increased visibility and the complicated cultural conversation about homosexuality.

Complications from AIDS—Media Representations

In many ways, 1980s media represented society's somewhat schizophrenic attitudes toward homosexuality. The work of gay activists in the 1970s continued to translate into changing media representations of gays and lesbians into the 1980s. However, the cultural backlash brought on by GLBT political gains and deepened by fears about AIDS would challenge this progress, delaying fuller recognition of gays and lesbians in mainstream media until the 1990s.

Gay men received a wave of new media attention in the wake of the AIDS crisis. Early press attention to AIDS was marred by the deeply homophobic makeup of U.S. society. Early reports of the disease began appearing in newspapers by the 1980s, but most editors were nervous about giving attention to the story as it seemed to involve primarily gay men. In general, a disease identified as the "gay cancer" met with about as much interest from the press as it had from government health officials. Despite a growing death toll, the *New York Times* did not make it a front-page story until 1983. Because the *New York Times* set the agenda for newsworthiness, other news outlets including television networks were slow to cover the growing epidemic. When stories did appear, they generally focused on promiscuity as its cause and constructed gay men as a threat to the health of the nation. A great deal of the coverage focused on what Gross (2001) calls the "raunchy" elements of gay subculture and polarized gay men into two camps, "victims" or "villains." As victims, they were seen as pathetic sufferers of their own behavior, and, as villains, they were constructed as predatory creatures bent on spreading disease. Streitmatter (2009) describes one such egregious characterization of gay men in a 1985 *Life* magazine story titled "Now No One is Safe from AIDS." Its cover featured the picture of a woman, a soldier, and a young couple with an infant, all presumably heterosexual and the next potential victims of AIDS. Like many other stories, the *Life* coverage vilified gay men as pathological carriers and transmitters of AIDS, despite the existing evidence that AIDS was linked to certain behaviors and required blood-to-blood contact.

AIDS activists had been outraged by the initial lack of news coverage in the early years of the AIDS epidemic, but were incensed equally by coverage that demonized gay men and did little to dispel myths about the disease. Gay activists would draw upon their strengthened networks in the gay community to pressure news outlets to change their reporting practices. Most notably, in 1985, a group of activists in New York, including Vito Russo, formed the Gay and Lesbian Alliance Against Defamation (GLAAD) to respond to what they viewed as sensationalized and homophobic AIDS coverage by the *New York Post*. Following the lead of earlier media activism, GLAAD used street activist strategies to draw attention to negative coverage and to secure meetings with publishers and producers to demand change.

Broader changes in media coverage of AIDS would only come, though, after the 1985 public declaration by Rock Hudson that he was dying from the disease. Hudson was one of the best-known movie and television stars of the time, having played romantic leading roles in the 1950s and 1960s. He was the first major celebrity to publicly announce he had AIDS, and his announcement and death later that same year would thrust AIDS into the headlines like never before (Dyer, 2001). According to Alwood (1996), the number of news stories about AIDS in American newspapers increased by more than 250% in the last half of 1985.

This heightened attention to the AIDS crisis would spill over into fictional media, as well, with network television, independent film, and mainstream cinema providing a range of gay characters dealing with AIDs. Quite often, these depictions worked to dispel fears and combat prejudices about the disease. The earliest mainstream representation of AIDS was the 1985 made-for-TV film *An Early Frost*, which tells the story of a gay Chicago attorney who comes home to reveal his sexuality and positive HIV status to his family. The film fits within the "disease of the week" formula of TV movies popular at the time and, like most made-for-TV movies, sticks to a fairly conservative middle ground on social issues by personalizing them rather than politicizing them (Gross, 2001). Nonetheless, it offered a remarkably sympathetic portrayal of an HIV-positive gay man to a television audience of millions.

The first widely distributed Hollywood film involving AIDS would come out four years later. *Longtime Companion* (1989) was not the first film dealing with AIDS, but earlier films like *Buddies* (1985) were limited to showings at a small number of urban arthouse theaters. *Longtime Companion*, which won the GLAAD Media Award for Outstanding Film, follows seven friends as their lives are impacted by AIDS. The film's title was a reference to the *New York Times* policy against acknowledging homosexual relationships in obituaries, instead referring to a surviving partner as a "longtime companion." The film received critical acclaim for focusing on the effect of AIDS on the lives of gay people, rather than their straight friends and family (Gross, 2001). Movie critic Roger Ebert (1990) also applauded the film for featuring gay characters with complex identities that go beyond just their sexual orientation.

While press, television, and film treatment of AIDS certainly was important to the broader cultural conversation about homosexuality in the 1980s, media representations of gay people were not limited to these depictions. Television offered new gay characters, especially in series with a strong focus on melodrama, including daytime soap operas, and, most famously, on the popular campy nighttime soap opera *Dynasty* (1981–1989). Independent film producers also were producing gay- and lesbian-centered stories like *Desert Hearts* (1985) and *Parting Glances* (1986). Such films were a precursor to what B. Ruby Rich (1992) would dub "New Queer Cinema," a series of fictional films and documentaries in the early 1990s that depicted unapologetic and even subversive visions of gayness. The following two decades would see an acceleration of GLBT visibility across all forms of media that few likely could have predicted.

▶ CONCLUSION

This chapter overviewed the emergence of sexual identities, the growing cohesion of communities organized around those identities, the activist efforts of those communities, and the shifting representations of media depictions instructive of historically specific understandings of GLBT identities. Beginning in the mid- to late 1800s, a new scientific interest in sexuality, as well as changing socio-economic conditions, led to a new understanding of sexuality. A person's erotic desires and sexual behaviors coalesced into a sense of identity, both imposed on people by the medical community, but also defined and expressed by growing pockets of urban gay subculture. Marked gender inversion in media characters, particularly effeminate men, alluded to, but did not name, this emerging homosexual identity. Beginning with World War II, gays and lesbians were afforded increasing opportunities to connect with each other; however, they increasingly became targets of legal and social persecution. Media depictions reinforced cultural attitudes about homosexuality, labeling gays and lesbians as "perverts." In the face of this hostility, the homophile movement emerged, creating organizations to offer social support for gays and lesbians and also to fight for greater social acceptance. Groups began publishing their own newsletters and magazines to help spread information throughout the gay community. Such networks also existed for transsexuals, who, because of the high-profile case of Christine Jorgensen, were becoming more visible.

The 1960s and 1970s saw the emergence of the gay liberation movement, when GLBT people called for the radical overthrow of an oppressive heterosexist system. This movement eventually shifted its focus to securing equal rights under an ethnic minority understanding of gay identity. Depictions of gayness in the media began to grow more diverse during this time. Familiar tropes of homosexual villains and victims still were in place, but new and more sympathetic representations of gay people and gay communities began emerging. This was, in part, because of growing media activism by GLBT organizations. The coming of AIDS in the 1980s was devastating to gay communities, as homophobic fears stalled an appropriate response by the federal government, resulting in the mushrooming of AIDS into a national epidemic. However, the government's inaction bolstered gay activism to a new level, drawing new people and financial resources to the cause. AIDS also brought a new level of gay visibility in the media, making homosexuality no longer a topic to be whispered about. The strong foundation for gay politics and visibility solidified in the AIDS era would have lasting consequences for advancing the GLBT agenda and GLBT visibility in the following decades.

▶ REFERENCES

Abrams, M. (2007, June 5). The real story on gay genes. *Discover Magazine*. Retrieved from http://discovermagazine.com/2007/jun/born-gay.

Alwood, E. (1996). *Straight news: Gays, lesbians and the news media*. New York, NY: Columbia University Press.

Centers for Disease Control. (1983). Acquired immunodeficiency syndrome (AIDS). *Morbid Mortal Weekly Rep, 32*, 465–467. United States: CDC.

Chauncey, G. (1994). *Gay New York: Gender, urban culture, and the making of the gay male world, 1890–1940*. New York, NY: Basic Books.

D'Emilio, J. (1992). *Making trouble: Essays on gay history, politics, and the university*. New York, NY: Routledge.

D'Emilio, J. (1998). *Sexual politics, sexual communities: The making of a homosexual minority in the United States, 1940–1970*. (2nd ed.). Chicago, IL: University of Chicago Press.

Doherty, T.P. (1999). *Pre-code Hollywood: Sex, immorality, and insurrection in American cinema, 1930–1934*. New York, NY: Colombia University Press.

Doty, A. (1993). *Making things perfectly queer: Interpreting mass culture*. Minneapolis, MN: University of Minnesota Press.

Duggan, L. (1993). The trials of Alice Mitchell: Sensationalism, sexology, and the lesbian subject of turn-of-the-century America. *Signs, 18*, 791–814.

Dyer, R. (2001). *The culture of queers*. New York, NY: Routledge.

Ebert, R. (1990, May 25). Longtime companion. *RobertEbert*. Retrieved from http://www.rogerebert.com/reviews/longtime-companion-1990.

Entman, R. (1993). Framing: Towards clarification of a fractured paradigm. *Journal of Communication, 43(4)*, 51–58.

Gross, L. (2001). *Up from invisibility: Lesbians, gay men, and the media in America*. New York, NY: Columbia University Press.

Hall, R. (1928). *The well of loneliness*. London: Jonathan Cape.

Jagose, A. (1996). *Queer theory: An introduction*. New York, NY: New York University Press.

James, S. (2010, November 25). A near-forgotten casualty of AIDS: The Haight's gay identity. *New York Times*, A25A.

Katz, J.N. (1976). *Gay American history: Lesbians and gay men in the USA*. New York, NY: Crowell.

Katz, J.N. (2007). *The invention of heterosexuality*. Chicago, IL: University of Chicago Press.

Krafft-Ebing, R. (1886). *Psychopathia sexualis*. Philadelphia, PA: F.A. Davis Company.

McGarry, M. & Wasserman, F. (1998). *Becoming visible: An illustrated history of lesbian and gay life in twentieth century America*. New York, NY: Penguin Studio.

McIntosh, M. (1968). The homosexual role. *Social Problems, 16*(2), 182–192.

Meem, D.T., Gibson, M.A., & Alexander, I.F. (2010). *Finding out: An introduction to LGBT studies.* Thousand Oaks, CA: Sage Publications Inc.

Meyerowitz, J. (1998). Sex change and the popular press: Historical notes on transsexuality in the United States, 1930–1955. GLQ: *A Journal of Lesbian and Gay Studies, 4*(2), 159–187.

Reed, C. (2007, May 17). The Rev. Jerry Falwell: Rabid evangelical leader of America's 'moral majority.' Retrieved from http://www.theguardian.com/media/2007/may/17/broadcasting.guardianobituaries.

Rich, B. Ruby (1992). New queer sensation. *Sight & Sound, 2*(5), 30–34.

Rubin, L. (2004). Is this a white country, or what? In M. Anderson & P.H. Collins (Eds.), *Race, class, and gender: An anthology* (5th ed.) (pp. 410–418). Belmont, CA: Wadsworth.

Russo, V. (1987). *The celluloid closet* (revised ed.). New York, NY: Harper & Row.

Rutledge, L.A.W. (1992). *The gay decades: From Stonewall to the present: The people and events that shaped gay lives.* New York, NY: Plume.

Schiavi, M. (2011). *Celluloid activist: The life and times of Vito Russo.* Madison, WI: University of Wisconsin Press.

Sears, C. (2006). Cross-dressing in the 19th-Century San Francisco Press. In L. Casteñeda & S. Campbell (Eds.), *News and sexuality: Media portraits of diversity* (pp. 1–19). Thousand Oaks, CA: Sage.

Sommerville, S. (2000). *Queering the color line: Race and the invention of homosexuality in American culture.* Durham, NC: Duke University Press.

Streitmatter, R. (1995). *Unspeakable: The rise of the gay and lesbian press in America.* Boston, MA: Faber and Faber, Inc.

Streitmatter, R. (2009). *From "perverts" to "fab five": The media's changing depiction of gay men and lesbians.* New York, NY: Routledge.

Stryker, S. (2008). *Transgender history.* Berkeley, CA: Seal Press.

Williams, W. & Retter, Y. (Eds.). (2003). *Gay and lesbian rights in the United States.* Santa Barbara, CA: ABC-Clio, LLC.

Visibility

When it premiered in 2009, almost 10 million viewers tuned into the FOX series, *Glee* (2009–2015). Helmed by openly gay producer Ryan Murphy, *Glee* explored the world of high school "losers" who found community and meaning by participating in the school's glee club. The show's quirky aesthetics, melodramatic plots, campy humor, musical numbers, and celebration of difference made it especially appealing to GLBTQ youth. The show featured not one, but a number of gay teen characters, who along with their straight counterparts, navigated love, longing, and growing up. Fans of the show took to Twitter, Tumbler, Facebook, and fan fiction sites to celebrate the romance between gay teens Kurt and Blaine or between lesbian Santana and bisexual Brittany, respectively dubbed "Klaine" and "Brittana." In 2012, during the show's third season, *Glee* introduced an African-American, transgender woman character, played by Alex Newell. Newell was discovered by *The Glee Project* (2011–), a spinoff reality competition show with the coveted prize of an appearance on *Glee*. During the height of *Glee*'s popularity, its first three seasons, the show was capable of pulling in up to 12 million viewers, sold numerous downloads of the songs covered by the Glee Club on iTunes, mounted a successful touring stage version of the show, inspired an active and vocal fan base through social media platforms, and encouraged fans to identify themselves, in a play on the word "geeks," as "gleeks." It is doubtful that those advocating for improved media coverage in the early 1990s might have predicted a show that not just represented, but celebrated, GLBTQ identities. There can be no doubt that the past 20 years have given rise to an era of unprecedented visibility for GLBTQ individuals, communities, and issues.

While increasing visibility often is celebrated in the mainstream press, by activist organizations, and even by academics, the past two decades also have witnessed a growing concern about the potential costs of visibility. How scholars evaluate the impact and meaning of visibility depends on a few factors, including their theoretical and methodological approaches to the study of media, their theoretical assumptions about sexual identities, and their theoretical commitment to either assimilation or undoing heteronormativity as the end goal of activism. While some scholars concentrate on whether images are negative or positive, a key goal of this chapter is to explore how we can move beyond "positive" and "negative" as the language of evaluation in order to consider how and why particular versions of GLBTQ identity circulate at any one time.

This approach leads to what we call the "yes, but" approach to thinking about visibility. On the one hand, this means acknowledging the tremendous advances and improvements that increased visibility has brought to the everyday lives of GLBTQ people. On the other, it means insisting that as media consumers, users, and producers we remain vigilant to the complex ways that media can contribute to forms of discrimination, hatred, and persistent devaluation of sexual identities rendered outside the norm. Before this, the chapter will explain some reasons for the increase in GLBTQ characters and themes across a range of media. Next, it will consider the unique aspects of the relationship between visibility and sexual identities. From there, the chapter will explore the potentials and limitations of stereotype analysis. Finally, we will move beyond stereotypes to consider the different bases from which scholars evaluate media visibility.

▶ THE VISIBILITY GENERATION

If you were born in the late 1980s forward, you have grown up in an era of unprecedented visibility for GLBTQ individuals, communities, and issues. No doubt some of you found the world described in Chapter 2 a strange one. If it once was possible to never see gays or lesbians in the media, today it is difficult *not* to see gays and lesbians, and increasingly bisexuals and transgender individuals. References to various forms of sexual and gender identities appear in TV shows, movies, magazines, popular music, video games, books, the news, and the Internet. While there are many reasons for the growth of gay visibility, this section will focus on two interrelated reasons. First, the increasing success of activist organizing for recognition of and rights for lesbians and gays has had a tremendous impact in shaping the kinds of political visibility that arose. Second, important changes in the media industries involving new technologies and the shifting practices of advertisers, programmers, and audiences created a fertile ground for the emergence of new forms of mediated GLBTQ visibility.

Political Recognition

The AIDS crisis, as introduced in Chapter 2, was a potent demonstration of the lack of rights held by sexual minorities in the United States. The political response of GLBT activists was key to gaining necessary social and political investment into fighting the disease. By the 1990s, the more fiery politics of the era were overtaken by an increasingly well-funded and -organized gay and lesbian movement dedicated to pursuing those rights that would allow sexual minorities full inclusion in U.S. social, political, and cultural institutions, including the right to military service, the addition of sexual identity as a protected category in local and state civil codes, and the right to marry. These goals were pursued through both legal challenges and political activism. Throughout the 1990s, gay and lesbian politics was marked by a swinging pendulum of growing recognition as deserving of rights and successful political maneuvers to squelch such rights. The new millennium, however, brought a string of legal victories that began to resolve this tension, offering the GLBTQ population uneven, but increasing, access to American social institutions.

The 1992 election season marked a watershed moment in gay politics. On the one hand, numerous Democratic candidates, from the local to the Presidential level, actively courted gay and lesbian voters, who were able to celebrate the victory of Bill Clinton as President. On the other hand, Republicans turned gay rights into a wedge issue in order to get out voters, especially fundamentalist Christians, to support anti-gay rights efforts. The clash between these groups centered on two key debates at the national level, access to the military and marriage rights. While Clinton had promised to end the ban against gays and lesbians serving in the armed forces, tremendous political pressure led in 1994 to Don't Ask Don't Tell (DADT), a policy that prevented the military from asking about the sexual orientation of service members, thus allowing gays and lesbians to serve, but under the constant threat of discharge if their sexuality was discovered.

GLBTQ activists increasingly used the court system as a way to address discrimination and won two key victories that would help set the stage for the fight over gay marriage. In *Romer* v. *Evans*, decided in 1996, the Supreme Court overturned a Colorado voter referendum that forbade any town or the state to add civil rights protections for gays and lesbians. While the Court had upheld such laws in the past, in this case the Court struck down the referendum, arguing that in singling out gays and lesbians the law was an unfair burden. The ramifications of this ruling were felt more fully in the 2003 landmark case of *Lawrence* v. *Texas*, in which the Court ruled that Texas's law against sodomy was unconstitutional because no state could make a law that singled out a behavior simply because the majority found it distasteful. These rulings were based on the increasing recognition that there was no compelling legal basis for singling out gays and lesbians with rules prohibiting certain activities and behaviors.

Activists across the country organized at the state level to legalize gay marriage. 1993 brought a key victory for activists when a court in Hawaii ruled that forbidding people of the same sex to marry each other was unconstitutional. Federal legislators responded to what they saw as a threat to the sanctity of marriage with the Defense of Marriage Act (DOMA), passed in 1996. Because existing federal laws mandated that states should legally recognize marriages from other states, all states would be forced to accept gay marriages even if only one state actually legalized them. By specifically banning any federal recognition of same-sex marriages, DOMA allowed states that forbid gay marriage the right to not recognize same-sex marriages performed in states where it was legal. Activists continued to pursue marriage rights, but in the face of DOMA used terms like "civil union" and "domestic partnership," instead of "marriage."

The pace of change in the new millennium, especially the teens, has been rapid. In 2011, the Obama administration finally dropped the DADT policy and also announced that it would no longer enforce DOMA. Legal cases challenging the constitutionality of the law found support at the federal court level. In 2013, in *United States* v. *Windsor*, the Supreme Court officially decided that federal law could not limit marriage to being between a man and a woman. Since that time, state courts continually have ruled state laws against gay marriage also are unconstitutional. By the time you read this, gay marriage may well be legal across the United States.

Media Visibility

These political victories are strongly connected to the increase in media visibility that seemed almost unimaginable even at the beginning of the 1990s. This rise in gay visibility, especially increasingly sympathetic portrayals of gays and lesbians, owes a great deal to GLBTQ activists. As discussed in Chapter 2, the post-Stonewall gay rights movement made agitation for better representation part of their activism. However, activism alone cannot account for these changes. Also significant were a series of key changes in technology, the structure of media industries, and advertisers' conceptions of audiences. This led to a fragmented media market of proliferating choices supported by smaller audiences than in the past. The media and advertising industries responded to this reality by increasingly emphasizing narrowcasting: designing media products that spoke to small subsets of the broader audience.

The proliferation of GLBTQ images during the 1990s was perhaps most obvious on television, where this new visibility emerged in large part because of changes in the television industry. By the 1990s, the traditional world of television had been forever turned upside down by the increasing popularity of cable. The accelerated fragmentation of audiences across multiple channels led to the gradual loss of national audiences from the big four broadcast networks (ABC, CBS, FOX, and NBC). At the same time, advertisers increased their pressure on the television industry to develop narrower target demographics. One group that advertisers were eager to reach was what Ron Becker (2006) calls the SLUMPY (Socially Liberal, Urban Minded Professionals) class. Advertisers were seeking ways to reach this lucrative young demographic willing to use its disposable income on consumer items. The result was hip, urban network programs that included gay characters, such as *Friends* (1994–2004). Smaller networks, such as the WB and CW, used gay themes as part of their teenage-oriented lineup, including programs like *Buffy the Vampire Slayer* (1997–2003) and *Dawson's Creek* (1998–2003). The GLBT market also was targeted directly. Between 2001 and 2005 several established media companies launched gay cable television channels, including Viacom's still operating LOGO channel. We will talk more extensively about the relationship between advertisers, advertising, and GLBTQ identities in Chapter 4.

The most groundbreaking television shows, however, were the broadcast television series *Ellen* (1994–1998) and *Will & Grace* (1998–2006). The world of television was rocked in 1997 when Ellen DeGeneres simultaneously came out in real life and in her self-titled sitcom, becoming the first lead gay or lesbian character on television. The show lasted only one more season, unable to bear both studio nervousness and public scrutiny of being the only show with a GLBTQ character as the lead. *Will & Grace*, the first program to feature two lead gay male characters, premiered in the 1998–1999 television season, merely a few months after *Ellen* went off the air. Centered around the relationship between gay Will and straight Grace, the show found instant and long-lasting success with audiences, airing an impressive eight seasons. In addition, the actors were not associated with their roles. Eric McCormack, the actor playing Will, made frequent mention of his wife in interviews and public events, while Sean Hayes, who played the flamboyant Jack, refused to publicly comment on his sexuality.

While networks placed gay and lesbian characters in sitcoms, premium cable television, less regulated than broadcast television or beholden to advertisers, offered more graphic representations of sexuality and sexual identity in series such as *Queer as Folk* (2000–2005) and *The L Word* (2004–2009). Bisexual and transgender characters on television are still rarely seen, though they have become more regular features in queer-themed shows, including *Glee* (2009–) and *The L Word* (2004–2009). Most recently, streaming video service Netflix earned several Emmy nominations for its subscription-funded "television" series *Orange is the New Black* (2013–), including a nomination for Laverne Cox as Best Supporting Actress in a comedy series, breaking ground as the first out transgender actress nominated.

GLBTQ visibility also heightened in film by the 1990s, with an even broader range of representations than television, in part because of independent production companies. As described in Chapter 2, the early 1990s witnessed the production, screening, and recognition of a growing number of independent films about gay life, dubbed the

FIGURE 3.1 Ellen DeGeneres comes out to the world
Source: Time magazine April 14, 1997.

New Queer Cinema. Films including *The Living End*, *Swoon*, and *R.S.V.P.* all premiered in 1992, and film festivals around the globe, including in cities around the United States. Toronto, Berlin, and London offered special panels and discussions by younger queer-identified filmmakers and screenings of their work. Although film critic and scholar B. Ruby Rich (1992) noted that these films largely were focused on the work of white men, she still acknowledged the significance of them. Made in the wake of the AIDS crisis, these films offered a significantly different take on AIDS than television had in the 1980s by centering on the experience and voices of gays and lesbians. While significant in the gay and lesbian community, the New Queer Cinema was not made for or widely marketed to mainstream audiences. However, the films did have a great deal of impact on later filmmakers, who found more success exploring queer themes, such as Kimberly Peirce in *Boys Don't Cry* (1999) and John Cameron Mitchell in *Hedwig and the Angry Inch* (2001), most recently adapted into a Tony Award-winning musical on Broadway.

During this time, however, gay and lesbian characters also became more common in mainstream Hollywood film. The commercial and critical success of *Philadelphia* in 1993, which cast Tom Hanks as a lawyer suing his own law firm after they fired him for having AIDS, broke through taboos about the commercial viability of gay characters in films. The commercial success of the film certainly was boosted by Hanks' win of the Oscar for Best Actor in a Leading Role that year. Taking note of the critical and financial success of gay-themed mainstream films like *Philadelphia,* as well as the growing financial viability of independent cinema thanks to alternative distribution platforms like cable, DVDs, and new media, several Hollywood production companies established "indie houses" or special projects divisions to produce gay-themed content. This new "Gay Indiewood" produced high-production-value, GLBTQ-themed films backed by big studio marketing budgets (Knegt, 2008). The highest grossing of these films include *Far from Heaven* (2002), *The Hours* (2002), *Kinsey* (2004), *Monster* (2003), *Brokeback Mountain* (2005), and *Capote* (2005), all of which were targeted to both niche GLBTQ and mainstream audiences.

The Internet and popular music have proved the most adept and willing to directly target GLBTQ audiences. The shrinking costs of media production enabled by technological change and relative ease of distribution on the Internet have allowed for a proliferation of content. GLBTQ individuals increasingly turned to it as a source of connection, a place to build community, and a site to explore stories, images, and relationships that do not fit within conventional mainstream media. GLBTQ visibility on the Internet appears across social media, websites, blogs, amateur YouTube videos, and an increasing number of professionally produced web series. Popular music continues to be a key resource through which GLBTQ individuals can define their experiences and find supportive voices. The growing decentralization of the music industry since the 1990s has created opportunities for different kinds of artists to reach out to segmented audiences. Pop stars like Lady Gaga and Katy Perry courted gay audiences with musical odes to self-empowerment. We will discuss more about the Internet and popular music as important spaces for GLBTQ media production in Chapter 5.

Despite a seeming explosion of GLBTQ visibility over the past 20 years, it is important to remember that not everyone is exposed to this visibility equally (see Textbox 3.1). As detailed above, a great deal of this increasing visibility is owed in part to changes in the media industry in the past 20 years, especially the growing multi-channel universe of television, the increasing profitability of independent and "Indiewood" cinema, and the growth of the Internet as an alternative platform for producing and distributing media. Advertisers' recognition of the potential profitability of GLBTQ-themed programming for broader audiences has also been important. However, such content is targeted to these fairly narrow demographics. The industry changes of the 1990s have resulted in a world in which media no longer need to appeal to everyone. As a result, it becomes easier and easier for people to live in their own media echo chambers, filtering out television, film, music, and web content that does not suit them. On the flip side, the increased GLBTQ visibility is easily accessible to any and all who desire it. Assessing the nature of this new visibility has become increasingly important. But before that we need to consider why visibility is important.

BOX 3.1   Tracking Visibility

Since Chapter 1, we have stressed continually that GLBTQ visibility has been highly uneven. The most visible faces of the GLBTQ population have been white gay men. But who comes next? For this activity, you will examine a range of popular media, performing a rudimentary content analysis, to take a snapshot of the current state of diversity *within* GLBTQ media representations. First, working with a group, as a class, or on your own, brainstorm all of the GLBTQ characters you remember from the movies or TV. As you brainstorm, begin noting the following variables for characters:

- ▶ gender
- ▶ race/ethnicity
- ▶ economic class
- ▶ age
- ▶ number of GLBTQ characters per movie/show.

Next, add to your own data with some Internet research. You can find lists of GLBTQ characters in television and film at www.glaad.org. If you click on the "Resources" button you will find the most recent versions of the movie *Studio Responsibility Index* and *Where We Are on TV* reports. Incorporate this data with what you developed through your brainstorming. Finally, consider what audiences are exposed to these images. You can find information about television ratings and audiences at www.tvbythenumbers.com and details of movie numbers at www. boxofficemojo.com.

Drawing on these basic counts, consider the following questions:

Images
1. Who has gained the most visibility?
2. Who is left behind?
3. How does this relate to the broader patterns of visibility of other minority groups?
4. What general picture of the GLBTQ population emerges from this pattern? Did you find any surprises?
5. How might this pattern shape our understanding of the GLBTQ population? What assumptions might we make based on this pattern?

Audiences
6. What television channels feature the greatest number of GLBTQ characters? What are the overall ratings for these shows?
7. What movie studios are releasing films with GLBTQ characters? What are the audience sizes for these movies?
8. What kinds of audiences are being targeted?
9. How large are the media audiences engaging to GLBTQ content? Based on the information you gather, can you create a snapshot of the demographics of those audiences?
10. Overall, how broad or narrow are the audiences for GLBTQ visibility? Why does this matter?

▶ WHY VISIBILITY MATTERS

As the above discussion and Chapter 2 make clear, much of the history of the making of modern sexual identity has occurred in tandem with the rise of modern electronic media. Gays and lesbians, then bisexuals and transgender individuals, have fought for recognition in order to combat the relative invisibility of GLBTQ individuals and communities in the media. Visibility matters in two key ways, one common to all minority groups, and the other unique to GLBTQ identities. First, for many groups in society, media visibility is considered an important form of social and political recognition. Second, for GLBTQ people, media representation is often a vital source for self-recognition and identity formation.

The significance of visibility was recognized in the 1970s through the concept of symbolic annihilation. Symbolic annihilation, first termed by George Gerbner and Larry

Gross (1976), was further elaborated by feminist media scholar Gaye Tuchman (1978). Symbolic annihilation can refer to an absence of representations, underrepresentation of a particular social group, or a markedly strong pattern of negative representations. Writing in the 1970s, Tuchman developed this concept to describe a situation in which most media presented a world filled with men in the most important positions. According to Tuchman, the symbolic annihilation of women in the media created the de facto sense that they were secondary citizens. Scholars have used the concept of symbolic annihilation to study the representation of other groups, such as African-Americans or Asian-Americans, in order to link the lack of or narrow media visibility to their lack of social and political recognition.

While the symbolic annihilation of women and minority groups emphasized their relative political and social invisibility, for the GLBTQ population the stakes of this erasure are even higher. While women and minority groups might see either their absence or very limited images of themselves in the media, they can nonetheless see themselves in the world. Simply put, women see other women and African Americans see other African Americans as members of their families, in school, in their communities, etc. GLBTQ individuals often grow up around heterosexuals, and it is quite possible that they do not encounter people like themselves in their existing social worlds (Gross, 2001). In this case, symbolic annihilation will at the very least reinforce the idea that the GLBTQ population is made up of second-class citizens, but, far worse, perpetuate their social invisibility. Whereas the absence of women in the media indicates a tremendous power imbalance and contributes to their devaluation, the absence of GLBTQ individuals can create the sense that they simply do not exist. For example, activist Vito Russo (1987), introduced in Chapter 2, remarked in *The Celluloid Closet*,

> The big lie about gays and lesbians is that we do not exist. The story of the ways in which gayness has been defined in American film is the story of the ways in which we have been defined in America. . . . As expressed on screen, America was a dream that had no room for the existence of homosexuals.
>
> (p. xii)

GLBTQ visibility is significant because, for many people, such representations are the point of first contact with GLBTQ identities. For instance, sexual minorities, unlike racial, ethnic, or religious minorities, typically are not raised in families and communities that share their minority identities. GLBTQ people by and large come to their identities later in life, and not always in supportive situations. In fact, a declaration of their identity can lead to rejection by friends and family members. Even if GLBTQ people do have a social support system available to them, they certainly are aware of the continuing social stigma of gay, lesbian, bisexual, and transgender identities. Cultural acceptance of sexual minorities, particularly gays or lesbians, has undoubtedly increased in recent years, yet coming to terms with one's own identity still involves anxiety, shame, and isolation for many GLBTQ individuals. Because many GLBTQ persons may have grown up with limited or no models of people with variant sexual identities in their own lives, media often fill that void (Calzo & Ward, 2009; Gomillion & Guilano, 2011). Jennifer Reed (2009) surveys the growing presence of both lesbian characters and lesbian celebrities in the media and argues that the

> creation of a public lesbian presence has untold effects in that lesbian subjectivity becomes a possibility that did not exist in the same way before. If it exists as a publicly acknowledged reality, people have the opportunity to identify with it. The obvious material consequences include the fact that women come out younger, see other lesbians to identify with, and find a more comfortable and roomy place in which to build a self, and community.
>
> (p. 308)

GLBTQ visibility also is important for straight and cisgender persons who have little to no personal exposure to GLBTQ people and rely heavily on the media to understand those identities. Simply put, many people's first experience with GLBTQ people comes through the media rather than personal experience. The fact that many people might not know GLBTQ individuals in their daily life gives media images an extra weight, strongly shaping impressions of a group of people with whom they may not have direct experience (Schiappa, Gregg, & Hewes, 2005; 2006).

While visibility cannot take the place of politics, activism, community building, and interpersonal forms of support, there can be no doubt that mediated representation is a key form of social and political recognition that indicates the relative social worth of a particular group of people. Representation itself becomes a form of power, portraying certain social relations as natural and justifiable. If we do not see GLBTQ people in the media, then, at the least, we might not even be aware of their existence, which might cause special pain to queer youth trying to make sense of their experience. At worse, it justifies continued discrimination and even violence. While in the next section we will examine critiques of the current state of GLBTQ visibility, it is important to realize that even if scholars think that progress has been uneven, they nonetheless agree that it is *significant*. The significance is indicated in the titles of several book-length studies that document the rise of gay visibility through the 1990s and early 2000s, including Larry Gross's (2001) *Up from Invisibility*, Suzanna Danuta Walters, (2003) *All the Rage: The*

Story of Gay Visibility in America, and Richard Streitmatter's (2009) *From "Perverts" to "Fab Five": The Media's Changing Depiction of Gay Men and Lesbians.*

▶ APPROACHES TO VISIBILITY

Given the importance of visibility and its unique relationship to GLBTQ identities, it is important to find ways to understand, examine, and evaluate the meaning and possible impact of such visibility. As discussed in Chapter 1, the study of media takes place across a range of scholarly traditions, and therefore encompasses a number of approaches. However, most of these traditions are interested in the meaning and impact of representations on minorities. While there are important differences between them, in this section will discuss the dominant way of thinking about media images: stereotype analysis. We will examine the ways scholars approach the question of stereotypes and some of the methods they use to examine them. Next, we will introduce you to some of the key critiques of stereotype theory. While not rejecting the study of stereotypes, these criticisms call into question the assumptions that guide more straightforward stereotype analysis. The key point in this discussion is to think about what we might gain by moving past a binary logic of "positive" and "negative" in order to develop a richer exploration of meanings of visibility.

Stereotypes

Most of us are familiar with the concept of stereotypes. We understand stereotypes as widely circulated, constantly repeated, reductive or even, untrue images or ideas about a particular social group. For example, there are stereotypes of women with blonde hair as dumb, African-American men as lazy, fraternity brothers as drunk jock types, Asian-Americans as good at math, and lesbians as more masculine than feminine. Stereotypes often are central to the study of media visibility. Walter Lippmann (1922) used the term to describe the "pictures in our heads," the process of categorization we use to make sense of a complex world (p. 18). People use generalized conceptual categories to "place" new situations and people into some category that helps them move through the world without having to size up every single situation and person as radically new and particular (pp. 53–62). More recently, social psychologists have argued that stereotypes are best understood as "schemas" in our head, informed by sources such as the media, that "prime" us to see individuals we encounter based on those schemas rather than our immediate observation of them. While Lippmann, and even social psychologists, do not see the process of stereotyping as inherently bad, they do believe that such categorizations can distort our ideas about social groups or situations. The stereotype, therefore, is approached as either a misrepresentation or misperception of reality that has the power to negatively influence different social groups. Media often are seen as a key site for the circulation of stereotypes, exposing audiences to potentially harmful ideas about minority social groups, which shape how they are seen by others.

Scholars and activists have identified a broad range of stereotypes about the GLBTQ population. For example, Chapter 2 detailed how the most enduring stereotypes of gays and lesbians in media can be traced back to the early understanding of homosexuality as a form of gender inversion. Since that time, representations of gays and lesbians have been marked by stereotypical references to femininity in the case of gay men and masculinity in the case of lesbians. These enduring stereotypes abound in representations of gay men, from Albert Goldman in *The Birdcage* (1996), Jack on *Will & Grace* (1998–2006), Cameron on *Modern Family* (2009–), Kurt on *Glee* (2009–), and even in reality programming, including contestants on *Top Chef* (2009–), *Project Runway* (2004–), and the *Amazing Race* (2001–). In some ways the connection between women and masculinity has dissipated over time so that today the use of gender inversion in the representation of lesbianism is less pronounced. For example, while Ellen DeGeneres in her public persona presents herself as less feminine than typical female Hollywood stars, her ads for *Cover Girl* indicate that she is far from mannish. The popular Showtime series *The L Word* (2004–2009) featured a cast of characters who largely adhered to conventional Hollywood beauty norms. In part, this can be traced to the wave of "Lesbian Chic" in the early and mid-1990s. Celebrated in magazines, movies, and even television shows, lesbians became more visible, but primarily through the stereotype of the "lipstick lesbian," who rejected the older stereotype of the butch or mannish lesbian. Bisexuals frequently are stereotyped as sexually promiscuous and as a danger to stable relationships. For example, media reports of the breakup of film star Johnny Depp from his longtime girlfriend Vanessa Paradis laid the blame on Depp's costar, Amber Heard, because she is an open bisexual (Anderson-Minshall, 2012). MTV's *A Shot at Love with Tila Tequila* (2008–2009) further exploited this stereotype. These images are criticized as inaccurate and distorted pictures of sexual minorities that do not accurately reflect their real lives.

The study of stereotypes can be conducted in a number of ways. A common method from the social sciences is quantitative content analysis, a research method focused on looking for representations that fit within pre-established categories. These categories usually are narrowly defined features of media texts, such as the presence or absence of particular social types (women, housewives, African Americans, gay men), stereotypes of a particular group that are assumed to be inaccurate or harmful (effeminate gay men, women as housewives, etc.), particular acts (violent acts, sexual acts), or kinds of relationships between characters. For example, Raley and Lucas (2006) explained their method for the study of stereotypes of gays and lesbians in television:

> [t]he shows were content analyzed for a number of variables related to the
> characters. The variables included the gender, race, sexual orientation of the
> recorded characters, the number of jokes with homosexual themes said by
> the characters, the number of times the character engaged in a display of
> affection with another character, and whether the character interacted with
> children.
>
> (p. 28)

Content analysis is an important technique for revealing broad patterns of representation, for comparison of representations across specific moments in time, and for activist groups challenging the limited nature of their representations. Qualitative researchers also examine stereotypes, sometimes asking the same or similar questions as quantitative researchers but, as we will discuss later, other times asking very different questions.

Because content analysis of stereotypes produces quantifiable results about such patterns, it is the kind of analysis often used by advocacy groups, including the Gay and Lesbian Alliance Against Defamation (GLAAD). As described in Chapter 2, GLAAD was formed in 1985 by a group of activists in New York, including Vito Russo, to respond to what they viewed as sensationalized and homophobic AIDS coverage by the *New York Post*. Today, GLAAD is one of the best-known and best-funded GLBT activist organizations in the United States. GLAAD's mission is to:

> amplif[y] the voice of the LGBT community by empowering real people to
> share their stories, holding the media accountable for the words and images
> they present, and helping grassroots organizations communicate effectively.
> By ensuring that the stories of LGBT people are heard through the media,
> GLAAD promotes understanding, increases acceptance, and advances
> equality.
>
> (About GLAAD, 2014)

Not only does GLAAD serve as a watchdog for negative portrayals of GLBTQ persons, it also organizes the annual GLAAD awards to "recognize and honor media for their fair, accurate and inclusive representations of the lesbian, gay, bisexual and transgender community and the issues that affect their lives." (See Textbox 3.2 for a discussion of the growing criticism about the links between GLAAD and Hollywood.)

One of the organization's regular activities is tracking media visibility, including the yearly publication of the *Where We Are on TV* report, taking account of the current state of visibility, primarily in television. This is the report you used in the Tracking Visibility activity (Textbox 3.1). GLAAD performs an accounting of the number of gay, lesbian, bisexual, and transgender characters on television, drawing specific comparisons between the diversity they find on the screen and the diversity they find in real life, and also using numbers as a sign of progress, or lack thereof. For example, the report of the 2011–2012 season "found that 2.9% of series regulars are lesbian, gay, bisexual or transgender (LGBT), down from 3.9% in 2010 and 3% in 2009" (GLAAD, 2012). In addition to counting the overall number of characters, GLAAD compares the relative diversity of such characters against U.S. demographic data. They note, for example, that, "while there have been improvements in terms of the gender divide, women still only account for 43% of series regulars on primetime broadcast television while making up more than half the U.S. population" (GLAAD, 2012). In addition, they examine the ethnic diversity of GLBTQ characters on television. The purpose of such work is to advocate for increased gender and racial diversity that better matches societal reality.

BOX 3.2   Advocacy for Whom? GLAAD and Its Critics

When it was founded in 1985, GLAAD was a group of local chapters spread around the United States and run almost exclusively by volunteers. Since that time, GLAAD has become a national organization, with 46 full-time employees and a $7 million budget (Graham, 2005). It increasingly is recognized as among the most powerful advocacy groups in Hollywood. However, GLAAD is not without its critics. Its increasing power and budget have led to key questions regarding exactly for whom and for what GLAAD is advocating.

Vincent Doyle (2005), who spent time inside GLAAD's organization while conducting an ethnographic study, suggests that GLAAD's shift from its grassroots street activist beginnings to its professionalization of media activism during the late 1990s is indicative of the broader shift that was happening in GLBT activism as radical liberationist movements of the 1970s shifted into identity politics of inclusion. Doyle contends that GLAAD's new leaders and staffers, who increasingly came from professional media and marketing backgrounds, made it their key focus to cultivate good relationships with media decision makers. In adapting a "We want in!" slogan calling for increased visibility for GLBT people, GLAAD was willing to accept the largely narrow diversity of those representations. He writes,

> As media professionals, they had internalized the limits and rewards of the advocacy structure set up by the media companies to manage and contain the dissent of marginalized or underrepresented groups. Instead of seeing visibility as a precarious,

(Continued)

ambivalent, conditional, revocable and market-driven achievement, then, they labored under the impression that they were responsible for great changes in the way the media represents people.

(pp. 213–214)

As Doyle makes clear, GLAAD has been perfectly willing to advocate for "acceptable" representations of the GLBTQ population that are less likely to ruffle the feathers of advertisers or even draw negative publicity.

GLAAD also increasingly has been criticized for its financial relationship with the very media companies over whom its mission is to serve as watchdog. Gay activist, writer, and talk-show host Michelangelo Signorile attacked GLAAD for what he viewed as its lack of immediate and clear outrage when ABC cancelled upcoming live performances by Adam Lambert after Lambert, an openly gay former *American Idol* (2009) winner, kissed a male keyboardist during the 2009 American Music Awards. Signorile (2010) wrote in his column for *The Advocate*, "If GLAAD wants to be a real leader in quashing gay bias in the media, it must stop taking money from the companies whose programming it scrutinizes and must speak out quickly and forcefully when incidents occur." As affection between men continues to be underrepresented in advertising-supported television, it becomes the kind of controversial content with which GLAAD does not want to associate itself.

GLAAD's autonomy once again came into question in 2011 after its then president, Jarrett Barrios, sent a letter to the Federal Communications Commission (FCC) supporting the controversial proposed merger between AT&T and T-Mobile. He suggested that the merger would improve access to the Internet for GLBTQ people; however, some suggested that GLAAD had been influenced by financial contributions (AT&T is one of its donors) and AT&T executive Troup Coronado, who served on GLAAD's board of directors. Coronado and seven other board members left GLAAD following the controversy (Martinez, 2011).

GLAAD's close ties to the entertainment and communication industries raise a number of questions. While we earlier directed you to GLAAD's reports in order to examine the broader state of GLBTQ visibility, this time we ask you to visit the website to consider the kind of advocacy work in which GLAAD is engaged. Answer the following questions:

1. How does GLAAD define diversity? Is there evidence that GLAAD is focused on increasing the diversity of media representations of GLBT people?
2. What type of activism is done by GLAAD's field teams?
3. Who currently serves in leadership and board positions for GLAAD? How closely are they tied to the entertainment industry? Is this problematic? Are there advantages?

4. Examine GLAAD's financial documents from the prior year (available on their website) and check their rating on charitynavigator.org. How much is their executive director compensated? How is their money spent? Who are their biggest donors?

5. Who exactly does GLAAD serve? Does it represent the full diversity of the GLBTQ population or a narrow segment? Or, does it seem to be serving the interests of the entertainment and communication industries?

Studies of stereotypes generally work to identify negative representations that might be inaccurate, distorted, or just limited in the way a social group is seen in the media. Quantitative and qualitative researchers share a belief that media stereotypes limit the way we make sense of people who are not part of the dominant culture and believe that more complex, positive representations will lead to greater social and political acceptance of the GLBTQ population. In this belief that improved representations will lead to greater recognition, scholars sometimes turn to earlier models of ethnic representations as a starting point. These models suggest media reflect and reinforce the status quo by limiting the representations of those in society who have less economic and social power. Scholars propose that representations of minorities move through a progression of representational stages that begin with negative or non-existent representations and over time move toward more positive representations.

For example, Clark (1969) proposed three "stages" that representations of ethnic minorities on television must first pass through—"non-recognition", "ridicule", and "regulation"—before reaching the final stage of "respect." "Non-recognition" describes a phase in which the minority group simply is not depicted in television. The "ridicule" stage suggests a period in which minority characters on television are made fun of for the benefit of the presumed white audience. The "regulation" stage involves representations of minorities in positions associated with the maintenance of law and order (e.g., police detective, member of the military, intelligence officer). Hart (2000) and Raley and Lucas (2006) both have applied Clark's model to representations of gay characters.

Hart (2000) found that gay men remained in the non-recognition stage until television began reflecting the social issues of the 1960s, at which point they entered the second stage, ridicule. He cites "stereotypes of gay men," which include use of derogatory language on talk shows, effeminate characters in comedy, and pedophilic gay characters in dramas (p. 63). Hart credits the gay liberation movement for the shift to television's move to a regulation stage in the 1970s, before the 1980s AIDS epidemic contributed to less positive representations. However, Hart contends that representations of gay men in the 1990s finally entered Clark's final stage of respect. Raley and Lucas (2006) are less optimistic than Hart in applying Clark's stages of representation to television. Using content analysis, they suggest that, while gays and lesbians clearly have moved beyond the non-recognition stage, representations fall within the ridicule and regulation stages. They also suggest that bisexuals remain in the non-recognition stage. Neither study examined television's portrayal of transgender characters.

Applying a model like Clark's to media representations of GLBTQ characters can help to illustrate the broad changes in representations over the past 50 years. Quantitative studies of media stereotypes help us understand the broad patterns of representation that shape how we see social groups. Qualitative studies help us see how stereotypes operate in more specific contexts. Such studies can form the basis of advocacy work based on improving the ways groups are seen. In advocating for more positive images, scholars and activists are clear that visibility matters to how we see people who are not part of culturally dominant groups, and that developing more positive, realistic, and diverse representations of any group can lead to increased social and political tolerance of social diversity. However, as we will discuss below, stereotype analysis has some important limitations that suggest that there are good reasons for expanding our approaches to the study of visibility.

Critiques of Stereotype Analysis

The examination of stereotypes has been central to a consideration of the ways that media texts reproduce inequalities in society. All of us who have grown up in our saturated media culture certainly are aware of the fact that stereotypes, or some sort of typing, are key to creating media images that make sense to widely divergent groups of individuals, each coming to the media with particular experiences of the world. However, scholars trained in media studies and influenced by critical cultural theories, as discussed in Chapter 1, seek to complicate our understanding of stereotypes and argue that there are some key weaknesses in making them the basis of the study of visibility. Scholars criticize, first, the view of stereotypes as inaccurate distortions of the reality of social groups and, second, the presumption that stereotypes have a clear meaning that can be evaluated as negative or positive. Instead, scholars argue that we examine the *work* that stereotypes do in circulating particular definitions about gender and sexual identities, especially in cases where such differences cannot clearly be marked by vision alone.

A key critique of stereotype analysis is the tendency to examine stereotypes as distortions of some reality of a particular social group. The assumption here is that there is some independent, verifiable "reality" of any identity group that we can all agree on, and that identity itself is stable and fixed. However, some scholars argue that there is no inherent "truth" of identity that can be distorted by a stereotype. For example, feminist media scholar Liesbet Van Zoonen (1994) argues that in trying to determine how they were "distorted" by stereotypes, it would be impossible for scholars to ever agree on the "truth" of what women are. "Women" as a category is simply too large, complex, varied, and contingent to ever decide on a single truth of what "women" are or even should be. In addition, many stereotypes have some connection to some aspect of a social group. For example, we might note it is common to negatively stereotype lesbians as more masculine than feminine. Yet, there are a number of lesbians who proudly and confidently call themselves "butch." If we state this as a negative stereotype, what are we saying about women who self-identify with the label?

Second, content analysts tend to see media meanings as clear and indisputable, regardless of the social experiences of particular audience members or even of the context of a particular image. Stereotype analysts tend to argue that media meanings are fairly stable and singular. For example, content analysis of media images depends upon the idea that audiences can agree on a single and clear meaning of media images. However, media studies scholars point out that this often misses the complexity of most images. In Chapter 1 we discussed Stuart Hall's (1973) model of encoding and decoding. What this model stresses is that media texts often contain more than one meaning, while audiences themselves decode those meanings in different ways depending on their social position. When it comes to examining visibility in media texts, then, media studies scholars apply a qualitative textual approach, defined by McKee (2003) as "an educated guess at some of the most likely interpretations that might be made of [a] text" (p. 1). In other words, they take into consideration that a text's meaning is never stable and that different groups might "read" it in different ways.

In critiquing some of the underlying assumptions of quantitative stereotype analysis—that identity is fixed and that the meaning of media images is clear—media studies scholars further note that the evaluation of some images as negative and others as more positive can end up leading to confusion. For example, we can consider the representation of sexual promiscuity among gay men. It is true that in our culture, which historically has associated monogamy with certain forms of class and gendered acceptability, to be stereotyped as promiscuous can be understood to be negative. Certainly during the AIDS crisis, the strong connection that media texts made between gay male promiscuity and death contributed to the slow government response and lack of public sympathy. Yet, might we imagine ways in which some people might actually view representations of promiscuity in a positive light? Take the case of *Queer as Folk* (2000–2005), which originated in Great Britain and was adapted by Showtime for American TV in 2000. Compared to network offerings like *Ellen* (1994–1998) or *Will & Grace* (1998–2006), the program was marked by its frank depictions of gay male promiscuity, drug use, and open discussion of AIDS. This led some critics to argue the program replayed negative stereotypes of gay men, which largely reconfirmed society's worst ideas. However, for many viewers, including some scholars and critics of this show, such representations more fully resonated with their lived experiences than those found in the more clean-cut broadcast network programs (Streitmatter, 2009). In other words, the accusation that the show negatively stereotyped gay men led to the implicit judgment of promiscuity in the gay community.

Stereotypes as "Work"

Of course, stereotypes are a reality of our media environment. In fact, media texts take all kinds of "shortcuts" to convey a lot of information in the most economical way possible. However, getting stuck in the endless loop of whether they are negative or positive can ultimately be a limiting way of approaching visibility. Another way to think about ste-reotypes is to examine the kind of "work" they do in supporting or challenging broader systems of power relationships. As we discussed in Chapter 1, some scholars who study media tend to view its impact as being primarily about its effect on the perception, atti-tudes, and even actions of individuals. However, we also read about the critical cultural approach to media that considers the broader historical, cultural, and social significance of media. One of the central concepts that these scholars draw on is the theory of ide-ology. Ideology has many definitions, but it most commonly refers to a dominant set of ideas, including values, beliefs, historical stories, and ideas about social roles, that work to maintain an existing set of power relations. Italian theorist Antonio Gramsci used the term "hegemony" to refer to the process through which leaders rule not through force, but through gaining consent to a set of ideas that circulate as common sense. These are ideas that seem so "natural" that no one asks questions about them.

Media also are seen as a key part of the process of creating norms. There is a subtle distinction between the theorization of norms and ideology. Growing out of Marxism, theories of ideology often are concerned with the ways that top-down power structures are maintained. Growing out of the work of Foucault, theories of normativity are con-cerned with questions of power as both repressive *and* productive. As you recall from Chapters 1 and 2, discourses about sexuality did not *repress* sexual behavior, but instead actually *created* sexual identity categories that people use in the construction of their identities. While the Marxist and Foucaultian perspectives have some important differ-ences, many media scholars work with both sets of terms somewhat interchangeably, allowing the combination to offer a richer view of the relationship between media and identity. What both theories do is invite us to think of media not as a discrete part of our social, cultural, and political systems that say something about the "real" world out-side of them, but as a key social institution for the circulation of discourses that shape, reinforce, and even challenge dominant ideologies and/or norms.

By circulating various discourses, media can be understood as doing social or cultural "work" around important issues. Richard Dyer (1993) argued that the work stereotypes do is to create boundary definitions between social groups, and between behaviors that are valued by society and those that are not. Stereotypes condense complex cultural knowledge into easily identifiable "types" of people in ways that ask us not the think about social power. For example, we can think of the stereotype of African-American men as poor and lazy. A stereotype analysis would note that this is a negative stereotype of African-American men that contributes to their social ostracism. However, a media studies scholar might note that the truth is that many African-American men *are* poor, but that the stereotype works to make us think of economic disparity as resulting from personal failures rather than broader patterns of racism in American society that have historically limited opportunities for black men. That is to say, the stereotype works to pathologize black men rather than critiquing social power structures. In this case, it is not the stereotype alone that needs to be improved; i.e., seeing African-American men as rich and hard-working still will prevent us from seeing the bigger problem of structural social inequalities. Stereotypes are an exercise in social power; they define groups within terms set by the dominant groups in society. Reversing the stereotype does not necessarily alter that fact.

When it comes to categories based on behaviors, the use of stereotypes becomes more complicated because they are necessary to maintain a boundary where visual confirmation alone is not possible. Dyer (1993) wrote that

> The role of stereotypes is to make visible the invisible, so that there is no danger of it creeping up on us unawares: and to make fast, firm and separate what is in reality fluid and much closer to the norm than the dominant value system cares to admit.

(p. 16)

For example, today you might think that there is a natural connection between young girls and the color pink and young boys and the color blue thanks to dominant stereotypes. Walk into any toy store or baby section of a major retailer and girls' toys and clothes will all be in shapes of pink and light, pastel colors, while boys' toys and clothes will be in blue and darker, primary colors. But, the use of pink for girls and blue for boys is a fairly recent arrangement. Why be so concerned with such a strict color differentiation? Because our culture currently is concerned with drawing a sharp distinction between the male and female, the use of these colors makes it seem as if from birth our biological sex determines our gender identity. The stereotype helps keep that boundary in place. Fixing cultural or social processes as natural "facts" is referred to as reification. That is, the idea that colors are used to reinforce a cultural definition of the difference between the sexes is treated as if the color distinction is proof of a natural distinction.

As Dyer (1993) points out, the fact is that, without *some* sort of typing work, we might never *see* GLBTQ characters in the media. The further reality is that much of what scholars and advocates see as stereotypes emerges from the practices of GLBTQ communities, who historically have relied on visual codes to make themselves recognizable to each other. The desire to expunge the stereotype as negative also might be rejecting part of GLBTQ history and/or identity. Rather than settling for an evaluation of a stereotype as positive or negative, it is more productive to think about *what* aspects of the stereotype are considered negative, how those aspects link up with broader ideas about gender and sexuality, the historical development of the stereotype, the cultural norms supported by the stereotype, and even the relationship between the stereotype and the social group it represents.

We can think of this in relationship to the sissy stereotype. If we ask any of our classes about negative stereotypes of gay men, a number of students invariably will mention the "sissy" figure. One of the most enduring images of gay men in Western culture, the "sissy" is effeminate, vain, over-emotional, and, worst of all, flamboyant. Across the space of the last hundred years, the sissy often has served as *the* image of gay men's failed masculinity. The roots of this stereotype are found in the work of sexologists, discussed in Chapter 2, who conflated gender and sexuality to assert that homosexuality is a form of gender inversion. Sexologists did not see this as necessarily bad, but in popular discourse the idea of inversion was taken to be a sign of the failure of gays and lesbians to fulfill the "natural" expectations of gendered behavior. Since the 1970s, activists and scholars have been critical of this stereotype as a negative portrayal of male homosexuality.

Historically, the sissy figure has acted as a dividing line between homosexual men and heterosexual men. As the need to make that boundary more clear became important, so, too, did the stereotype grow more "negative." For example, as you might recall from the *Celluloid Closet* (1995) documentary, in the 1930s and 1940s the sissy was a fairly harmless figure; he was the "dandy" or the wardrobe man in a traveling show. The humor aimed at him was gentle, and no one ever whispered the word "homosexual." But by the end of World War II, the need to bring back troops from the homosocial environment of the military and stimulate economic demand by advocating marriage and family growth meant that by the 1950s the line between straight and gay men became sharper. Increasingly, the sissy functioned as deceitful, devious, murderous, or purely for laughter. The sissy's femininity helped make sure that no man could be mistaken as homosexual simply by virtue of his being masculine. After all, what "normal" man would bear such hatred by exposing himself as even remotely feminine if he was anything other than heterosexual?

What exactly is being criticized in this stereotype? The thing that is reviled is *femininity*. It functions as part of patriarchy to view anything feminine as less than worthy. After all, the same line between gay and straight men was maintained between men and women, so that the divide between the genders also was strictly maintained. The fact is that there are gay men who are effeminate. As Richard Dyer (1993), who refers to the effeminacy of men as "in betweenism," argues, "this negative use of the types should not blind us to the fact that ideas of in betweenism have been used by gay people themselves, not only in subcultural practices but in historically progressive activism" (p. 36). That is to say, effeminate gay men often have stood at the forefront of gay activism. More than this, however, the fact is that simply by being "in-between" masculine and feminine, the sissy's very presence challenged the presumed naturalness of the divide between them. (See Textbox 3.3 to examine the potential of the sissy to trouble masculinity in hopeful ways.) In addition, for the many years that homosexuality, either through explicit or implicit censorship, could not be discussed in movies or television shows, effeminacy served as a source of knowing *identification*, deploying codes recognizable in gay subcultures.

BOX 3.3   Rethinking the "Sissy"

FIGURE 3.2 Kurt Hummel joins the football team
Source: *Glee*, Season 1, Episode 15, "Preggers," 2009, FOX
Broadcasting Company.

(Continued)

Today, people continue to refer to the sissy as a negative stereotype. In fact, even within some segments of the gay community, feminine men are reviled and treated as an obstacle to political progress. For those gay men who want "in" to dominant culture, including dominant notions of masculinity, the effeminate gay man is an embarrassment. But, the sissy also offers a potent critique of masculinity. His appearance has the power to upend the seeming naturalness of the link between male bodies and masculinity. In addition, the sissy's often biting humor further denies norms of heterosexual culture. In this sense, the sissy can be seen as offering a utopic alternative to more destructive forms of masculinity. An example of this is found in the "Preggers" episode of *Glee* (Falchuk, 2009). The effeminate Kurt Hummel tells his father that he is on the football team when he is caught filming himself and his friends performing Beyonce's "Single Ladies" dance. Caught in a lie, Kurt must now try out for a position. It turns out that Kurt is a freakishly good kicker on a very bad team. Though cruelly and persistently teased by his teammates for his effeminacy, Kurt eventually leads the team to victory when he convinces his fellow players to confuse the opposing team by performing the "Single Ladies" dance—the very act that had gotten him in this situation in the first place. Of course, viewers never see Kurt on the team again, but for a short while the show rephrases the understanding of the sissy and shows how opening up masculinity might just be a good thing after all.

To examine the kind of "work" the sissy figure does, watch an episode of a television show that features a recognizable "sissy" character, including *Glee* (2009–2015), *The New Normal* (2012–2013), or *Will & Grace* (1998–2006). You might also consider the web series *Husbands* (2011–). As you watch, keep the following questions in mind:

1. What behaviors allow you to recognize the characters as a sissy?
2. What role does the sissy character play in the narrative?
3. How does this sissy character get along with other men in the narrative?
4. In what ways does the sissy character ask us to rethink what it means to be a man?
5. Drawing on the above discussion, what "work" is the sissy character doing in establishing a line between gay and straight masculinity?

Stereotype analysis remains an important way of studying visibility. However, as we have suggested here, there are some key limitations to the approach. At a basic level, stereotype analysis works to measure media images against an empirically verifiable reality. As the critiques make clear here, the end result can be a superficial analysis that fails to consider stereotypes in their broader historical and cultural contexts. Even models of progress do not accurately account for such contexts. Thinking of representations in terms of "stages" also has its limitations. For instance, it presumes a progressive model in which representations will necessarily become better over time. However, media representations of GLBTQ people are linked to particular socio-historical moments full of competing discourses about sexuality and gender. As we saw in Chapter 2, history is not a simple linear march of progress for sexual minorities. Additionally, cultural discourses about sexuality and gender are never univocal, which oftentimes plays out in a complex range of media representations. Such models are based on the idea that representations influence individual attitudes, and that improvements will come by changing attitudes toward a social group. But what counts as improvement? If we want to move beyond the idea of negative and positive as the language for evaluating visibility, then on what basis *do* we make judgments? In the next section we will consider the ways that different ideas about the political aims of visibility shape such evaluations.

▶ VISIBILITY FOR WHAT?

How people evaluate the meaning of visibility depends on a number of factors, including their perspective on sexuality, their view of the relationship between media and identity, including the theoretical and methodological approaches in media, and in the underlying assumptions made about sexual identity as either natural or constructed. A key distinction in how scholars and critics make sense of media visibility is what they think the ultimate goal of GLBTQ activism should be. On the one hand are those seeking the assimilation of gay, lesbian, bisexual, and transgender individuals into mainstream society. Activists and scholars with this goal in mind evaluate images on the basis of to what extent they promote inclusion into society. On the other hand are those scholars and activists, usually working within a queer political perspective, who evaluate visibility on how far it goes in questioning dominant norms, our very framework for thinking about sexuality, and imagining a world free from heteronormativity and all its attendant oppressions.

A great deal of stereotype research is founded on an implicit assumption that assimilation is the end goal of GLBT identity politics. The idea that gays and lesbians, especially, should be treated as equal to, and thus "like," heterosexuals is implicit in evaluations that rely on terms like "negative" and "positive" and in calls for more accurate representations. As discussed above, evaluations of negative or positive are often made on the basis of how close representations of GLTQ characters are to the representations of heterosexual characters. To the extent that characters seem to fit into the dominant norms of culture, they are seen as politically progressive and key to changing the opinions of individual viewers.

Scholars influenced by queer theory often are critical of the assimilationist thrust of many contemporary representations. In theorizing sexual identities as fluid, they consider the ways that media help open up certain possibilities for what it means to be gay, lesbian, bisexual, or transgender. Taking a queer theoretical approach, scholars examine the more complicated ways media visibility either reinforces or challenges dominant discourses of sexuality, and offer ways of thinking about texts that seek to get past the positive/negative bypass and to move beyond thinking of visibility as a panacea for homophobia. This is an approach that seeks to move beyond identity politics in the narrow sense, in order to examine the broader discourses and practices that situate a narrow definition of acceptable sexuality as normal and other forms of sexual practices and identity as inherently deviant.

One approach involves examining the ways particular representations work to maintain heteronormativity. As you will recall from Chapter 1, heteronormativity describes the way in which heterosexual privilege is completely woven into the fabric of society. The concern here is less with the stereotyping of individual characters than it is with the broader structures of representation. Drawing from cultural studies methods, the theoretical aim of such a project is to examine more fully the ways that the presence of gay characters or even a gay community does not guarantee that a particular representation does much to challenge the dominant heterosexual/homosexual binary, and thus the dominance of heterosexuality. For example, we can consider the case of the popular ABC sitcom *Modern Family* (2009–), featuring gay couple Mitch and Cameron. On the one hand, there is a great deal of popular discussion about the extent to which the two fall into stereotypes, with some arguing that they challenge stereotypes because Cameron is both flamboyant *and* a former athlete. At the same time, however, both men are vain, over-emotional, and sometimes fall into the sissy stereotype. It is clear we could go back and forth on this issue without ever finally settling on whether these characters are negative or positive (see Textbox 3.4).

 **BOX 3.4**   Evaluating the Meaning of Gay Marriage in Television

Recent legal victories and growing social acceptance for gay marriage increasingly have found their way into media representations. Gay weddings and gay marriage have become common. Many of these weddings are seen as signs of acceptance, and in some advocacy discourse, recent court victories are seen as the "arrival" of gays and lesbians into mainstream American culture. Therefore, it is no surprise

FIGURE 3.3 Cam and Mitch say "I do"
Source: *Modern Family*, Season 5, Episode 23, "The Wedding," 2014,
American Broadcasting Company.

that some viewers and advocacy groups were happy to see one of America's favorite television gay couples, Mitch and Cam from ABC's *Modern Family* (2009–) tie the knot in the two-part, fifth season finale (May 14 and 21, 2014). In a blog post on the GLAAD website, "Why the #ModernWedding Matters," Jeremy Hooper (2014) praised the show for making an important contribution to the growing acceptance of gay marriage, especially the realistic way the program has handled the issue of gay marriage. There can be no doubt that, from an assimilation perspective, *Modern Family* deserves to be celebrated.

But, what if we were not persuaded that assimilation was the best end goal for gays and lesbians? Yep, Lovaas, and Elia (2007) distinguish between assimilationist and radical views of gay marriage. Assimilationists argue that gay marriage extends civil rights and social acceptability, provides social stability, and civilizes gay men the same way that heterosexual marriage civilizes straight men. The radical position is that marriage itself is a flawed institution, that the fight for marriage negates the value of different kinds of relationship, allows both Church and State to define the kinds of relationships people can have, and reinforces heteronormativity. Jack Halberstam (2012) argues that the benefits of gay marriage primarily accrue to white, middle-class gays and lesbians at the expense of considering the ways that racism and class impact the GLBTQ population. A radical view critiques the fight

(Continued)

for gay marriage for denying the rich range of relationships and forms of "family" organization that people can build for themselves.

Examining the case of the *Modern Family* (2009–) wedding, or any show featuring a gay wedding, consider some of the following questions:

1. How are the gay or lesbian characters positioned as parallel to all of the other heterosexual couples in the program?
2. What kinds of gender roles do the members of the same-sex couple perform? Is there a recognizably "masculine" and "feminine" partner?
3. Do we see the same-sex couple engaging in as much affection as opposite sex couples in the show?
4. Does the show offer an assimilationist or radical view of marriage?
5. What kinds of relationship possibilities are closed down by the idea of marriage in the show?

In addition, scholars increasingly pay attention to what Lisa Duggan (2003) termed homonormativity, which "is a politics that does not contest dominant heteronormative assumptions and institutions but upholds and sustains them while promising the possibility of a demobilized gay constituency and a privatized, depoliticized gay culture anchored in domesticity and consumption" (p. 50). Duggan argues that the modern mainstream movement has abandoned its quest for radical change and instead is content to advocate for the rights of GLBTQ individuals to live their lives just like straight people. In addition, these goals are focused primarily on the goals and needs of white, middle- and upper-middle-class, educated people, primarily men. The media rarely allows for visibility of non-white, working-class, or poor individuals who embrace a set of values that might be at odds with mainstream heteronormative ones. The point is not that this is necessarily bad, but that it is a very narrow and limiting view of GLBTQ life that positions gay men as invested in straight culture without thinking about how heterosexual culture might benefit from an engagement with queer cultures. The queer theoretical perspective, therefore, allows us to consider the idea that gay, lesbian, or transgender characters can exist in a text, but they are made sense of through the lens of heteronormativity. The point is not to examine whether the characters are positive or negative, but to consider to what extent they reinforce and challenge the norms of heterosexuality. Finally, it can help us move beyond the more specific visibility of GLBTQ identified characters to consider the sometimes surprising ways that all kinds of texts might reinforce heteronormativity, but also challenge it.

▶ CONCLUSION

There can be no doubt that the explosion in visibility has contributed to a seeming sea change in attitudes, especially toward gays and lesbians, but increasingly to bisexuals and trans men and trans women. Simply put, today's young people have tools to make sense of themselves and understand themselves in new ways that were not available only a generation ago. In this chapter, we have asked you to consider different ways of thinking about media visibility. We started with a concept almost everyone is familiar with: stereotypes. For most of us, the very thought of the term usually signals that we see something "negative" in a media text. In seeing stereotypes as negative, scholars, activists, and everyday people often seek to find ways to move us to more positive representations. However, we asked you to engage with some criticisms of stereotype research, which point out that it often can end in an endless loop: It's positive! It's negative! No, it is positive! Who can tell anymore?

As an alternative, we suggested that thinking about what stereotypes *do* is more productive. Placing them in their larger social, cultural, and historical context allows us to think about the ways that stereotypes are linked to broader patterns of power, and allows us to see them in ways that the negative/positive binary makes us miss. Finally, we considered alternative ways of evaluating visibility by thinking more critically about the sometimes unstated assumptions critics have about the goals of GLBTQ politics. Those seeking full inclusion of sexual and gender minorities into mainstream American culture will evaluate media texts differently than those who want to challenge the dominant discourses and norms of that mainstream. In thinking through a queer political perspective, we ask a different set of questions about visibility, ones that allow us to see visibility in complicated ways.

We end with the position we explained in the beginning: a "yes, but" approach. No one will deny the tremendous gains that have been made in terms of GLBTQ political and cultural recognition *and* media visibility. But, such gains cannot undo almost a century of harm, and the roots of heterosexism and homophobia remain deep in our culture. The idea that media visibility can undo that past or serve as a panacea for homophobia ignores the ways that GLBTQ visibility has been shaped by our heterosexual culture. As Sender (2012) argues, "[b]ecoming visible . . . enters GLBT people into regimes of representation that have not always been kind" (p. 217). As you move through the rest of this book, you will consider ways that the marketplace, the logics of the closet, comedy, and concerns over sex and gendered bodies can work to contain and limit the ways we might imagine GLBTQ identities. At the same time, you will also learn the ways that GLBTQ individuals and communities have turned to media as a source of support, identity building, and community recognition.

▶ REFERENCES

"About GLAAD". (2014). Retrieved from http://www.glaad.org/spiritday/textpurple.

Anderson-Minshall, D. (2012, December 24). Tabloids blame the bisexuals. *The Advocate* (June edition). Retrieved from http://www.advocate.com/artsentertainment/people/2012/06/24/tabloids-blame-bisexuals-june-edition.

Becker, R. (2006). *Gay TV and straight America*. New Brunswick, NJ: Rutgers University Press.

Calzo, J.P. & Ward, L.M. (2009). Media exposure and viewers' attitudes toward homosexuality: Evidence for mainstreaming or resonance. *Journal of Broadcasting & Electronic Media, 53*(2), 280–299.

Clark, C. (1969). Television and social controls: Some observation of the portrayal of ethnic minorities. *Television Quarterly, 9*(2), 18–22.

Doyle, V. (2008). "But Joan! You're my daughter!" The Gay and Lesbian Alliance Against Defamation and the politics of amnesia. *Radical History Review*, 100, 209–221.

Duggan, L. (2003). *The twilight of equality: Neoliberalism, cultural politics and the attack on Democracy*. Boston, MA: Beacon Press.

Dyer, R. (1993). *The matter of images: Essays on representation*. New York, NY: Routledge.

Falchuk, B., Brennan, I. (Writers) & Murphy, R. (Director). (2009, September 23). Preggers [Television series episode]. In I. Brennan, D. DiLoreto, B. Falchuk, & R. Murphy (Executive Producers), *Glee*. New York, NY: Fox Network.

Ganz, M., Lloyd, C., & O'Shannon, D. (Writers) and Statman, A. (Director). (2014, May 21). The Wedding, Part 2 [Television series episode]. In P. Corrigan, S. Levitan, C. Lloyd, J. Morton, D. O'Shannon, J. Richman, B. Walsh, Bill Wrubel, & D. Zucker (Executive Producers), *Modern Family*. Los Angeles, LA: American Broadcasting Company.

Gerbner, G. & Gross, L. (1976). Living with television: The violence profile. *Journal of Communication, 26*, 172–199.

GLAAD. (2012). *Where we are on TV: 2011–2012*. Retrieved from http://www.glaad.org/publications/whereweareontv11/overview.

Gomillion, S.C. & Giuliano, T.A. (2011). The influence of media roles models on gay, lesbian, and bisexual identity. *Journal of Homosexuality, 58*, 330–354.

Graham, C. (2005). Growing pains at GLAAD.advocate.com. Retrieved from http://www.advocate.com/news/2005/04/11/movement-crisis-growing-pains-glaad?page=full.

Gross, L. (2001). *Up from invisibility: Lesbians, gay men, and the media in America*. New York, NY: Columbia University Press.

Halbertsam, J.J. (2012). *Gaga feminism: Sex, gender and the end of normal*. Boston, MA: Beacon Press.

Hall, S. (1973). *Encoding and decoding in the television discourse*. Birmingham, AL: University of Birmingham, Centre of Contemporary Cultural Studies.

Hart, K.R. (2000). Representing gay men on American television. *Journal of Men's Studies, 9*, 59–79.

Higginbotham, A., Karlin, B., & Richman, J. (Writers) and Levitan, S. (Director). (2014, May 14). The Wedding, Part 1 [Television series episode]. In P. Corrigan, S. Levitan, C. Lloyd, J. Morton,

D. O'Shannon, J. Richman, B. Walsh, Bill Wrubel, & D. Zucker (Executive Producers), *Modern Family*. Los Angeles, LA: American Broadcasting Company.

Hooper, J. (2014, May 14). Why the #Modern Wedding Matters. *GLAAD*. Retrieved from http://www.glaad.org/blog/why-modernwedding-matters.

Knegt, P. (2008). *Forging a gay mainstream: Negotiating gay cinema in the American hegemony.* (Unpublished master's thesis). Concordia University, Montreal, Quebec, Canada.

Lippmann, W. (1922). *Public opinion.* New York, NY: Harcourt Brace Jovanovich.

Martinez, J. (2011, June 19). GLAAD chief resigns, but fallout continues. *Politico*. Retrieved from http://www.politico.com.

McKee, A. (2003). *Textual analysis: A beginner's guide.* Thousand Oaks, CA: Sage Publications.

Raley, A.B. & Lucas, J.L. (2006). Stereotype or success? Prime-time television's portrayals of gay male, lesbian and bisexual characters. *Journal of Homosexuality, 51* (2), 19–38.

Reed, J. (2009). Lesbian television personalities—A queer new subject. *Journal of American Culture, 32* (4), 307–317.

Rich, R. (1992). New queer sensation. *Sight & Sound, 5* (2), 30–34.

Russo, V. (1987). *The celluloid closet: Homosexuality in the movies.* New York, NY: HarperCollins.

Schiappa, E., Gregg, P.B., & Hewes, D.E. (2005). The parasocial contact hypothesis. *Communication Monographs, 72* (1), 92–115.

Schiappa, E., Gregg, P.B., & Hewes, D.E. (2006). Can one TV show make a difference? *Will & Grace* and the parasocial contact hypothesis. *Journal of Homosexuality, 51*(4), 15–37.

Sender, K. (2012). No hard feelings: Reflexivity and queer affect in the new media landscape. In K. Ross (Ed.), *The handbook of gender, sex and media* (pp. 535–551). Hoboken, NJ: Wiley & Sons, Ltd.

Signorile, M. (2010, January 12). GLAAD reconsidered. advocate.com. Retrieved from http://www.advocate.com/politics/commentary/2010/01/12/glaad-reconsidered.

Streitmatter, R. (2009). *From "perverts" to "fab five": The media's changing depiction of gay men and lesbians.* New York, NY: Routledge.

Tuchman, G. (1978). Introduction: The symbolic annihilation of women by the mass media. In G. Tuchman, A.K. Daniels, & J. Benét (Eds.), *Hearth and home: Images of women in the mass media* (pp. 3–38). New York, NY: Oxford University Press.

Van Zoonen, L. (1994). *Feminist media studies.* London: Sage Publications.

Walters, S.D. (2003). *All the rage: The story of gay visibility in America.* Chicago, IL: University of Chicago Press.

Yep, G.A., Lovaas, K.E., & Elia, J.P. (2007). A critical appraisal of assimiliationist and radical ideologies underlying same-sex marriage in LGBT communities in the United States. In M.M. Jenkins & K. Lovaas (Eds.), *Sexualities & communication in everyday life: A reader.* Thousand Oaks, CA: Sage Publications.

Consumer Culture

A 1994 IKEA furniture commercial is credited as being the first American television commercial to include overt representations of gay men. The commercial, which featured two men shopping for a living room table together, received significant backlash from conservative groups, and one or more individuals made bomb threats to IKEA stores. Fast forward to present day, and we find more and more companies willing to defy conservative protests by including gay and lesbian representations and overtly supporting GLBTQ causes. For instance, on Gay Pride Day 2012, Kraft Foods' Oreo took a stand in America's culture wars by posting on its Facebook page a chocolate sandwich cookie with rainbow-colored filling. The photo was accompanied by the text, "Proudly support love!" Within two days, the posting generated more than 220,000 likes and over 36,000 comments. It also landed the rainbow-colored Oreo on the *Colbert Report* (2005–2014) as the subject of one of Stephen Colbert's tongue-and-cheek commentaries that mocked the "homosnaxual" and its "consensual double stuffing." That Kraft would transform its family-favorite cookie into a symbol of gay equality demonstrates the sea change in companies' attitudes about targeting gay and lesbian audiences since that IKEA commercial less than two decades earlier. However, as we have learned, progress is an uneven process, with some people benefiting more than others. Sometimes, so-called progress also comes at a political price, as is the case in marketplace recognition of GLBTQ consumers.

This chapter will explore the multifaceted relationship between sexual identities and consumer culture. In the first half, we will consider the gay and lesbian market, including when and how it emerged as a distinct market segment, and the three primary ways advertisers attempt to appeal to gay and lesbian audiences. In the second half, we will consider the social and political implications of marketplace recognition of gays and lesbians. You will notice very little attention to the transgender community in this chapter. While transgender individuals have become increasingly visible in the media, they typically are not recognized as a distinct consumer market. As you will read below, social groups need to be recognized as a potential market before advertisers become interested in them. For many transgender people, "passing" as a gender different from their biological sex at birth is important, which typically prevents them from being identified as a market distinct from other similarly gender-identified consumers (i.e., cisgender men and women). Similarly, bisexuals typically are not treated as a unique set of consumers; marketers likely presume bisexual consumers will be reached through advertising to both mainstream and gay and lesbian audiences. A small number of advertisers have begun to incorporate transgender models or allude to bisexuality; however, such depictions typically are more about generating "buzz" than reaching those consumers (see Textbox 4.1).

BOX 4.1   "Gendernebulous" Fashion Advertising

In 2010, the fickle world of fashion was rocked by two fresh new faces, Andrej Pejic and Lea T. The following year, the Serbian-born Pejic graced the covers of 14 magazines, and the Brazilian-born Lea T became the poster model for Givenchy. While their bodies fit the prepubescent model of the typical female supermodel, they have garnered headlines well outside the fashion world. Both are transgender fashion models. Pejic has been described as "the first 'female' supermodel not in possession of a vagina," and Lea T, who first posed with male genitalia partially exposed, since has undergone sex-reassignment surgery. Pejic and Lea T, appear to be on the cutting edge of a new trend in modeling that includes other transgender models like Stav Strashko, Filipa Tav, and Carola Marra. These models are not the first transgender individuals to walk the runway; however, what makes them different from those who have come before is that their success does not come *in spite* of their gender identity, it comes *because* of it.

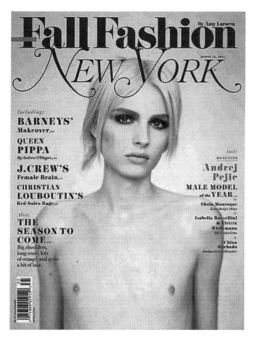

FIGURE 4.1 Transgender model Andrej Pejicc named Male Model of the Year
Source: *New York* magazine, August 22, 2011.

The popularity of MtF transgender models may reflect less a broader cultural acceptance of gender transgressive sexualities than the next logical step in the androgynous codes of high fashion. Fashion reflects societal change, particularly with regard to sex and gender. As gender roles evolve, these shifts play out in the world of fashion in styles that challenge traditional notions of gender and sexuality. Since the 1920s, fashion has embraced androgyny both in terms of its fashion as well as its models. The trend was heightened in the 1990s with androgynous models like Kate Moss and their embodiment of prepubescence. The prepubescent body, lacking the curves of femininity or the muscularity of masculinity, provides an androgynous canvas for fashion designers. Modeling agencies specializing in androgynous models even emerged, including a Dutch modeling agency appropriately named Androgyn. Androgynous models meld strong masculine bone structures with the slimness of femininity.

(Continued)

The idea of biological men representing idealized feminine beauty might be considered a mere extension of this trend. For example, Pejic served as inspiration for designer Jean Paul Gaultier's men's and women's wear shows. In the men's show, "a pistol-packing, bare-chested Pejic wore a sleek black suit as 'James Blonde,'" and in the women's show Pejic sported a couture bride's dress, eventually worn by Rihanna at the Grammys (Associated Press, 2012).

Transgender models reflect an increasing fluidity of gender; however, they simultaneously can reinforce narrow ideals of gendered beauty that few can attain. This is particularly a problem for so many transgender people who suffer the most because their bodies, in fact, fall outside of societal norms. As one GLBTQ program coordinator told the *New York Times*, "It's important to advocate for sustained media attention, not just celebrating people who attain a particular beauty standard that reinforces gender norms, which are a source of a lot of difficulty for trans people in the first place" (Van Meter, 2010).

While male-born female fashion models have drawn significant media attention, female-born male fashion models are virtually invisible. One recent exception is Elliott Sanders, a female model who in 2012 made the decision to cut her hair, bind her breasts, and begin modeling male fashion (Whitelocks, 2013). Compare articles written about some of the male-born female fashion models like those profiled above with stories written about Sanders. Consider the following questions:

1. Why are there fewer female-bodied male fashion models than male-bodied female fashion models?
2. What aspects of Sanders' personal life are included in stories about her? How does this compare with the personal information in stories about Pejic or Lea T?
3. How does Sanders' androgyny compare to that of Pejic or Lea T? What physical qualities might be identified as masculine, and what features are more traditionally feminine?
4. Both Pejic and Lea T have posed for nude photographs (Lea T did so before and after her surgical transition). The photos emphasize the "gendernebulous" quality of their bodies. Would nude photos of Sanders have the same effect?
5. Does Sanders reinforce narrow gender ideals for men in the same way that male-born women's fashion models reinforce female gender ideals? Why or why not?

▶ THE GAY MARKET

It should go without saying that people sexually attracted to others of the same sex purchased commodities long before the identity labels of gay, lesbian, bisexual, or transgender had even been imagined. In fact, mainstream print ads dating back to 1917 depict overt references to homosexual relationships, indicating that companies, including Ivory Soap and Standard Plumbing Fixtures, acknowledged the presence of gay consumers (Branchik, 2007). However, advertisers did not conceive of a "gay market," per se, until decades later. Consumer markets are customer groups defined by a common set of traits. These shared characteristics may be demographic, psychographic, behavioristic, or geographic, and they allow marketers to view a group of individuals as a collective group to be targeted.

The emergence of the gay market generally is traced to the 1960s and is tied to two related factors. First, marketers began shifting their strategies away from trying to reach a mass audience of consumers, instead targeting segmented groups. Peñaloza (1996) suggests this shift resulted from "increasing levels of competition for the mass market, shifts in demographic growth rates and geographic patterns of residence for the U.S. population, and increasing availability of specialized media products" (p. 15). This shift in marketing strategy happened during the same period in which the United States saw a dramatic increase in social activism. Second-wave feminism, civil rights, and the gay liberation movement were based on an identity politics model in which the groups' identities provided recognition of their second-class status, which served as the catalyst for collective political change. As detailed in Chapter 2, the gay liberation movement solidified and made visible a *national* gay community, imagining themselves as a single subculture, like ethnic minorities. Some of the gay publications that grew out of that political movement also played a crucial role in encouraging national advertisers to view the GLBTQ community as an untapped commercial market.

The gay and lesbian market challenges traditional conceptions of a "market segment," which require that, to be identified as such, a group must be "identifiable, accessible, and of sufficient size" (Fugate cited in Peñaloza, 1996, p. 10). Not only is the gay and lesbian market not always visible, even determining who is and is not gay or lesbian can be a challenge. As described in Chapter 1, sexuality may be defined by sexual attraction, sexual behavior, or sexual identity. While academics may argue over whether gay and lesbian consumers collectively constitute a "market," as Baker (1997) puts it, "the proof that the market exists is that marketers . . . *believe* that it exists; commercial interest, is, after all, what defines a market" (p. 11, italics in original). In effect, all "markets" can be thought of as projections of advertisers' conceptions of people grouped together by identifiable characteristics. (Textbox 4.2 explores the emergence of the gay "Bear Market.")

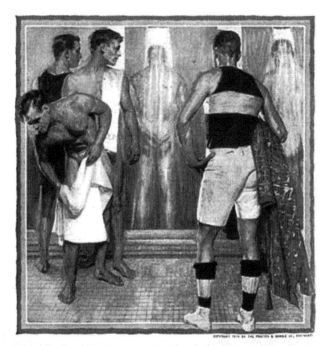

NOT the least of the pleasures of a hard game is the bath that follows it. For it is just after the final whistle, when you realize for the first time how warm you are and how your skin is chafing, that the cooling, soothing, refreshing qualities of Ivory Soap are most appreciated.

The mild, smooth, copious Ivory lather feels grateful to the sweating skin and tired muscles. Just a few moments' stand under the rushing water removes every particle of soap and dirt. A brisk rub-down leaves the body aglow with health, and muscles and nerves in perfect trim.

It is this ability to cleanse thoroughly without irritation to the skin that makes Ivory Soap so popular with all athletes. In it quality and purity combine to produce cleanliness pleasantly and perfectly under every conceivable condition.

IVORY SOAP. . . [IVORY] . . . IT FLOATS

99 44⁄100 % PURE

FIGURE 4.2 1917 Ivory Soap advertisement

Since the 1980s, advertisers have been led to believe that the gay and lesbian market is an ideal market. Economist Lee Badgett (2001) has identified three flawed assumptions on which this favorable construction of the market is based:

> Lesbians and gay men make up an affluent, well-educated, professional elite, occupying positions of power and influence in the workplace and society at large. . . . Gay people have no family responsibilities to hamper their job

advancement or accumulation of wealth. . . . Gay people are hedonistic and consumption-oriented, an ideal niche market for upscale products.

(pp. 1–2)

The problem is that this perfect marketer's dream, painted as such by market researchers is just that—a dream. These gay market myths grew out of studies conducted by companies like Simmons Market Research Bureau and Overlooked Opinions, which found gays and lesbians were disproportionately wealthy and educated. However, gay marketing companies were drawing their research pool from gay and lesbian newspaper subscription lists, resulting in a significantly skewed sample. Therefore, the "snapshot" of the gay market being sold to advertisers is more like a Photoshopped reconstruction. By 1993, Yankelovich Partners had more scientific data, that found that the income of gay men was similar to that of straight men, and the earnings of lesbians only slightly higher than straight women (Baker, 1997). Badgett (2001) had similar findings in her book-length study of the economic lives of gay men and lesbians. Nonetheless, the myth of the lucrative gay market persists still today.

BOX 4.2   The Bear Market

As part of a move by marketers to cater to increasingly niche markets, the gay and lesbian market has become hyper-segmented. An example of this tendency is the attempt to cater to the bear community of gay men. Bear culture emerged in the 1980s as a response to idealized gay masculinity present in gay culture and was popularized further by marketing and popular culture. Bears are identified in large part by their physical appearance, including "beards, bellies and body hair." However, early members of the bear culture suggest that what brought bears together was a desire for acceptance, after being made to feel othered in a gay community that valued svelte bodies and urban male fashion.

Where some saw a collective sexual identity, others saw a potential new market of consumers. Two members of the bear culture, Steve Harris and Mike Goldberg, founded *A Bear's Life*, "the first national glossy magazine specifically targeted at the bear community" (Campbell, 2006). Unlike the earlier *Bear Magazine* (1987–), a sexually explicit magazine distributed to a geographically localized audience, *A Bear's Life* positioned itself as a lifestyle magazine and secured national advertisers like Blue Moon, Coors Light, Progressive Insurance, and Rogaine. The magazine

(Continued)

led to a companion web series, *A Bear's Life* TV, with video versions of stories found in the print edition.

In targeting potential advertisers, Harris and Goldberg argued that the bear community was an overlooked and underserved market:

> These men are more comfortable wearing jeans and flannel shirts than Armani suits, more likely to drive a truck than a BMW, enjoy drinking beer, attending football games, going camping and engaging in other activities traditionally identified as masculine. These men are rejecting any limitations on gay identity and redefining what it means to be gay. As such, they no longer identify with many of the images advertisers have historically employed when marketing to the gay community.
>
> (*A Bear's Life* Press Kit, quoted in Campbell, 2006)

Following in the trend of early gay market research, the founders presented the bear market as a highly attractive demographic. They touted an average household income of $102,000. However, their claims were based on surveys collected from attendees at bear social events in the United States and Europe. Respondents' attendance at such events certainly skewed the demographic toward more affluent gay men.

Although the bear community emerged in resistance to the gay masculinity that had become idealized in consumer culture, bear culture, too, has become shaped by commercialism. As noted by Les Wright, an author of two books about bear culture,

> The internet and bear media have taken control of mediating who or what a bear is. Belonging to the bear community seems to be about going to commercial bear events, buying bear-favored stuff, taking vacations at bear events, etc. . . . to be a bear means to have money and spend it in a certain way.
>
> (quoted in Shell, 2011)

Additionally, marketing to the gay culture has emphasized the visual component of bear culture, some say at the expense of some of the initial codes and values in what began as a group defined by inclusivity. At its base, hyper-segmentation is drawing lines around ever smaller groups of people in order for marketers to target them. Such market logic operates in direct opposition to bear culture's original mission of inclusion.

In 2012, the *New York Times* published a story about bear culture, titled "The Brotherhood of the Bears" (Moskowitz, 2012). The story describes photographer Alan Charlesworth's work capturing images of bears whose bodies are strikingly different than the idealized depictions of gayness found in mainstream media.

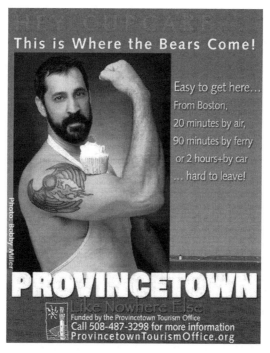

FIGURE 4.3 Provincetown advertisement
Source: A Bear's Life magazine, Fall 2010, Issue 21.

Compare Charlesworth's images of bears with those found in bear-targeted advertisements. Consider the following questions:

1. How are the men depicted in Charlesworth's photographs similar to or different from representations of bears in advertisements?
2. How is the bear community depicted in each?
3. If advertisements continue to be one of the few media spaces in which bears are depicted, what impact could that have on gay men looking for models of gayness with which to identify?

When advertisers first began recognizing gays and lesbians as a market of consumers, mainstream companies had to weigh the potential benefits of reaching gays and lesbians with the potential risks of offending straight audiences. Today, companies increasingly see the advantages of depicting gay and lesbian characters in their advertisements in both gay and mainstream media; however, until the late 1990s, companies were much more cautious about having their companies' brands associated with the gay and lesbian community. The gay rights movement of the 1970s had been met with a conservative backlash, resulting in a culture war in which few companies wanted to find themselves in the middle. Religious-right organizations like Focus on the Family, Moral Majority, and the Family Research Council spread their anti-gay, "family values" message through conservative radio, documentaries, and even direct mailings. Some groups, like the American Family Association (AFA), targeted corporations it believed supported what the FRC had coined the "homosexual agenda." This included television networks and their advertisers. During the 1980s, the AFA successfully lobbied companies to pull commercials from television programs depicting gay characters (Southern Poverty Law Center, 2005).

As social attitudes about gays and lesbians have changed over time, so, too, have the strategies marketers use to appeal to them as consumers. The first national companies willing to test out the gay market did so through direct marketing in gay publications and mailers. Some companies also began surreptitiously targeting gays and lesbians in mainstream publications through gay-vague advertising. Today, however, an increasing number of national companies openly target gays and lesbians in mainstream advertising in hopes of gaining the support of the GLBTQ community and their liberal allies. Below, we explore the different strategies designed to reach the gay market.

Marketing in Gay Publications

By the late 1970s, gay-targeted publications recognized the untapped revenue from national advertisers but faced the difficult task of convincing mainstream companies to target their audiences directly. As described in Chapter 2, the early gay press was rooted in the work of gay and lesbian rights organizations. As such publications became more prevalent during the gay liberation movement of the 1960s, they were limited primarily to local or regional audiences. They also were restricted in their sources of advertising revenue, relying on local and regional businesses like gay bars and alternative bookstores, as well as income from personal ads. To grow in size, gay-targeted newspapers and magazines would need the financial backing of national advertisers; however, for national advertisers to be convinced that gay publications were "safe" territory, content changes would have to be made.

One of the magazines credited with luring national advertisers to the gay market is *The Advocate*. The publication began in 1967 as the newsletter for PRIDE (Personal Rights in Defense and Education), a Los Angeles-based group organized in response to police officers' violent treatment of GLBT people (Streitmatter, 1995). What was then called the *Los Angeles Advocate* is credited as being "America's first gay newspaper" (p. 87). The publication initially was limited by geography and small print runs of only 500 copies. However, within two years, circulation had more than quadrupled, and papers were being distributed in large metropolitan cities around the country, including Boston, Chicago, Miami, New York, and Washington. Streitmatter (1995) notes that in less than 10 years, the publication, which was renamed *The Advocate*, "was being recognized by the publishing industry as one of the dozen fastest-growing magazines in the country, gay or straight" (p. 185).

Initially, *The Advocate* was funded through advertising from Los Angeles or East Coast gay establishments and through personal ads. The personal ads and other overtly sexual content of the newspaper, including pornographic photo spreads, had kept national companies fearful of having their brands associated with the magazine and the gay and lesbian community. After investment banker David Goodstein purchased *The Advocate* in 1974, the newspaper began excluding sexually explicit content from the main portion of the magazine and shifted its focus from political stories to lifestyle features. By the late 1970s, music and alcohol companies began advertising in gay publications like *The Advocate*; however, the AIDs epidemic of the 1980s scared off most mainstream advertisers who feared association with the gay community. In an attempt to go after national advertisers, in 1992 *The Advocate* became a slick lifestyle glossy, similar to other emerging magazines like *Genre* (1991–2009) and *Out* (1992–). The redesign came the same year that "a research firm attached a specific figure to how much America's estimated 18 million gay and lesbian adults were pumping into the nation's economy each year: $514 billion" (Streitmatter, 1995, p. 314). Although an inflated number, it was enough to get the attention of mainstream national advertisers.

Advertising in gay-targeted publications allowed companies to market to gays and lesbians without attracting the attention of straight consumers. However, the method was not foolproof, because conservative groups would target companies directly targeting the gay market with highly publicized boycotts. Therefore, by the early 1990s, only companies least at risk of boycotts from conservative groups were willing to test the waters of the gay market through direct advertising. Absolut Vodka and Phillip Morris were among the corporations advertising such "*sin* products" in gay-targeted magazines (Wilke, 2006). Gay men's assumed high disposable income also was attractive to other entertainment and travel companies. By 1992, such ads made up almost half of the advertising content in *The Advocate* (Phillips, 2012). Other advertisers included companies like Columbia Records, Pay-Per-View, Green Mountain Coffee, and Metro-Goldwyn-Mayer (MGM) studio. Eventually, other industries began following on the coattails of these gay-advertising pioneers. By 1997, automobile, finance, phone service, and clothing and apparel companies all advertised in the three major gay lifestyle magazines.

As corporations increasingly recognized the appeal of the gay market, direct-mail advertising became another avenue to reach gay audiences. Marketers, though, first had to identify households with gay consumers, which is not necessarily an easy task. In addition to buying mailing lists from gay publications, companies sometimes relied on stereotypes to determine likely gay homes. For instance, marketers might buy mailing lists from theaters and orchestras to identify men who had only a single-person season membership or target men who subscribed to fashion or gardening magazines. Clearly, this was not a foolproof method, nor did it necessarily protect companies from conservative backlash, as AT&T discovered in its attempt at a direct-mail campaign in 1994. The long-distance company was the first in its industry to go after the gay market, although Sprint and MCI would follow suit. AT&T followed its first ad in *The Advocate* with a direct-mailer as part of their "Let Your True Voice Be Heard" campaign. The mailer drew the attention of the trade publication *Advertising Age*:

> The six-panel brochure, mailed to an undisclosed number of consumers who appeared on subscription lists of gay publications, includes a photo of two men accompanied by the caption: "When David's away on business, we like to stay close. I love to know what he's doing and what's on his mind." Another photo shows a man and his mother, who's quoted as saying: "Even though Paul lives a coast away, I love knowing how his life is going. His father and I always look forward to his calls."
>
> (Fitzgerald, 1994, p. 8)

Like other direct-mail campaigns of the time, AT&T also used imagery and language associated with the gay rights campaign. This included rainbow graphics and use of the color purple, as well as phrases like "be proud" and "come out." The single mailer from AT&T would be the last for its "True Voice" campaign after socially conservative organizations were made aware of it and began protesting the company. After the incident, it took AT&T five more years to decide that the benefits of targeting the gay market outweighed the risks and again began advertising directly to gay and lesbian audiences (Phillips, 2012). Direct marketing to gays and lesbians through direct mail or in gay publications initially was a strategy for reaching gay and lesbian consumers without drawing the attention of straight audiences; however, the backlash that some companies like AT&T received left many companies fearful of directly targeting the gay market.

"Gay Vague" Advertising

One way that companies have attempted to reach gay audiences without attracting the attention of straight readers is with "gay vague" or "gay-window advertising" in mainstream publications. Such ads often avoid overt heterosexual markers like a man and woman wearing wedding rings that might close down multiple interpretations of characters' sexuality. Instead, the ads include more ambiguous representations like a single individual or a crowd shot without clearly marked couples. Gay-vague advertising relies on ambiguity to allow, and sometimes encourage, different audiences to interpret the same advertisement in different ways. This is an intentional use of advertising's polysemic quality, the idea that media texts, including ads, include codes that carry multiple meanings in order to appeal to a broader audience. A brief discussion of semiotics will help clarify how gay-vague advertising works.

Semiotics is the study of signs and how meaning is made from them. A sign can be anything that has meaning attached to it, and it consists of two aspects: the signifier and the signified. A signifier is the material thing—symbol, sound, image, etc.—that represents an object or concept. That object or concept represented by the signifier is called "the signified." For example, the word "book" is a signifier for the object you are reading right now, which is the signified. Similarly, think what image comes to mind when you hear the word "rose." The word (the signifier) and concept it conjures in your mind (the signified) jointly make up a sign. Semiotics also considers how meaning operates by examining the relationship between a sign's signifier and signified. The fundamental, or one-to-one, relationship between the signifier and the signified is the sign's denotative or literal meaning. However, signs also carry a connotative meaning, an idea or feeling that has become associated with its denotative meaning. For example, the denotative, or literal, meaning of the word "rose" is a woody perennial with green leaves, thorns, and fragrant flowers in a range of colors. By comparison, the connotative meaning associated with the rose in Western cultures is "love" or "romance," particularly if the rose is red. The denotative difference between a red and yellow rose might only be a matter of pigmentation, but the connotative difference (love v. friendship) may make a world of difference to the receiver.

Semiotics helps us to understand how gay-window advertising allows different groups of people to make different meanings from the same signs in an advertisement. As explained in Chapter 1, codes are the signs in a text, including the technical elements, people, and objects, that carry cultural meaning. Media producers cannot control the way that audiences interpret the texts they produce; however, they are able to include codes that limit the likely connotative meanings made by audiences or ones that are intentionally ambiguous. For example, the codes of an ad that depicts a man in a tuxedo and a woman in a long, white dress standing together in front of a man wearing clergy vestments and holding a Bible strongly connote heterosexual marriage in Western cultures. Alternative interpretations would be possible, but unlikely. By comparison, an ad depicting two young men wrestling in a living room is open to more interpretations because of the multiple connotations this act might carry for different audiences—youthful play, athleticism, competition, or homoeroticism. In gay-window advertising, advertisers rely on this ambiguity, but sometimes go so far as to include codes that carry connotative meaning for the

FIGURE 4.4 Abercrombie & Fitch advertisement featuring Patrick and Anthony Wayne (father and son), in affectionate poses in *Vanity Fair* (September 1996)

gay and lesbian community that straight audiences might initially miss or not even be aware of. Examples might include references to "being proud" or the use of purple text. However, as signifiers of gay culture have become more visible in mainstream culture, their use in advertisements is more likely to attract the attention of straight audiences.

Because gay-window advertising generally relies on the ambiguity of its codes, it can be difficult to know for sure when advertisers are engaging in the strategy. For example, in the 1990s, Abercrombie & Fitch made advertising headlines for an eight-page spread in *Vanity Fair* that some considered an obvious case of gay subtext, but the clothing manufacturer insisted this was not their intention. The black-and-white photos depicting two men in affectionate poses onboard a sailboat were taken by Bruce Weber, a photographer known for shooting nude males. Similar ads by the clothing company depicting "beefy, shirtless men" were appearing in *Out* at the time (Wilke, 1996). The president of the advertising company that created the ads suggested the ads never were meant to suggest homosexual overtones. In fact, the men depicted in the spread were the son and grandson of John Wayne, a Hollywood icon made famous by his leading roles in westerns in the 1950s and 1960s. *Advertising Age* writer Michael Wilke was criticized by at least one reader for his description of the ads as having "gay overtones." In a letter to the editor, the reader shared her own interpretation of the ads:

> The photographs capture a real and tender moment between a father and son and if Mr. Wilke chooses to read into that, then that's his own prejudice coming out. There is nothing homoerotic about this campaign . . . and to state it as fact is not only wrong, it's irresponsible.

Still today, this ad campaign is debated by users of *Commercial Closet*, an on-line catalog of GLBTQ advertising portrayals. Some user posts applaud what is interpreted as a clear overture to the gay community and others criticize such interpretations, suggesting the ad should not even appear on the website. (Textbox 4.3 describes *Commercial Closet* and its rating system for advertisements.)

BOX 4.3   Commercial Closet

The Commercial Closet Association boasts an on-line library of over 4000 television and print advertisements featuring GLBTQ representations. The non-profit organization's founder, Michael Wilke, is a veteran advertising journalist who covered gay marketing for publications like *Advertising Age*, *Adweek*, the *New York Times*, and *The Advocate*. Inspired by Vito Russo's book (1987) and documentary, *The Celluloid Closet* (1995), which profiled the tragic trajectory of gay and lesbian representations in film, Wilke named his project Commercial Closet. Launched in 2001, the database, now housed at www.adrespect.org, gathers relevant ads from around the world. The site is more than just a repository, however. It gives advertising awards for positive GLBTQ-related ads, provides "dos and don'ts" for companies incorporating GLBTQ representations, and rates the positive or negative inclusivity of the commercials in its expansive library.

Commercial Closet's editorial staff determines an ad's "AdRespect" score. The score is determined by an algorithm tied to the themes present in the ads:

$$z = \frac{100p + e\,(85 + y) + 60s + 0n}{n}$$

(Continued)

In this equation, p = the number of positive themes in the ad; e = the number of equal themes in the ad; s = total number of caution/stereotyped themes in the ad; n = number of negative themes in the ad; and x = number of total themes present in all categories (n + p + e + s). The website offers examples of positive, equal, caution/stereotyped, and negative themes.

An example of a commercial that received the full 100 points for its AdRespect score is a 2005 ad for 1–800-contacts featuring drag queens. Commercial Closet's editorial staff gave the commercial high marks for "gay pride," "GLBT empowerment," "racial diversity," and "real GLBT person." Farther down the AdRespect scale is the 2002 Budget truck rental ad entitled "Disco." In this ad, Budget executives are brainstorming new strategies, including providing help "loading and unloading" their moving trucks. One executive suggests roller skates to accelerate the loading and unloading of trucks, and the viewer sees men with facial hair wearing short shorts and roller skates, skating to disco music. The ad received an AdRespect score of 48 for themes of camp/drag (even), sissies (caution/stereotypes), and GLBT punchlines (negative).

Commercial Closet's AdRespect score is an example of content analysis that attempts to draw attention to negative or positive GLBTQ representations, as discussed in Chapter 3. Two of the drawbacks of the language of stereotypes are that it assumes a "true" representation that does not align with stereotypes and it assumes a single and clear meaning in media texts. Some of the comments left on Commercial Closet demonstrate how rating GLBTQ representations may be more complicated than it might seem. For instance, the one comment on the ad from 1–800-contacts that received a 100% AdRespect score is that "it's cheap bottom feeder humor" (David Byrd). By comparison, the "Disco" ad from Budget, which received low marks from Commercial Closet, received fairly high praise from viewers. Most of the comments attacked the AdRespect rating: "To be honest, this seemed to be more of a parody of 'sexy girl troupe' promoters than of effeminate or transsexual men" (Gavlas, n.d.). "[T]he men themselves were far removed from any gay stereotype in their build, haircuts, etc. Only their queeny behavior could be called stereotypically gay. It just didn't strike me as a negative ad, and left me laughing, not grumbling" (Brickmore, n.d.). As these comments demonstrate, determining what a positive or negative GLBTQ representation is may depend on the particular perspective of the viewer.

To see how your interpretations compare, randomly select five ads from Commercial Closet without looking at the AdRespect score. Watch the ads and note what you believe to be positive, negative, or neutral about the ad. Then, compare your notes with a classmate who has watched the same ads. Finally, compare your perceptions of the commercials with those of Commercial Closet's editorial staff and then viewers' comments. Answer the following questions:

1. How do your perceptions compare with those of your classmate and of Commercial Closet's editorial staff?
2. What does your comparison with others' perceptions of the same commercials say about the complications of visibility and stereotypes raised in Chapter 3?
3. If you were to develop your own rating system for ads, what factors would your system include?

▶ From Gay Vague to Gay Vogue

Increasingly, companies are being more overt in their overtures to the gay market, finding the benefits of a GLBTQ-friendly reputation outweigh the risks of potentially turning off socially conservative consumers. While companies who include gay and lesbian representations in their advertisements still risk the threat of boycott by conservative groups, doing so can generate a positive buzz among both GLBTQ consumers and some of the most financially attractive straight consumers. For example, the department store JCPenney embraced the controversy it stirred up in 2012 with its friendly overtures to the gay and lesbian market and saw the financial payoff for doing so. The company, already having been boycotted by the conservative group One Million Moms (OMM) for signing lesbian comedian and talk show host Ellen DeGeneres as its spokesperson, included a depiction of lesbian mothers in their May catalog. The ad for Liz Claiborne clothing showed two women hugging each other, their daughters, and their grandmother. In tribute to Mother's Day, the catalog copy reads:

> You'll often find Wendi, her partner, Maggie, and daughters elbow deep in paint, clay or mosaics. "Even as babies, the girls toddled around in diapers, covered in paint," said Wendi. They come from a long line of artists, which includes grandma Carolyn. Visiting her art studio in Granbury, Texas is a favorite outing. And, like any grandma, this one loves to bake—pottery, that is.

FIGURE 4.5 JCPenney celebrates Mother's Day and Father's Day in 2012

Not unexpectedly, the ad received more negative attention from OMM, but generated buzz in both mainstream and social media. Penney embraced the publicity, releasing a statement to ABC News that reaffirmed the controversial content of the catalog, saying that it celebrated "women from diverse backgrounds who all share the heartwarming experiences of motherhood." The following month, JCPenney included two gay fathers and their family in their ads in honor of Father's Day. The text read: "First pals: What makes Dad so cool? He's the swim coach, tent maker, best friend, bike fixer and hug giver—all rolled into one. Or two."

The decision to portray gays and lesbians in ads is no longer just a strategy for attracting gay and lesbian consumers. It also allows companies to simultaneously target the SLUMPY class (Socially Liberal, Urban Minded Professionals) discussed in Chapter 3 (Becker, 2006). There is evidence that the strategy worked in the case of JCPenney's Mother's and Father's Day ads. According to the research service YouGov BrandIndex, customers' opinions of the company surpassed those of its competitor Kohl's after the ads drew national attention (AdRespect 1999; 2012). Other companies targeting SLUMPY consumers also have succeeded in generating a positive buzz for unapologetically including gay and lesbian representations in their marketing campaigns. The

home furnishing retailer Crate and Barrel included in its *January Inspiration 2013* catalog a section called "Us & Always," which included two men enjoying a candlelit dinner together. The catalog text promised more than just a good meal: "Spend a Saturday
night at home, cooking together, dining together. Music, candlelight and a good bottle
of wine, and you can have the table as long as you like." The nature of the men's relationship also was made clear by the free downloadable dinner playlist of songs like "When
We First Met," "I'm in Love," and "This Is for Real." The gay couple does not seem out of
place with the heterosexual couples featured in the same catalog, all attractive, professional thirty-somethings meant to appeal to a lucrative young demographic willing to
use its disposable income on consumer items (i.e., the SLUMPY class).

A second, more ambiguous, use of GLBTQ representations in mainstream advertising is in advertisements that might be labeled as "queer chic." Gill (2007) explains how
queer chic differs from more overt mainstream gay and lesbian representations like the
ones described above: "What is striking is the way in which queerness is aestheticized and
fetishized in advertising, rather than being treated as merely a different sexual identity"
(p. 100). Advertisements from Abercrombie & Fitch increasingly fit this description as
they have become more "gay" and less "vague," depicting nude men together in the shower
and men appearing to strip in front of other men. In fact, Abercrombie & Fitch's racy
catalogs are delivered to homes in shrink wrap, reminiscent of mail-order pornography.

Particularly popular in advertising are racy representations of female-to-female sexual
attraction, which was popularized in the 1990s by Hollywood films like *Basic Instinct*
(1992). While these "lesbian chic" ads can be interpreted as liberated female sexuality, they
often echo men's woman-on-woman fantasies found in male pornography. Michael Wilke
(2006), founder of *Commercial Closet*, describes one such ad for Bison Brand Vodka:

> It shows three women and a man sitting in the grass of a park at night,
> playing Spin the (empty vodka) Bottle. The women have long hair and are
> wearing more makeup than clothing. Two of the gals are staring passionately
> into each other's eyes, about to liplock, as the skinny guy watches and the
> other gal covers her naked breasts. The tagline is "A little grass, a little vodka.
> Nothing wrong with that."
>
> (Wilke, n.d.)

This ad makes a clear association between the sexual possibilities that become more
likely with the help of alcohol to lower inhibitions. However, the no-holds-barred sexual environment is not for the pleasure of the two women engaging in it, but for the
man left watching. As Reichert, Maly, and Zavoina (1999) point out, lesbian chic ads contain any erotic pleasure of women's touching or kissing by presenting women as the
object of heterosexual male fantasy/desire. As these examples demonstrate, the polysemy of advertisements complicates our ability to even identify what can be counted

as a representation of gay men or lesbians or which mainstream ads are attempting to appeal to gay and lesbian audiences.

▶ IDENTITY, POLITICS, AND CONSUMER CULTURE

Marketers' recognition of the gay market, along with their attempts to court gay and lesbian consumers, no doubt has contributed to the increased GLBTQ visibility in the media more generally. It also can be validating for GLBTQ people to have their collective economic power recognized by more and more companies. Additionally, the market power that a minority group wields can influence the political power they hold, and vice versa. However, market recognition and social/political equality are not synonymous, and the former can come at a cost to those individuals who fall farthest outside the margins of acceptability. Below, we explore the complicated intersection of sexual identities, politics, and consumerism.

Identity and consumption are connected in two interrelated ways. The first is on the personal level, the idea that through our everyday consumption of goods we construct our personal identities. The second is at the more abstract level, the relationship between particular social groups and their construction as viable markets by advertising companies. The way that a market is constructed, targeted, and represented ultimately may influence how people understand their own personal identities. As described in Chapter 2, consumption and the broader consumer culture have played a significant role in sexual identities from their initial emergence as cultural categories in the late 1800s. At the level of personal identity, gay people needed a way to mark their sexuality as a signal to other gay people, in the process, identifying themselves as part of emerging gay subcultures. They would often do so through the clothing that they wore, tying their self-expression to an activity of consumption. In New York, for instance, gay men signaled their sexuality by wearing red clothing, particularly neckties (Chauncey, 1994). Consumption, though, allowed for more than a code for identification. It also opened up an entire "gay world." Chauncey recounts one man's description of his introduction to this new world in New York City:

> [My friend] brought me around . . . taught me the language, if you will, took me to places. I found out that there were gay restaurants, that there were gay clubs, that there was a gay beach, that there3 was a *gay world*.
> (Chauncey, 1994, p. 277, emphasis in original)

This was a world accessible to those with money; it was a world—and an identity—accessible through consumption.

At the broader level of identity, the shift from a production culture to a consumer culture played a key role in the emergence of sexual identities as social categories. As detailed in Chapter 2, gay subcultures in large urban centers, like New York City, only became possible when men could earn their own wages and no longer had their economic survival tied to a family unit. As these subcultures emerged, sexual minorities began to view themselves as a collective and understood themselves as an oppressed social group in need of civil rights protections. As you read in this chapter, the emergence of gay identity politics in the 1960s contributed to the recognition of gay people as an identifiable consumer market. This has resulted in a complicated relationship between sexual identities, consumer culture, and gay politics. As Chasin (2001) explains, "market mechanisms became perhaps the most accessible and the most effective means of individual identity formation and of entrance into identity-group affiliation for many gay people" (p. 24). As a result, capitalism and its resultant consumer culture provide the basis for group formation, a necessity for collective political rights action.

The Marketplace as Political Battlefield

The marketplace long has served as a battlefield for political and social rights, as evidenced by the civil rights movement of the 1960s. Peñaloza (1996) writes that historically civil rights have been fought for

> at the lunch counters, in bus and retail service, in hotel accommodations, and in socially acceptable standards of dress. In this sense, the marketplace may be viewed as an important domain of social contestation whereby disenfranchised groups engage in ongoing struggles for social and political incorporation.
>
> (p. 16)

The gay rights movement has embraced this model of marketplace political activism, long targeting companies that support anti-gay politics and rewarding companies supportive of GLBTQ equality. An early example is the orange juice boycott organized by gay activists in 1977, when pop singer and Florida Citrus Commission spokeswoman Anita Bryant became a vocal proponent of repealing local ordinances protecting gays and lesbians from discrimination. Her organization, Save Our Children, fed into homophobic fears, particularly of gay men, by depicting them as child molesters and sexual perverts (McGarry & Wasserman, 1998). Some gay bars responded by taking screwdrivers off their menus and replacing them with an alternative drink called the "Anita

Bryant," made with apple juice. The boycott made national headlines and gained the support of some celebrities.

Boycotts from GLBTQ groups continue to be a political weapon in the marketplace. For example, in 2010, discount store Target's donation of $150,000 to a group supporting a socially conservative gubernatorial candidate in the company's home state of Minnesota resulted in a social-media-based boycott. Facebook groups like "Boycott Target Until They Cease Funding Anti-Gay Politics" sprang up,' on Twitter, @Target-Boycott tweeted phone numbers for Target executives under the heading "Bigot of the Day," and a YouTube video showing a mother of a gay son returning more than $200 in Target purchases and then cutting up her Target credit card went viral. Although Target denied any connection to the 2010–2011 controversy, in 2012 the company began selling Gay Pride T-shirts on its website, with 100 percent of sales going to Family Equality Council, an advocacy group for GLBTQ parents and their families.

Increasingly, companies have supported pro-gay causes in order to gain a reputation of being gay-friendly. In 2012, one of Minnesota's largest employers, General Mills, announced its opposition to a proposed constitutional amendment to ban same-sex marriage. That same year, Microsoft and Starbucks backed a bill that would extend marriage rights to gays and lesbians in the companies' home state of Washington. These same companies joined with more than 250 other companies in 2013 to file a friend-of-the-court brief urging the Supreme Court to overturn the Defense of Marriage Act (DOMA). The brief argued that DOMA was financially costly, because different policies have to be instated for different employees.

Companies also can gain a pro-GLBTQ reputation by financially supporting gay-rights organizations. In 2013, the Gay and Lesbian Alliance Against Defamation (GLAAD) listed five corporations as having made cumulative donations of at least one million dollars. Among this elite "visionary circle," as GLAAD terms this giving level, are companies known to target the gay market: Absolut Vodka, Anheuser-Busch, IBM, MillerCoors, and Wells Fargo. The same is true of the Human Rights Campaign's (HRC) "platinum partners": American Airlines, Citi, Diageo (spirits, beers, and wines), Microsoft, and Nationwide. The HRC also thanks major sponsors of its fundraising events on its Facebook page, spreading the word of their support of gay causes.

Corporate donations toward GLBTQ causes reflect an expectation from gay and lesbian consumers, particularly young ones, that companies should work to gain their loyalty (Gudelunas, 2011). Two decades ago, GLBTQ consumers could buy the book *Cracking the Corporate Closet* to research the workplace policies and to find records of companies in fields ranging from aerospace to entertainment (Baker, Strub, & Henning, 1995). Today, consumers can turn to online searchable databases, like the HRC's "Buyer's Guide" to identify gay-friendly companies.

Advertising's Model Minority

Not only are consumerism and politics tied up in the flow of money between corporations and pro-gay or anti-gay causes, their connection also has implications for GLBTQ people, as their sexual identity is increasingly defined by consumer culture. Chasin (2001) explains that consumer institutions increasingly have replaced other institutions that have played a key role in GLBTQ identity and community formation. For example, GLBTQ people now draw from television, film, digital media, glossy magazines, and all of their associated advertising to understand their sexual identities. These have replaced the socializing and community-building function of house parties and drag balls that historically had been largely invisible to non-GLBTQ people. In the process, consumer culture has solidified a gay identity that uses as its model that identity most attractive to advertisers—upper-class, white gay men. As a result, identity-based marketing behaviors and their connection to identity politics largely has magnified the power of those already most privileged and inhibited widespread social change tied to a more radical queer agenda.

Concerns about the relationship between the gay market and gay politics tie into broader concerns about the contemporary identity politics model of advocating for GLBTQ rights. One point of concern for some GLBTQ supporters is that not all markets are created equal. That is, markets only are valuable and, thus, targeted if they are financially lucrative. Based on market research as well as cultural perception, upper-class, white gay men are at the top of the marketing chain. Lesbians—outside of lesbian chic advertising—have been largely invisible. This is because they have been more difficult to imagine as a marketing niche. Part of this perception is based in research and part in mere stereotype. Even though lesbians earn higher salaries than their straight counterparts, their earning power is unequal to that of gay men (Badgett, 2001). Also, historically the popular mythos of lesbians is that they are less consumption-conscious than gay men. While marketing practices are beginning to change, lesbians historically have not been sought after and therefore have not been as visibly present in advertising.

These omissions in representations occur because any time a group is consolidated into a market based on a single aspect of their identity—in this case, sexuality—other differences become flattened or invisible. The gay market becomes homogenized, and only the most "respectable" members of that community are allowed to represent it. As with other media representations of gays and lesbians, marketers search for the most palatable representation of gayness available. As a result, sexualities that are non-white, non-male, non-upper class remain largely invisible. As Gluckman and Reed (1997) explain, "today, the sword of the market is slicing off every segment of the gay community that is not upper-middle class, (mostly) white, and (mostly) male"

(p. 7). Those images that do appear in mainstream advertising also adhere to hetero-normative ideals that would be least offensive to mainstream sensibilities. For exam-ple, the JCPenney Mother's Day catalog and Father's Day ads that caused such a stir limit the potential threat of the homosexual "other" by positioning the lesbian couple and gay men within familiar familial arrangements. Both ads depict white, middle- to upper-class couples and emphasize their normalcy, with descriptions to which other straight families may relate. This is not surprising given that advertising always pres-ents idealized representations; however, this is a very narrow representation of gay and lesbian experiences.

Additionally, gay media that historically have offered a space to marginalized people and behaviors have succumbed to market pressures and now present largely sanitized and narrow assimilationist versions of homosexuality. Gay media initially emerged as a space for alternative voices, ones that were not present in mainstream media. *The Advocate* and other gay press publications often served as newsletters where political information could be disseminated within the GLBTQ community. As described earlier, before *The Advocate* changed ownership in the 1970s, it also was known for its explicit personal ads and advertisements, many of which fea-tured images of naked men. The personal ads, a precursor to today's digital "hook-up" websites, made up a large portion of the publication's revenue at the time and were a favorite with readers. Hundreds of ads would fill dozens of pages with witty, racy content. Streitmatter (1995) describes the "gay lexicon," or insider language, of these ads:

> Readers knew that an ad beginning, "Are you getting your share?" was not talking about a guy's share of financial profits, and one offering "MEXICAN HOUSEBOYS. Live-in type" was suggesting the men would do more than wash windows. Likewise, savvy *Advocate* readers knew that when an ad stated, "Turn On, Tune In, Turn Over," the last reference was to a man readying himself to be the receiving partner in anal intercourse.
>
> (p. 104)

When Goodstein purchased *The Advocate*, he relegated such advertisements to a sepa-rate pull-out section as not to offend potential readers and advertisers. In an interview with the *New York Times*, Goodstein celebrated these changes boasting, "We've come a long, long way. . . . We are being desleazified" (quoted in Sender, 2004, p. 32). Similar shifts have happened in digital media, as websites like Gay.com and PlanetOut have become a means to sell advertising rather than to bring together isolated and disen-franchised gays and lesbians. Gay media have followed the same trajectory as main-stream media, being gobbled up by larger media conglomerates, whose first concern is financial gain. At one point, the company PlanetOut Partners owned the two leading GLBTQ websites, Gay.com, and PlanetOut.com, as well as the two leading GLBTQ magazines, *Out* and *The Advocate*. As Gamson (2003) argues,

> the Internet has been a major force in expediting, amplifying, and solidifying historical processes that began to take hold in the 1980s: the transformation of gay and lesbian media from organizations answering at least partly to geographical and political communities into businesses answering primarily to advertisers and investors.
>
> (p. 260)

Gay media have become more homogenized and concerned with infotainment, consisting of popular culture, fashion, and consumerism.

The shifts in gay media that have resulted, in part, because of marketers' recognition of the gay market, may have been business decisions, but they carry political implications. First, the sex-positive aspect of gay male culture increasingly has been erased, replaced with constructions of gayness that fall closer to the "charmed circle" of sex described in Chapter 1 (Rubin, 1999). As a result, those spaces originally reserved for people with marginalized identities increasingly erase images of gayness that cannot be aligned with advertisers' desired market conception. Second, gay publications have replaced political content with lifestyle content less offensive to advertisers' sensibilities. As a result, gay identity increasingly is aligned with consumption choices rather than a political agenda. (Textbox 4.4 asks you to imagine what content in a gay-targeted publication like *The Advocate* might include if it was not constrained by market forces).

BOX 4.4   GLBTQ Publications as Activism

As detailed in this chapter, many gay-targeted publications have shifted away from their original activist mission in an attempt to secure national advertisers. Sender (2001) suggests the vision of gayness found in *The Advocate* after its transition into a gay lifestyle glossy reflects a marketer's construction of gayness rather than the lived realities of many gays and lesbians:

(Continued)

FIGURE 4.6 Actor Sean Hayes, famous for the role of Jack McFarland on *Will & Grace*, on the cover of *The Advocate* (April 2010, Issue 1037)

What could be more tempting for advertisers, publishers, editors, and readers alike than to imagine a world in which gay people are not in continual struggle against the depressing, frightening, unjust limitations of a heterosexist and homophobic society but may adopt a gay-specific way of living in which taste, style, and body perfection are achieved through the peculiar freedoms of self regulation?

(p. 95)

Because glossies like *The Advocate*, *Out*, and *Curve* have become synonymous with gay publications, it can be difficult to imagine what type of content a more radical gay magazine might include. This activity asks you to propose a new GLBTQ-targeted publication with political, rather than economic, goals. If you are unfamiliar with alternative gay publications, familiarize yourself with some of the ones found in the online Queer Zine Archive (qzap.org). Next, think about what an overtly political GLBTQ publication might look like if it had significant financial backing without having to worry about being palatable enough for advertisers. Working as part of a group or on your own, determine the following:

1. Who is the target audience for your publication? How is this audience different from consumers of existing gay lifestyle publications?
2. What would be the most important content to include in the publication? How would you organize the content?
3. How would the cover design reflect your political mission, content, and intended audience?

After answering these questions, create a sample cover for your publication. You can use publishing software like Adobe InDesign or Microsoft Publisher or more basic word processing software like Microsoft Word. Another option is to hand-sketch your sample cover.

▶ CONCLUSION

This chapter considered the complex intersection of gay identity, politics, and consumer culture. It explored the emergence of the gay market in the 1960s, linked both to shifts in marketing strategies to reach smaller niche markets and to the solidification of a national gay identity made possible by the gay liberation movement. By the early 1990s, market research firms were heralding gays and lesbians as a dream market, largely based on flawed research methods that led to an overestimation of the buying power of many gays and lesbians. As national advertisers first sought to reach this new target market, some tested the waters in gay publications like *The Advocate*, balancing potential financial gains with the risks of alienating their straight consumers by brand association with gays and lesbians. Companies also began targeting gays and lesbians in mainstream publications with "gay vague" advertising meant to appeal to gay consumers without drawing notice from straight viewers. More recently, advertisers are achieving financial benefit from overt depictions of gays and lesbians, which generate a positive buzz both with gay and lesbian consumers as well as their financially attractive SLUMPY counterparts. In addition, some advertisers are incorporating a queer aesthetic in their advertisements, particularly in the form of lesbian chic depictions.

This chapter also considered ostensible progress in marketplace visibility within a broader framework of GLBTQ identity and politics. Marginalized groups long have used the marketplace as a battlefield for social and political rights. This includes the GLBTQ community, which historically has supported GLBTQ-friendly companies and pressured companies that support anti-GLBTQ causes with negative publicity. However, some critics increasingly are wary of the intertwining of consumer culture and sexual identities. They contend that the gay market identity constructed by marketers is a narrow and depoliticized one.

▶ REFERENCES

AdRespect Advertising Education Program (1999). Ad library: Bison brand vodka "Spin the Bottle." Adrespect.com. Retrieved from http://www.adrespect.org/common/adlibrary/adprintdetails.cfm?QID=581&ClientID=110 64.

AdRespect Advertising Education Program. (2012). *Creativity. Oil paints. Freedom of expression.* Retrieved from http://www.adrespect.org/common/adlibrary/adprintdetails.cfm?QID=4835&ClientID=1 1064.

Associated Press. (2012, February 9). He's the gender-bending beauty who has become the fashion world's hottest property . . . but is model Andrej Pejic getting overexposed already? *MailOnline.* Retrieved from http://www.dailymail.co.uk.

Badgett, M.V.L. (2001). *Money, myths and change: The economic lives of lesbians and gay men.* Chicago, IL: University of Chicago Press.

Baker, D. (1997). A history in ads: The growth of the gay and lesbian market. In A. Gluckman & B. Reed (Eds.), *Homo economics: Capitalism, community and lesbian and gay life* (pp. 11–20). New York, NY: Routledge.

Baker, D., Strub, S., & Henning, B. (1995). *Cracking the corporate closet: The 200 best (and worst) companies to work for, buy from, and invest in if you're gay or lesbian—and even if you aren't.* New York, NY: Harper Business.

Becker, R. (2006). Gay-themed television and the SLUMPY class: The affordable, multicultural politics of the gay nineties. *Television & New media, 7*(2), 184–215.

Branchik, B.J. (2007). Pansies to parents: Gay male images in American print advertising. *Journal of Macromarketing, 27*(38), 25–36.

Brickmore, R. (n.d.). Visitors' comments: Disco. *AdRespect.* Retrieved from http://www.adrespect.org/common/adlibrary/adlibrarydetails.cfm?QID=911&ClientID=1 1064.

Byrd, D. (n.d.). Visitors' comments: Drag show. *AdRespect.* Retrieved from http://www.adrespect.org/common/adlibrary/adlibrarydetails.cfm?QID=2857&clientID=11064.

Campbell, J.E. (2006). The evolution of the gay market: Constructing the dream consumer. *Advertising & Society Review, 7*(4). Retrieved from http://muse.jhu.edu/journals/asr/v007/7.4unit11.html.

Chasin, A. (2001). *Selling out: The gay and lesbian movement goes to market.* New York, NY: Palgrave Macmillan.

Chauncey, G. (1994). *Gay New York: Gender, urban culture and the making of the gay male world, 1890–1940*. New York, NY: Basic Books.

Ellin, A. (2012, May 3). Million moms rips JCPenney on gay "culture war." *ABC News*. Retrieved from http://abcnews.go.com/blogs/business/2012/05/million-moms-rips-jcpenney-on-gay-culture-war.

Epstein, R. & Friedman, J. (Producers and Directors). (1995). *The celluloid closet*. Culver City, CA: Sony Picture Classics.

Fitzgerald, K. (1994, May 16). AT&T addresses gay market. *Advertising Age, 8*. Retrieved from LexisNexis Academic.

Gamson, J. (2003). Gay media, inc.: Media structures, the new gay conglomerates, and collective social identities. In M. McCaughey & D.M. Ayers (Eds.), *Cyberactivism: Online activism in theory and practice* (pp. 255–278). New York, NY: Routledge.

Gavlas. (n.d.). Vistors' comments: Disco. Retrieved from http://www.adrespect.org/common/adlibrary/adlibrarydetails.cfm?QID=911&ClientID=1 1064.

Gill, R. (2007). *Gender and the media*. Cambridge, UK: Polity.

Gluckman, A. & Reed, B. (1997).The gay marketing moment. In A. Gluckman & B. Reed (Eds.), *Homo economics: Capitalism, community and lesbian and gay life* (pp. 3–9). New York, NY: Routledge.

Gudelunas, D. (2011). Consumer myths and the gay men and women who believe them: A qualitative look at movements and markets. *Psychology & Marketing, 28*(1), 53–67.

McGarry, M. & Wasserman, F. (1998). *Becoming visible: An illustrated history of lesbian and gay life in twentieth century America*. New York, NY: Penguin Studio.

Moskowitz, P. (2012, August 27). The brotherhood of the bears. *New York Times*. Retrieved from http://lens.blogs.nytimes.com/2012/08/27/the-brotherhood-of-the-bears.

Peñaloza, L. (1996). We're here, we're queer and we're going shopping!: A critical perspective on the accommodation of gays and lesbians in the U.S. marketplace. *Journal of homosexuality, 31*(1–2), 9–41.

Phillips, L. (2012). Moving beyond vodka, vacations and viaticals: How *The Advocate's* 1992 redesign contributed to the solidification of a new LGBTQ market segment. *Advertising & Society Review, 13*(2). Retrieved from Project MUSE.

Reichert, T., Maly, K., & Zavoina, S. (1999). Designed for (male) pleasure: The myth of "lesbian chic" in mainstream advertising. In M.G. Carstarphen & S.C. Zavoina (Eds.), *Sexual rhetoric: Media perspectives on sexuality, gender and identity* (pp. 123–133). Westport, CT: Greenwood.

Rubin, G. (1999). Thinking sex: Notes for a radical theory of politics of sexuality (2nd ed.). In R. Parker & P. Aggleton (Eds.), *Culture, society, sexuality* (pp. 150–187). New York, NY: Routledge.

Russo, V. (1987). *The celluloid closet* (Revised Ed.). New York, NY: Harper & Row.

Sender, K. (2001). Gay readers, consumers, and dominant gay habitus: 25 years of *The Advocate* magazine. *Journal of Communication, 51*(1), 73–99.

Sender, K. (2004). *Business, not politics: The making of the gay market*. New York, NY: Columbia University Press.

Shell, B. (2011, September 2). Bear necessities: An insider's look at an atypical gay culture and community. *The GA Voice.* Retrieved from http://thegavoice.com/bear-necessities-an-insiders-look-at-an-atypical-gay-culture-and-community.

Southern Poverty Law Center. (2005). A dozen major groups help drive the religious right's anti-gay crusade. *Intelligence Report, 117.* Retrieved from http://www.splcenter.org/get-informed/intelligence-report/browse-all-issues/2005/spring/a-mighty-army.

Streitmatter, R. (1995). *Unspeakable: The rise of the gay and lesbian press in America.* Boston, MA: Faber and Faber, Inc.

Van Meter, W. (2010, December 8). Bold crossings of the gender line. *New York Times.* Retrieved from http://www.nytimes.com/2010/12/09/fashion/09TRANS.html?pagewanted=all&_r=0.

Whitelocks, S. (2013, October 30). Blonde bombshell who cut off hair to work as male model reveals how she and her husband now get mistaken for a "gay couple." *Mail Online.* Retrieved from http://www.dailymail.co.uk/femail/article-2480168/Elliott-Sailors-female-works-male-model-gets-mistaken-husband-gay-couple.html.

Wilke, M. (1996, September 16). Gay overtones seen in Abercrombie ad: The Duke's descendants star in 8-pages shot by Bruce Webber. *Advertising Age, 20.* Retrieved from LexisNexis Academic.

Wilke, M. (2006). Understanding the gay and lesbian marketplace. *Advertising & Society Review, 7* (4). Retrieved from Project MUSE.

Wilke, M. (n.d.). Lesbian ads still more male fantasy. *AdRespect.* Retrieved from http://www.adrespect.org/common/print_page_body.cfm?Type=ReportDetail&QID=446 0&TopicID=344&Guide=&ClientID=11092.

Resistance

Desiree and Ingrid, "superficial, homophobic lesbians," certainly are in the running for the most dysfunctional couple. Desiree continually focuses on how "butch" Ingrid is, insisting that she is the prettier one and disturbed to find men are attracted to Ingrid instead of her. Ingrid continually reminds Desiree that she is unreliable because she is bisexual, and thus not exactly trustworthy. The web series *The Slope* (2010–2012) is the brainchild of independent filmmakers Desiree Akhavan and Ingrid Jungermann, and focuses on a lesbian couple navigating the unique complications of both lesbian relationships and life in Brooklyn, New York. Unlike the kinds of "positive" representations that visibility advocates might call for, a great deal of the humor comes from the ways the characters judge each other by stereotypes of various groups. In one particularly funny episode, the couples decide to make their own "It Gets Better" video (Akhavan & Jungerman, 2010). Desiree gives her usually shallow advice, which mostly consists of "don't be fat." A direct satire of Dan Savage, creator of the campaign, who is known for negative comments he had made about overweight men and women over the years, Desiree and Ingrid end up suggesting that their imaginary viewers make things better for themselves now. *The Slope* is full of in-group humor and references specific to some GLBTQ communities. The relationship it portrays is not one that mirrors heterosexual ones, but that specifically focuses on the ways that GLBTQ couples negotiate homophobia in themselves and in their relationships. This is content that speaks specifically to GLBTQ audiences.

Members of GLBTQ communities have historically grown up in a media environment that offered little visibility. Even in our current era of increased visibility, certain narrow constructions of GLBTQ identity are privileged. However, when we think about the relationship between GLBTQ communities and the media, we are never only talking about representations *of* those communities, but also about the ways that members of those communitities interact with, make sense of, use, and create media. Whether it is the elevation of movie and pop stars as icons by some gay men, the production of non-mainstream GLBTQ media made by and for various communities, or participation in fan cultures, GLBTQ individuals actively participate in all kinds of activities associated with media. This chapter will discuss this in relation to two interrelated practices, resistance and appropriation, related to two separate, but increasingly interrelated activities, production and reading.

Resistance can refer to a number of practices, from a thoroughgoing rejection and criticism of mainstream media products, including the production of alternative forms of media, to criticism of certain media practices and forms of engagement not expected or intended by popular culture producers. From independent films to web-based series, such as *The Slope* (2010–2012), that are made outside of the mainstream media, different kinds of texts emerge. Resistance also can refer to organized and specific forms of protest, including boycotts of media texts, the activities of GLAAD and other advocacy groups, and the growing use of the Internet and social media to directly talk back to producers. Appropriation refers to the practice of different cultural groups drawing from the cultural texts of other groups and using them in ways not necessarily intended by their original makers. As most mainstream media is largely produced by and for heterosexual audiences, this has meant that GLBTQ audiences historically have developed strategies of consuming and creating media in ways that drew from dominant cultural practices, while speaking to the interests of GLBTQ subcultures.

Both of these practices have been key to understanding the relationship between GLBTQ audiences and mainstream media as well as GLBTQ media production. From finding meaning and pleasure in a popular culture landscape hostile to their existence to working as active producers of film, music, TV, and Internet content, GLBTQ individuals have sought to at the very least make a home in, and at most actively critique and resist, the dominant culture. However, as this chapter also will demonstrate, while resistance and appropriation help us understand sexual minorities as producers, consumers, and users of media, not all use of media is resistant, not all forms of appropriation are necessarily progressive, and not all participatory media activity is necessarily transgressive or even liberatory. Over time, many GLBTQ individuals have been perfectly happy to consume media without attempting to make their own meaning.

▶ PRODUCTION AS RESISTANCE: GLBTQ-PRODUCED MEDIA FOR GLBTQ AUDIENCES

Up to now, we have considered questions of how GLBTQ people are made visible in media or about the power of advertisers to shape the kinds of images we see, but we have not considered the question of the media industries that make a great deal of mainstream content. For decades, the mass media such as film, television, and even the recording and radio industries were dominated by large corporations that acted as gatekeepers. Those seeking to produce media content had to work through one of these corporations in order to find funding to produce content and venues for exhibition of that content. This model of media largely worked by catering to large audiences and did not necessarily reflect the interests or needs of minority producers or audiences.

Larry Gross offered a model of media production in his 2001 book *Up from Invisibility* (see Figure 5.1). His linear model of the media system graphs the ways that historically most media have been made about the majority by the majority for the majority. The majority, in terms of production, have been primarily white, well-off, heterosexual men. The majority audience has been white, heterosexual, middle-class America. Media made about minorities also can be made by the majority for the majority, but media made by and about minorities usually was made primarily for minority audiences. Minority media production often was a shadow to the more fully funded, fully supported, and professionalized world of mainstream media production and consumption. Minorities rarely were able to speak for themselves in the mainstream and were instead spoken about. As the angled line in the model demonstrates, GLBTQ people existed in the world of majority media production, but largely served the interests of the majority stakeholders and thus produced content for majority audiences. Even if minority producers in mainstream media produced content that might reflect minority interests, that content always needs to "be palatable to the majority" (p. 150). This model demonstrates that, for the most part, the voices and concerns of the GLBTQ population largely were absent from mainstream media, and when they did appear were strongly shaped by the concerns of majority producers and audiences.

However, the new millennium has brought significant changes to the media industries, including the relationship between media audiences and the industry. This has ushered in the age of what media scholars, such as Henry Jenkins (2008), call convergence culture, marked by the collapse of the distance and distinctions between media/advertising corporations and audiences. Katherine Sender (2012) argues that it is useful to rethink the model about the relationship between majority and minority media production as no longer linear, but as more circular (see Figure 5.1). She argues that contemporary media are marked by a professional center, including "the bastions of traditional media: mostly news, sports, expensive fictional television shows

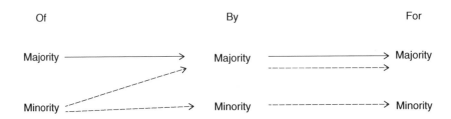

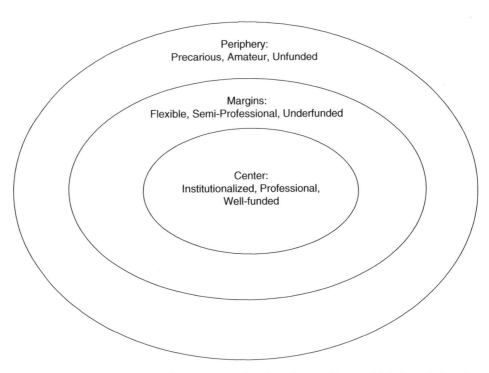

FIGURE 5.1 Linear model of media production (Larry Gross, 2001) and circular model of media production (Katherine Sender, 2012, p. 209)
Sources: Larry Gross, 2001, p.11, *Up from Invisibility: Lesbians, Gay Men, and the Media in America*, Copyright © 2001 Columbia University Press. Reprinted with permission of the publisher. Sender in K. Ross (Ed.), *The handbook of gender, sex and media* (pp. 207–225). Copyright © 2012 Wiley & Sons. Reprinted with permission.

and Hollywood movies" (p. 210). At the margins are "flexible, semi-professional, and underfunded" forms of production, including reality television (p. 210). While there are an increasing number of out gay and lesbian professionals producing media at the center, the representations largely reflect majority interests and are targeted at majority audiences. However, the underfunded margins, including on-line GLBTQ websites and other Internet activity, offer new, more expansive forms of representation. Another way this circular model differs from the linear model delineated by Gross (2001) is that, while the linear model did not allow for much influence of minority content on majority content, the circular model accounts for the ways that the center can take up products from the margins and produce them for majority audiences for a profit. There is far more flow between professional and non-professional media today than in the past, and minority-driven representations are more likely to be appropriated by the center, provided they can produce profit.

While no model can fully account for the variations and idiosyncrasies of the media production process and the place of GLBTQ individuals in it at any one moment, these two models do point out two things. First is the fact that structural constraints of the media industries have shaped both GLBTQ representation and thus forms of resistance. Second is that the nature of those constraints and forms of resistance have changed over time. As Chapters 2 and 4 have explained, print media have been a key site for minority media production involving the GLBTQ communities. Flexible, inexpensive, and more easily produced and consumed than film or television, newsletters, newspapers, magazines, zines, and comic books have been a key to the emergence of modern GLBTQ identity movements. These were forms of minority media production that were made specifically by and for gays and lesbians; minority media for minority audiences. We will look at resistant production in three other forms, music, film, and web and video series, to consider the ways that GLBTQ communities have created media that spoke specifically to their interests, experiences, and desires.

Music

Music is an area of cultural production that GLBTQ individuals have turned to as a space for resistance and community building. While the mainstream music industry was dominated for many years by large record labels, the relative flexibility and freedom for the performance, production, and even circulation of recordings outside of the mainstream industry, along with the long connection between music and forms of social protest, made music a vital part of GLBTQ subcultures. Like many conceptual terms, "subculture" is a contested term with several different definitions. Subcultures are loose cultural formations generally centered on the production and consumption of media, such as music, that stand in opposition to majority or center cultural forms. Embracing alternative styles and anti-normative attitudes, subculture participants define themselves both against the dominant culture and against other subcultures. As Halberstam (2003) argues, subcultures might be compared to the concept of community: "community, generally speaking, is the term used to describe seemingly natural forms of congregation. . . . Subcultures, however, suggest transient, extra-familial and oppositional modes of affiliation" (p. 315). Prior to the rise of gay visibility, alternative forms of music were key to building gay and lesbian identities and communities *as* subcultures. Since the 1990s, however, new forms of music have been central to building subcultures as alternatives *to* mainstream GLBTQ communities.

Gay and lesbian subcultures primarily have converged around two different forms of music since the late 1960s. Gay men have found community and connection through the production of, and congregation around, various forms of dance music, including disco and house. As a number of writers have demonstrated, disco and most other forms of dance music originated in gay, black, male club culture. Anthony Thomas (1989) explains that disco grew out of black gay clubs of the late 1960s and 1970s, where DJs would mix records by black artists together to maintain a seemingly endless stream of beat-based dance music. By the 1970s, the form migrated out of these clubs and was embraced by white gay men, and finally by mainstream culture, culminating in the widespread success of the *Saturday Night Fever* (1977) movie and soundtrack. However, as Thomas argues, disco's origins in black gay culture were ignored, and it was treated as a new cultural phenomenon and, in the process, stripped of a great deal of its original style. The result of this was house music, which emerged out of Chicago clubs, particularly The Warehouse. Faster and open to new forms of avant-garde dance music from Europe, house also took advantage of the growing use of synthesizers and beat machines to make cheap recordings. Since that time, the world of dance and electronic music has grown into ever-smaller niches, and dance and electronic music have been more fully appropriated both by young whites and by mainstream gay culture.

Women's music is rooted in folk and other forms of protest music and also is tied to the emergence of the second-wave feminist movement of the 1970s. Lesbian subcultures were formed in a sometimes uneasy relationship to the broader feminist movement. This form of music largely featured individual women who wrote songs that focused more on storytelling that spoke to the specific experiences of women, including lesbians, and contained explicit political critique of patriarchy, capitalism, and heteronormativity. While forms of dance music were co-opted by mainstream culture and became profitable forms of popular music, women's music remained more independent and was tied to smaller record labels, such as

Olivia Records, formed in 1973 by a woman's collective and dedicated to promoting women artists, or women's music artist Holly Near's Redwood Records started in 1973. Another key aspect of this subculture was the formation of women's music festivals, not only in the United States, but globally (Thomas, 1989). While dance music found mainstream success and women's music has retained its subcultural status, and beginning in the 1990s a new generation of women performers, such as Ani DiFranco and Melissa Ferrick, continued the tradition of creating their own labels and championing other artists.

With the growth of a more mainstream gay and lesbian presence by the late 1980s and the continued co-optation of gay and lesbian subcultural forms, new subcultures emerged, ones that embraced a stronger queer approach to identity and politics (Halberstam, 2003; Taylor, 2008). As mainstream gay and lesbian groups achieved more mainstream visibility and turned their attention to cultural legitimacy, others began to rebel against this. Whereas earlier music was tied to an era where most gay and lesbian cultural production was subcultural, queercore defined itself not only against mainstream heterosexual culture, but also against mainstream gay and lesbian culture. Queercore emerged in the 1980s as an offshoot of the punk movement. Working both against the dance-centered music of gay male culture, and the folk sounds of women's music, queercore was more than a music scene and included the production of zines, art, and other kinds of performances, such as slam poetry. Women performers in queercore played a part in the riot grrrl movement, a female-centered and feminist response to punk, and the creation of dyke subcultures. Bands like Le Tigre, fronted by Kathleen Hanna, Tribe 8, and Gossip, fronted by Beth Ditto, played with feminine gender norms, embraced forms of female masculinity, and adopted an in-your-face performance aesthetic not typically associated with women pop stars. Their music, lyrics, and performance spoke to the interests of women who did not embrace normative ideas of feminine respectability, and proclaimed a range of queer identities, from lesbian, to bisexual, to queer itself. Many of the women associated with this movement continue to play and, more importantly, continue to speak to the concerns of young queer women (Driver, 2007).

The production, circulation, and reception of music by GLBTQ subcultures continues today as music continues to play a vital role in creating forms of identity and affiliation. However, in the age of visibility a number of GLBTQ-identified artists have sought mainstream success in popular music styles. Most recently, a number of GLBTQ artists have worked to be out in the field of hip-hop. When R&B artist Frank Ocean came out of the closet as bisexual in 2012, revealing that his first love was a man, he received a great deal of support. In the meantime, out gay and lesbian hip-hop artists like Mykki Blanco and Brooke Candy are achieving levels of recognition and success unimaginable a decade ago (see Textbox 5.1).

BOX 5.1   Queering Hip-Hop

Mainstream media and blogs heralded 2012 as "the year hip hop went queer" (Lambe, 2012). Following President Obama's lead, superstar hip-hop artists, beginning with Jay-Z and followed by T.I. and P. Diddy, publicly endorsed their support of homosexuality. By 2013, Ryan Macklemore and Ryan Lewis's "Same Love"—a song that talks about legalizing same-sex marriage —became a radio hit and led to a performance at the 2014 Grammy Awards that featured a group marriage ceremony for 70 couples, including gay and lesbian couples.

The attention garnered by mainstream artists in a culture often hostile to gays and lesbians is noteworthy, but it also belies the long established presence of queer artists in hip-hop such as Invincible, Yo Majesty, and Deep Dickollective. In queer hip-hop, sometimes called homo hop, artists are gaining traction in the mainstream music industry and popular culture at large. Nevertheless, it remains difficult for GLBTQ-identified rappers to not only come out but also secure record contracts. For some artists, queerness is central to their artistic identity and output; for others, it is more peripheral.

Detroit is home to a number of hip-hop artists who identify as queer. Rebekah Farrugia and Kellie Hay (2103) spent several years studying and working with a women's hip-hop collective known as the Foundation. During that time, they worked with Miz Korona, one of the most-well-known artists in Detroit's underground hip-hop community. Beyond hip-hop circles she is known for her role as Vanessa, starring opposite Eminem in the biopic *8 Mile* (2002). While her talent for rapping is indisputable, music industry professionals have made it clear to Miz Korona that in order to succeed as a commercial artist she would need to adopt a more mainstream feminine appearance, including cutting her dreadlocks. Unwilling to alter her image, she has remained an independent artist with much notoriety in underground hip-hop communities internationally, but less mainstream success.

In 2012, Miz Korona made the decision to come out publicly. In her performance of "Who I Am," Miz Korona is defiant, telling audiences,

So take me for who I am
Cause I won't change for no woman
And I won't change for no man
I can only be who I am

However, as Farrugia and Hay note, the lyrics also address the struggles she encountered across the breadth of her social support systems, including home, church, and her neighborhood.

Growing up I was confused
They caught me kissing a girl
They told me straighten up, It's a cold, cold world
People won't accept that lifestyle that you living
and from that moment on I got used to pretending

Miz Korona's queer identity had not been central to her music. Instead, she used her "extremely witty and clever rhymes" primarily to address the "difficulties of inner city living such as substance abuse and the untimely death of young black men" (R. Farrugia & K. Hay, personal communication, November 1, 2013). However, today "her lyrics are powered by a much more personal statement about queer identity negotiations." Even so,

> when asked if she identifies as a queer hip-hop artist Miz Korona remarks, "I don't want to be labeled or put in a category as a queer hip-hop artist. I'd rather be known as a hip-hop artist who is openly queer."

Miz Korona's negotiation of her sexuality and the place of queerness in her artistic production highlight the tensions and complexities that queer hip-hop artists must negotiate. For this exercise, compare the musical performances of GLBTQ-identified hip-hop artists with those of heterosexual-identified artists. You can find the work of Miz Korona on YouTube, as well as GLBTQ artists like Le1f, Mykki Blanco, Big Freedia, Angel Haze, or Brooke Candy. Consider the following questions:

1. What are the dominant themes expressed in the music by both GLBTQ-identified and heterosexual-identified artists? What are the similarities and differences of those themes?
2. Do GLBTQ hip-hop artists perform masculinity and femininity differently than heterosexual hip-hop rappers? To what extent might they challenge the kinds of masculinity common in commercial hip-hop?
3. Do GLBTQ hip-hop artists offer new forms of musical expression that is less common in commercial, mainstream hip-hop performed by heterosexual-identified artists?

Film

The film industry, like other mass media industries, has long been dominated by powerful interests who produce movies for the majority, or center. As we will explore later, gays and lesbians working in Hollywood were able to encode certain forms of content for gay and lesbian audience members to decode; however, resistance through film often meant the production of less-polished products that often were exhibited in urban centers, sometimes at off hours, and, thus, never were widely circulated. Urban gay subcultures enjoyed the world of deviance explored in the exploitation films of the 1930s, which dramatized taboo topics. By the 1950s and 1960s, gay urban subcultures had access to physique films, which used bodybuilding and health as an excuse for displaying near-naked men on the screen (Benshoff & Griffin, 2005). Gay men also consumed and produced their own fan magazines devoted to male Hollywood stars (Gregg, 2010). However, it was the emergence of underground cinema in the 1960s and 1970s, so named because it was often screened late at night in urban areas, which led to the resistant production of movies that more explicitly dealt with GLBTQ themes.

Andy Warhol's films were key to this moment, as was a 1963 film that still remains a camp classic, Jack Smith's *Flaming Creatures* (1963). Featuring numerous multi- and varied-partner sex scenes, close-ups of genitalia, and enough gender play that Benshoff and Griffin (2005) wrote, "it becomes impossible to tell who is truly male and who is truly female, let alone who might be straight and who might be gay" (p. 120). The film was considered so controversial that it often was banned and even was the subject of Congressional testimony. The rise of avant-garde films led to the development of both hard-core pornography and another branch that critics called "loathsome" films, movies whose subject matter was deemed utterly tasteless and offensive from a mainstream perspective.

A key "loathsome" filmmaker was John Waters. In films like *Pink Flamingos* (1970) and *Female Trouble* (1974), Waters played with elements of camp (discussed later) to create movies whose plots, settings, characters, and situations defined norms of good taste and respectability. One of his key stars was Harris Glenn Milstead, who appeared in his film as his drag persona, Divine. Fat and outrageous, Milstead sometimes appeared as a man, but most usually as the female star. Waters' films gleefully challenged the boundaries of acceptability, upending the normative assumptions of heterosexual culture. For example, *Pink Flamingos* features a competition between two families over the dubious distinction of being the dirtiest. When Divine is declared to be the "filthiest person alive" by the press, the Marble family sets out to ruin Divine and her criminal family, while in the meantime running its own black-market adoption ring in which they kidnap young pregnant women and then sell their babies to lesbian couples. By the late 1980s Waters found more mainstream success with the more tasteful, yet still outrageous, 1988 camp classic *Hairspray*, which was remade as a Broadway musical, opening in 2002. The musical itself was turned into a mainstream Hollywood film in 2007.

In the early 1990s, the AIDS crisis brought about a new movement in independent cinema known as New Queer Cinema, as discussed in Chapters 2 and 3. These were independent films that began to achieve commercial success and, some argue, paved the way for the rise of gay visibility in the 1990s. Working to move beyond the binary of "positive" or "negative" characters, these films sought to tell complex stories of gay and lesbian identity, not only playing with characterizations, but also playing with the form of majority filmmaking (Benshoff & Griffin, 2005). Some of these films existed, in Sender's formulation, at the very margins of majority filmmaking, such as Sadie Benning's autobiographical sketches filmed with a toy Fisher Price Pixelvision camera. Derek Jarman's 1993 film *Blue*, completed months before his death from AIDS and after the filmmaker had begun to lose his sight, features a single image of a saturated blue screen and a soundtrack of actors and other directors discussing the significance of Jarman's work, as well as snippets of observations by Jarman himself. Some independent filmmakers were able to secure more funding and find exhibition space in urban centers, or increasingly through videotapes. These filmmakers self-consciously resisted the content and conventions of representing gays and lesbians in Hollywood, with directors like Todd Haynes, Gus Van Sant, Rose Troche, and Gregg Araki making films that represented a queer perspective, focusing on characters that mainstream film would consider unrespectable and pointedly criticizing heteronormativity.

Web and Video Series

The Internet also has proved important for the circulation of alternative media. As discussed by scholars like Henry Jenkins (2008), the Internet solves a key problem that faced alternative media producers: distribution. The barriers to distribution in film and television, and even music, traditionally have been high, with film studios, movie theater chains, and television and radio networks limiting the kinds of texts to which audiences are exposed. Films that once only were available to those living in urban areas, magazines and newsletters that once had limited circulations, and music made by and for GLBTQ audiences now have new spaces of circulation beyond the confines of geography or community infrastructure necessary to support an active gay community. Queer cinema found new audiences, first through videotape rentals, but most recently through streaming services like Netflix. Pornography is easily accessible, and where dating once relied on newspapers and magazines, today gay men, especially, use the Internet and mobile media as ways to connect for community, relationships, and sex. In the past decade, the Internet has also emerged as a key site for the circulation of alternative content, especially video content. This is witnessed in the rise of the web series. Web series are modeled after television series and often feature short episodes, usually running for 3 to 10 minutes, revolving around recurring casts and situations. The quality of web series varies immensely, from the low-budget, amateur productions at the periphery to mid-range, underfunded, but more polished presentations closer to the center, to more fully funded, professional series whose quality matches that of professional television productions that increasingly are becoming part of the center. What these series share is the ability to explore characters, themes, and situations not usually seen in commercially supported mainstream media.

At the professional end are series such as *Husbands* (2011–), *Venice* (2009–), *Hunting Season* (2012–), and *Neil's Puppet Dreams* (2012–). Co-created by veteran television producer and writer Jane Espenson, *Husbands* is billed as the first gay-marriage comedy. Beginning with a mismatched couple, one a closeted professional baseball player, the other an out gay celebrity, the two awaken in a Vegas hotel room and find themselves married the very night that gay marriage was made legal. Not wanting to set a bad example, the pair decides to give the arrangement a go. In many ways, *Husbands* deviates from more mainstream broadcast network fare. The program features more same-sex affection than is usually seen on the screen, openly deals with issues of homophobia, and makes its feminine partner the heart of the show rather than the object of its jokes. At the same time, it hardly is out of place with what one might expect to see in a situation comedy and, in fact, its creators expressed a strong desire for the show to be picked up by a television network. In 2013 they got one step closer when the program was picked up by CW Seed, a web-based offshoot of the CW television network.

While these more professionally based series push somewhat beyond the kinds of visibility that is typical in mainstream media, they also do not stray too far. Sometimes this is because they involve professional actors and producers who see these projects as ways to further their professional reputations, and other times because they actually want to see their web series picked up as a television series. On the more independent end are series that often feature content that has a harder time finding advertiser support or that might not appeal to mainstream audiences (see Textbox 5.2). Some of these series portray underrepresented groups of the GLBTQ community. For example, *Drama Queenz* (2008–) started by Dane Joseph while he was a graduate student at Columbia, tells the story of three black, gay male friends trying to make it in the New York theater world. The show received enough success that, by its second season, it brought on celebrity figures familiar to the black gay community, including transgender YouTube star Britney Houston, known for her parodies of music videos of black women artists. Quite a few web series center around the lives of lesbians.

BOX 5.2   Engaging GLBTQ Production

While gay and lesbian visibility have risen in the past two decades, mainstream representations are not necessarily directly aimed at GLBTQ audiences. The relative ease of access to digital production tools and low barriers of access to Internet distribution have made web series an exciting place for the creation and circulation of alternative content. While web series mimic some of the conventions of television series, such as organizing the narrative as "episodes," focusing on the personal lives of their characters, and using a serial format, most of these series exist removed from the center of actual television production, placing them outside of that center circle described by Sender (2012).

**FIGURE 5.2 Affectionate Cheeks and Brady from the web series
Husbands (CW Seed)**

For this exercise, you will work on comparing and contrasting two or three texts. First, choose a television program that features gay or lesbian characters in lead roles. Second, choose one of the more well-funded web series, such as *Husbands* (2011–) now distributed on the CW Seed website and supported by mainstream advertisers, or *Hunting Season* (2012–) on Logotv.com, and, finally, choose one of the more peripheral productions, such as *Drama Queenz* (2008–), which are often funded directly by viewers through fundraising sites, such as Kickstarter. For help locating web series, you can use the list maintained at televisual.org: http://tvisual.org/gaylesbian-web-series.

As you compare the two or three texts, consider the following questions:

1. How does the production quality vary between the texts in question?
2. What kinds of advertisements (or even product integration) surround each text?
3. How many main GLBTQ characters are there? How many straight characters?
4. Which characters get the most "screen time"?
5. What kinds of diversity are seen in each of the texts you choose?
6. Who is the implied audience?
7. What kinds of access to and familiarity with media might GLBTQ audiences need in order to access content specifically addressed to them?
8. What changes would you have to make to bring the periphery series closer to the center?

(Continued)

9. What changes could you make if the series closer to the center was at the periphery?
10. Finally, how do the differences in funding and production values link up with the way different groups are valued in society?

While there have been tremendous changes in the structure of the media indus-tries, as both Gross (2001) and Sender (2012) point out, majority media and center media usually are best funded, but most narrow in their representations of GLBTQ life. GLBTQ individuals have created media to resist these messages. Prior to the new millennium, Gross's model by and large accounted for the kinds of practices that took place. Minority media by gays and lesbians largely existed outside of the eyes of major-ity producers and audiences. There were important exceptions, such as disco and dance music, that showed some important movement between minority and majority media. The new millennium, however, has offered greater access to production, even if much of that is at the periphery. As our current era of GLBTQ media visibility is still narrow, these new forms offer a greater range of voices, and can reach out to audiences who once might have found little that directly addressed themselves. However, as the next section will show, the absence of visibility does not mean that GLBTQ individuals have not enjoyed media. Rather, they have developed complex sets of reading practices that allow for engagement with media on their own terms.

▶ READING AS RESISTANCE

As examined in Chapter 3, the explosion of gay and lesbian, and increasingly bisexual and transgender, visibility means that there are a growing number of media texts that directly speak to and about the experiences of the GLBTQ population. However, as both Chapters 3 and 4 point out, the range of expression still remains rather limited. Despite a history of absence, gay men, lesbians, bisexual, and transgender individuals long have engaged with media, but with media presumably made by and for heterosexuals. Under such conditions, GLBTQ audiences developed unique modes of engaging with popular culture texts from films and music to TV shows. While the "reading" of popular culture texts is a complex activity for all audiences, a number of theorists have pointed out that GLBTQ audiences bring to bear unique experiences and desires for making sense of texts and have developed ways to create positive meaning and pleasure in texts that are ostensibly heterosexual in content and address.

The complexity of these reading practices goes beyond Hall's (1980) theorization of encoding and decoding; the meanings people make are not merely negotiated or oppo-sitional, but involve modes of engagement that often create something sustaining from a culture that historically has not been kind to the GLBTQ population. Of course, many individuals and communities "poach" parts of media texts, taking "only those things that seem useful or pleasurable to the reader" (Jenkins, 1988, p. 86). Thinking more specifically about GLBTQ experiences, Brett Farmer (2005) discusses Sedgwick's theory of reparative reading, the idea that queer subjects "'succeed in extracting sustenance from . . . a culture whose avowed desire has often not been to sustain them'" (Sedgwick, 1997, as cited in Farmer, 2005, pp. 167–168). This involves a more purposeful form of engagement that moves beyond taking what is pleasurable, but *making* pleasurable and useful meanings from material that otherwise denies or reviles one's existence. It is important to realize, however, that not all attempts to gain pleasure are resistant. We can see this in the distinction scholars have made between two kinds of pleasure, plaisir and jouissance. Plaisir is generally considered as a "comfortable and comforting pleasure," while jouissance is thought of as "an ecstatic pleasure that involved disruption of and a momentary release from the social order; it is a temporary breakdown of subjectivity and therefore an evasion of ideology" (Ott & Mack, 2010, p. 245). Pleasure as jouissance can be considered a resistant practice, while pleasure as plaisir is much less so.

We will discuss four "reading" practices that offer various forms of resistance and pleasure to audiences. First, we will explore the pleasures of reading as the historical practice of looking for subtextual "codes" that hinted at, but never directly expressed queerness. Second, we will examine the practices of camp as a mode of finding pleasure in resistance to mainstream heteronormative culture. Third, we will consider queer readings as being tied to the circulation of ideas that challenge heteronormativity and offer readers queer pleasures. Fourth, we will explore the move from resistant reading to resistant "writing" in the emergence of fan cultures in our current age of participatory culture.

Active Decoders: Learning to Read Subtext

If you have had a chance to view the 1995 documentary film *The Celluloid Closet*, based on Vito Russo's book (1987) of the same title, you already have been introduced to the relationship between queer readers and subtext. As explored in Chapter 2, the era of classic Hollywood, a period from the mid-1930s through the 1960s, the Motion Picture Production Code specifically banned the representation of gays and lesbians from mainstream Hollywood movies. This did not mean that gay and lesbian characters and themes did not exist. Instead, images of gays and lesbians had to be "coded," that is represented beyond the surface content of the film text. As introduced in Chapter 1, codes are sign systems in texts that draw on shared cultural meanings. One way to study signs is through semiotic theory, which, as introduced in Chapter 4, conceives of language as a series of signs that have multiple levels of meaning. Denotation generally refers to the surface-level meaning, while connotation refers to the ways that signs can link to multiple meanings that might be recognizable to some audiences but not others. As Stuart

Hall (1980) famously argued in his seminal work "Encoding/Decoding," media texts often can contain more than one meaning, and audiences, based on their social position and familiarity with certain codes, can interpret those meanings in different ways.

In the case of Hollywood cinema, directors, screenwriters, and actors could use subtle hints to suggest to a knowing audience that a particular character or situation was not straight. Larry Gross (2001) notes in his model of media production, discussed above, that minority individuals often worked for majority media, and though the content produced had to be agreeable to majority audiences, this did not mean that they might not put in subtle cues for knowing audiences to pick up on.

Films might use double-entendres, gender inversion, stylistic choices, or what we might call stereotypical references to indicate homosexuality, such as a masculine female or a non-masculine, "sissy" male character. These methods are very similar to gay-vague advertising discussed in Chapter 4. Alfred Hitchcock often used coded meanings in his films. For example, the film *Rope* (1948) dramatized the story of Leopold and Loeb, known gay men killers. As the film could not mention this, it hinted at it by using various devices, including glances between the characters and conversations that hinted at a sexual relationship.

FIGURE 5.3 Connotative gun play in *Red River* (1948)
Source: The Celluloid Closet (1995).

D.A. Miller (1991) argued that such representations allowed plausible deniability and called connotation the "signifying practice of homophobia" (p. 125). Those involved with creating the coded message could deny it was so, while allowing the idea of homosexuality to remain always in the shadows. Because queer content could never enter the realm of denotation—i.e., could not be directly stated—it could only ever be hinted at through connotation. While it is true that the production of such connotative images was the result of homophobic practices, this does not mean that the processes of decoding were always a negative one for sexual minorities. In fact, the recognition of such cues provided a source of pleasure in and engagement with popular culture that indirectly validated the existence of gays and lesbians. In addition, the reading of such subcultural cues formed the basis of communal reading practices, which both drew from and created new forms of expression for especially gay and lesbian communities.

Camp: Finding Pleasure in Resistance

Camp is related to the practice of decoding subtext, that is, learning to decode connotative meanings. However, it also is about the very production of those connotative meanings. Camp is commonly understood as a mode of engagement with popular culture that grows out of the specific historical experiences of primarily gay men and is marked by the playful readings of popular culture that emphasize irony, humor, gender reversals, theatricality excess, and, as Susan Sontag (1964) famously argued, the elevation of style over meaning. While often containing criticisms of the dominant culture, camp nonetheless is motivated by a love of popular culture and by the search for spaces that puncture normative understandings of gender and sexuality. Full of witty, biting, often inappropriate, and caustic humor, camp involves an engagement with popular culture that tends to emphasize style over substance, with a particular joy taken in extravagance and excess. In general, objects open for camp readings are ones that are grand and serious in their attempts to tell a story, but generally fail or fall flat, and thus come off as ridiculous. Camp also is about relishing in the surfaces of things, be they movies or TV shows, stars, or certain performances. This is why certain kinds of old movies are often objects of camp. For example, *Glee* (2009–2015) can be read as camp. In addition to its over-the-top musical numbers and sometimes surreal plots, it offers the character of Sue Sylvester. Rude, arrogant, mean, prone to saying wildly inappropriate things, and mocking other characters' gender, racial, sexual, and ethnic identities, she perpetually upends normative decorum.

While the specific dates of its origins of camp are debated, it is fair to say that it emerged in the late 19th Century and developed over the course of the 20th Century as a response to periods of intense social homophobia and gender regulation. Camp builds on several aspects of gay and lesbian cultures shaped in response to that het-eronormativity and homophobia. Richard Dyer (1999) argues that camp grows out of specific adaptations gay men had to make in order to successfully move through society. He argues,

> We've had to be good at disguise, at appearing to be one of the crowd, the same as everyone else. Because we had to hide what we really felt (gayness) for so much of the time, we had to master the façade of whatever social set-up we found ourselves in. . . . So we have developed an eye and an ear for surfaces, appearances, forms—style.
>
> (p. 114)

A number of authors, including Dyer (1999) and Esther Newton (1999), author of *Mother Camp: Female Impersonators in America* (1979), an ethnography of drag culture, assert that camp developed as a form of defense. The witty, biting, and what can seem as inappropriate humor often is seen as an alternative to crying at being so reviled by mainstream culture. While there are any number of lists of the characteristics of camp, Newton (1999) identified three: "*incongruity, theatricality*, and *humor*. All three are inti-mately related to the homosexual situation and strategy. Incongruity is the subject mat-ter of camp, theatricality its style, and humor its strategy" (p. 103, emphasis in original).

A great deal of camp's humor and style comes through an ironic engagement with normative ideas of gender and sexuality. As most writers point out, this play with norms grows out of the experiences of gays and lesbians, who, based on their life his-tories, have unique insight into the arbitrary nature of gendered norms. Camp's play with gender norms especially is marked in gay, male subcultural engagement with female stars, or divas. Brett Farmer (2005) discusses the engagement with the diva as being more than mere resistance, arguing that it offers queer utopic sustenance. Key to its queer utopic potential is the way that diva worship disrupts the traditional binary categories related to gender, race, class, ethnicity, and even nationality. In challenging traditional norms of feminine behavior and class-based decorum, divas appeal to gay men as strong figures who create their own larger-than-life personas, often in the face of insurmountable odds. From the 1930s through the 1970s, opera singers and actresses served as icons of devotion. Sometimes worship was bestowed upon women who struggled in their own lives, and whose performances might be read as marked by that struggle. Judy Garland was especially admired, and the mel-ancholy-tinged "Over the Rainbow" is both utopic in its hope, but sad in its reflection on Dorothy's yearning for a better life. This melancholy connected to the shame that many gay men felt about their identities.

Other divas were worshiped for their theatricality. Pre-World-War-II screen actress Greta Garbo was a camp icon because, while she was fairly androgynous, her movie roles required her to be feminine. She deployed femininity *as* a disguise in many of her films, using it to fool and get the best of male characters (Newton, 1999). In other words, femininity was understood as performative rather than natural. A star like Bette Davis, popular from the 1930s through the 1960s, was an object of adoration because of the very artificiality of her acting. As Babuscio (1999) notes,

> The clipped voice, the strident walk, the raucous laugh, the hands that jab
> through space with ash-laden cigarettes—these stylised [sic] touches project
> an image of emotional authority, intelligence, and "masculine" self-sufficiency
> that serves as ironic commentary on the roles Davis was forced to play.
>
> (p. 125)

While the cultural situation that created the conditions for the kind of camp worship of the past has changed, today, contemporary music stars continue to earn the devotion of gay male fans. Usually these pop stars flaunt traditions of feminine decorum, such as Madonna and Lady Gaga, who have actively embraced and encouraged this devotion. Whole episodes of *Glee* (2009–2015), perhaps one of the campiest shows, have centered on the music and persona of these diva figures.

The gender play evident in gay male worship of the diva figure also comes into play in the practice of drag. Camp plays especially on the historical logics of passing and the complex codes of recognition negotiated for making oneself recognizable to other gays and lesbians, but pass as straight in the dominant culture. The most popular and recognizable form of this play is drag. Drag culture involves gay and lesbian performers donning hyper-exaggerated clothing indicative of their opposite gender: men dress as "queens," women dress as "kings." Drag performers might sing, lip-sync, or dance onstage, participate in competitions, and, in some urban areas, appear in public spaces. Judith Butler (1990) specifically references drag in her theorization of gender as performative, noting the ways that drag is best understood as an exaggeration of the ways that everyone plays with gender. This play with gender and other social roles is a central theme in Jenny Livingston's documentary of New York City drag ball culture, *Paris Is Burning* (1990). Examining the subculture of drag houses, informal communities providing support and "family" to young, often Hispanic or African-American, poor gay men and male-to-female transexuals, Livingston looked at the ways that drag performances point to the performativity of all social roles. Drag performers work to create authentic performances of various social types, including military men and prep-school kids, so that even male roles are performed in drag.

Today, drag has gone mainstream with the success of Logo TV's *RuPaul's Drag Race* (2009–). A parody of the seriousness of both *America's Next Top Model* (2003–) and *Project Runway* (2004–), contestants both create their outfits (à la *Project Runway*) and perform in them in a series of outrageous challenges (à la *America's Next Top Model* (*ANTM*)). *RuPaul's Drag Race* explores the world of drag while publicly enacting camp readings of popular culture. In the show, we get to meet the contestants out of drag and listen to how they conceive of and work on their performances. In true camp style, the show makes fun of the seriousness of fashion and modeling, revealing the performative nature of femininity and its fashions that both *ANTM* and *Project Runway* take seriously. For example, in a humorous play on the judging sequences on *ANTM* and *Project Runway*, the bottom two contestants are asked to "lip-sync for their lives" each week to dance songs popular in gay clubs. *RuPaul's Drag Race* plays with the camp traditions, and plays with codes and meanings that once were confined *mostly* to gay and lesbian subcultures, but also indicates the changing nature of camp. Once a cultural form that brought both pleasure and resistance in the face of intense homophobia, today, camp and other subcultural forms are increasingly part of the broader culture, and no longer necessarily tied to the culture of shame and stigma of homosexuality that led to the form's creation. The mainstreaming of camp humor will be explored in Chapter 7.

Despite its playfulness and often non-seriousness, camp historically has offered forms of political critique. In pointing out the artificiality of gender norms and puncturing the seriousness of certain class-based norms of taste and respectability, there can be no doubt that camp resists a great deal of mainstream culture's normalizing tendencies. As most observers of the phenomenon note, camp always is a communal activity; it requires a person performing camp, but also a reader who understands the performance (Newton, 1999). Historically, camp has been a central feature of community building and even protest, a tradition that continues today. For example, David Halperin (2012) discusses the yearly performance of a group of gay men who don the clothes and parody the performance of Italian widows during an annual Fourth of July drag festival in the gay male vacation mecca, Fire Island. Halperin argues that their hyperperformance of grief can be read merely as a superficial parody of the seriousness with which Italian widows perform mourning, but that it could be read as more. As widows, the Italian women's grief is treated with seriousness and respect as it speaks to heteronormative values, whereas the loss of gay men and their partners to AIDS was not. The performing "widows" embrace the real grief of loss, carving out political recognition and valuation of gay relationships.

Queering Readings: Finding Non-Heteronormative Pleasures

In the past 20 years, scholars have argued that queerness in popular culture should not be considered merely subtextual and have examined the ways that popular culture texts offer all sorts of moments of non-heteronormative meanings and pleasures that are open to all readers, not simply GLBTQ-identified readers. Alexander Doty (2000) has been especially influential, arguing that the intense homophobia of society has in fact *prevented* us from seeing the queerness that always has been around us. While the recognition of subtext and the creativity of camp played with hidden meanings only available to queer spectators, Doty argues that queerness has been on the surface all along, and only the intense heteronormativity of our culture has prevented us from acknowledging this fact. For example, Doty argues that *The Wizard of Oz* (1938) has remained popular with gay audiences, in part, because it could be understood as a lesbian coming-out narrative. Pointing to the history of the production of the film, he notes that any male love interest for Dorothy was written out in favor of an examination of her potentially erotic attachments to any number of women, including her Auntie Em, the Wicked Witch of the West, and the Good Witch, and her strictly platonic attachments to the variously gay-stereotyped Scarecrow, Tin Man, and Cowardly Lion. Doty asserts that, in the case of this film, the assumption that Dorothy is heterosexual is the alternative reading.

Doty (2000) also argues that presumably heterosexual texts can position all readers, regardless of their avowed sexual identity, to experience queer pleasures. He gives the example of the pleasures viewers gain from texts whose primary or most potent appeal is the bonds between women. Drawing on Adrienne Rich's (1980) theory of the lesbian continuum, which posits that women can experience a range of attachments to other women, from friendship to desire, he argues that texts that focus on relationships between women allow us to enjoy the emotional bonds between women. While the women characters identify as heterosexual and have relationships with men, the most significant and emotionally sustaining relationships they have are with other women characters. Examples of such texts include television shows such *I Love Lucy* (1951–1957), *Mary Tyler Moore* (1970–1977), *Laverne and Shirley* (1976–1983), *The Golden Girls* (1985–1992), *Designing Women* (1986–1993), *Sex and the City* (1998–2005), *Rizzoli and Isles* (2010–), and *Girls* (2012–). Doty notes that *Mary Tyler Moore* and *Laverne and Shirley* suffered strong ratings drops when the programs focused more on the relationships between the female characters and men than the friendship between the female characters. What is important to realize here is that a popular culture text does not need gay or lesbian *characters* to nonetheless offer a space for queer recognition, understanding, engagement, and, ultimately, pleasure (see Textbox 5.3).

FIGURE 5.4 Melanie, Joy, and Victoria providing moral support to each other in *Hot in Cleveland*
***Source:* Pilot, TVLand (2010).**

What makes a text queer? As the concept of queer readings suggests, it is not the ostensible presence of gay characters alone that makes a media text queer. As Chapter 3 noted, one of the limitations of the visibility paradigm is that it ignores the complexities of GLBTQ identity and life. Sometimes texts might feature gay or lesbian characters, but in ways that might not fully engage either the complexities of gay life, or in ways that challenge heteronormativity. A heteronormative story is one that emphasizes the centrality of opposite-sex relationships as the pinnacle of relational happiness, the pursuit of marriage and childrearing as key to future happiness, the importance of the nuclear family unit as the source of support and happiness, etc. At the same time, texts that offer no obvious reference to GLBTQ characters might, in fact, offer greater possible queer pleasures. As you read above, shows with female casts have the potential to offer queer pleasures. One such show is *Hot in Cleveland* (2010–), about the relationship of three middle-aged women, friends who have left behind the age bias of Los Angeles to pursue life in Cleveland, where they are "hot," and one older woman, played by former *Golden Girl* (1985–1992), Betty White. On the one hand, though not featuring any clearly identified gay or lesbian characters, the show speaks to queer audiences on a number of levels. First, the show offers a veritable smorgasbord of campy, interetextual references to other shows that have long had queer follow-ings. Betty White qualifies as a gay icon in her own right, having starred on both the *Mary Tyler Moore* (1970–1977) show and *Golden Girls*, while Valerie Bertinelli shot to youthful fame on *One Day at a Time* (1975–1984) and Jane Leeves on *Fra-sier* (1993–2004). Gay and lesbian audiences have embraced each of these shows. In addition, Wendie Malick plays a campy diva figure, a former soap opera drama queen who keeps trying to make it in movies. But the show also offers the kinds of non-heteronormative, queer pleasures discussed by Doty (2000) available to all viewers. The primary focus of the narrative is the friendship between the women, especially between the Bertinelli and Leeves characters.

What kinds of texts offer queer pleasures? Watch an example of a television show centered around the lives of women, including *Hot in Cleveland, Girls* (2012–), *Rizzoli and Isles* (2010–), etc., and consider the following questions:

1. What relationships are the most emotionally sustaining within the narrative? Are they between couples? Friends? Family? Who shares the most significant relationship in the program?
2. How closely do the characters' lives adhere to norms of middle-class respectability—i.e., single-family homes, stable romantic partnering, middle- to upper-middle-class comfort?
3. How closely do the characters adhere to gendered norms? In what ways do the characters violate gendered norms? You can think of appearance, age, sexual decorum, etc.

From Queer Pleasures to Queer Participation

Many of the practices discussed have developed historically, before our current age of visibility. This begs the question of whether these practices make any sense in our contemporary culture, where, especially gay men, but lesbians, and, to a lesser extent, bisexuals and transgender men and women live in a world of increased representa-tion that would seem to render resistant reading practices no longer necessary. In fact, since the rise of the gay and lesbian liberation movement in the 1950s, any number of cultural critics has predicted the end of camp, as it is a practice historically linked to homophobia. Yet, many of these practices not only survive, but also have grown more "open" and recognizable by a range of audiences. The madcap camp stylings of *Glee* (2009–2015), Lady Gaga's campy use of gay men as background dancers, the musical then film version of camp icon John Waters' film *Hairspray* (1988), and the success of the above-mentioned *RuPaul's Drag Race* (2009) indicate not only the enduring, but also growing, popularity of camp.

At the same time, any number of cultural producers continue to play with subtext, but often in a more overt way that speaks to important changes in the relationship between media audiences and producers in this age of convergence, marked by what Henry Jenkins (2008) calls "participatory culture." Today, media producers increasingly engage in and interact with fan cultures. Media audiences long have engaged in practices that are best labeled as fandom. More than simply watch a particular movie or TV show, fans increasingly *produce* their own text. Fans read and collect magazine and newspaper accounts of stars, movies, and TV shows, write and circulate stories that expand the story world of a TV show, novel, or movie, attend conventions, form clubs and other groups, and use social media sites such as YouTube, Tumblr, and Pinterest to circulate fan-created videos and GIFs emphasizing aspects of a program or movie most relevant to them. There can be no doubt that the Internet, and especially the interactivity of Web 2.0, have expanded greatly the scope and publicity of fan activities. What were once considered marginal activities have grown increasingly central to the media industries, which, in an age of fragmented attentions, work to build strong emotional investments between media properties and their audiences.

If GLBTQ themes have long been absent from mainstream media, they nonetheless have played a significant role in fan cultures. The first gay-themed fan fiction was written about the original *Star Trek* (1966–1969) series and featured a reimaging of Kirk and Spock as lovers rather than friends. This same-sex romantic and erotic pairing of characters represented as straight in the original text is known as slash fiction, as in Kirk/Spock. While the vast majority of slash fiction focuses on the pairing of men, there is a substantial subset of what is known as femslash, the pairing of two women. While this fiction was gay-themed, the earliest writers of slash fiction actually were heterosexual women. A great number of fan stories, videos, GIFs, and Tumblr pages recontextualize platonic friendships between same-sex characters as gay or lesbian romances. Melanie Kohnen (2008) examines the queer readings that heterosexual women make of the program *Smallville* (2001–2011). As Kohnen notes, a great deal of writing about queer spectatorship is based on the idea that people see queerly based on their queer identities. However, as we saw above with Doty (2000), queer pleasures are not limited to queer readers (see Textbox 5.4). Heterosexual *Smallville* fans engaged in HoYay!— Homoeroticism, Yay! readings, insisting on their interpretation of a romantic relationship between Lex and Clark as the dominant one. Kohnen (2008) argues that fans in one on-line community see the reading as so self-evident that they see the producers working overtime to deny the possibility. In other words, they need to continually add plot devices and love interests to *prove* that the characters are heterosexual instead of gay.

BOX 5.4   Slash Fiction

FIGURE 5.5 Slash fiction author Kate Butler
Source: **Photo courtesy of author.**

Much slash fiction actually is written by heterosexual audiences, especially women. Take the case of Kate Butler. Now an attorney, Butler has been writing slash fiction since she was a teenager. Since first discovering fan fiction in 1999, Butler has written hundreds of stories about characters from *Sailor Moon*, *CSI*, *Law & Order*, *Crossing Jordan*, and, most recently, Marvel comics. Her stories on Archive of Our Own (available at http://archiveofourown.org/users/the_wordbutler/) total over a million words. Her most popular solo work is a series of stories called *Motion Practice*, in which the Avengers are all attorneys. We asked Butler to explain her attraction to this genre:

Q: Why do you write slash fiction?
A: I write fan fiction generally because I like adapting a character's quirks and tragedies to a new situation. As for slash: dating back to my *Sailor Moon* (1995–2000) years, I've always found canon queer romances inherently more interesting than straight ones. But when I discovered that there are whole fan communities devoted to exploring relationships between same-sex characters . . . There's nothing in the world like loving the relationship between two characters and sharing that love with other people who also analyze and interpret how this fantastic connection might just turn into something more – especially when so many of the great slash relationships originate in the kind of spark that'd end in

(Continued)

happily ever after in a *Lifetime* movie.

Q: Why does slash fiction appeal to you as a heterosexual woman?

A: This question is asked a lot, actually. I personally think it's a combination of two things. First, there's a horrifying lack of diversity of *any* kind in media. Slash not only illuminates that fact but also strives to normalize the idea that a character can be complicated, important, *and* queer. It creates a bullhorn for otherwise underrepresented voices that we're unlikely to hear in "the canon" anytime soon. Second, women are constantly subjected to the same, tired *boy meets girl* tropes, and slash presents an opportunity to explore those tropes through a new lens. I think this process is really rewarding when you live in a world that is constantly (and loudly) communicating a very scripted, very heteronormative picture of romance. (And I firmly reject the school of thought that argues slash is straight women fetishizing queer relationships. As we say on the Internet: NOPE.)

Read some of Kate's stories or other samples of fan fiction writing. Then, working alone or in a group, outline your own slash fiction story. Consider the following questions:

1.   Why have you chosen a particular pair of characters to be read as queer? How does your fan reading go against the grain of the text, or to what extent does it seem to be invited by the text?

2.   How does a fan reading of two men or two women challenge our ideas of romance? What traits of men or women are stressed in slash romances that might not be in heterosexual romances?

3.   How does writing fan fiction help you think about the ways that heteronormativity shape ideas of romance and love in our culture. Do slash fiction stories challenge these norms, or do they reinforce them?

Since the 1990s, however, more self-identified GLBTQ individuals have begun to produce and share fan-produced content with each other, though the activity is still more prevalent among women, including lesbians. In many ways, fan fiction is a contemporary example of the queer reading practices of resistance and appropriation. In this way fan fiction is an important part of identity construction and can be a form of resistance against the limited representations of GLBTQ-identified individuals or more broadly of heteronormative ideas of romance and love. For example, lesbian fans of *Xena, Warrior Princess* (1995–2001) used fan fiction to create a space of agency. Engaging in fan fiction, especially the communal aspects, allowed fans to gain self-confidence and self-esteem, and therefore to see possibilities for queer futures for themselves (Hammer, 2010). In addition, fan fiction allows audiences to reimagine texts in ways that validate queer desires or remake texts that minimize same-sex desires and relationships. Fans of the soap opera *All My Children* (1970–2011) were active in producing videos that attempted to make up for what they saw as potential shortcomings in the program's representation of its only lesbian couple, Lena and Bianca (Ng, 2008). The "Lianca" videos edited together clips of lesbian couple Bianca and Lena in ways that sought to rewrite the couple's story arc. The videos intensified the emotional impact of the relationship by reordering the story elements to create the happy ending that the program denied them.

While these readings are consistent with a history of queer appropriation, the age of participatory culture has made media producers far more responsive to these readings. For example, in a nod to the numerous Tumblr pages and stories created by fans eager to see female friends Aria and Spencer as a couple ("Sparia"), the writers of *Pretty Little Liars* (2010–) used the first season finale (itself a campy ode to *Psycho* [1960]) to put the pair alone in a hotel room together and playfully discuss whether or not they should be a couple. In the most recent *Star Trek* (2009; 2013) films, the director and actors play with a long tradition of audiences reading Kirk and Spock as lovers, adding dialogue and looks between the characters that playfully acknowledge this slash tradition. The mega-successful *Pirates of the Caribbean* (2003) franchise features Johnny Depp as Jack Sparrow, a pirate whose purposeful play with masculinity and femininity allows for any number of readings of his sexuality (Fradley, 2012). Even programs made for and about GLBTQ audiences still play with subtext, as the Showtime series *The L Word* (2004–2009) did. As Candace Moore (2009) argued, though featuring a young cast, the program featured many references to more dated elements of lesbian culture in order to speak to multiple generations of lesbian viewers.

Programs like *Glee* (2009–) have been directly responsive to fans' reactions to the relationship between high-school cheerleaders Brittany and Santana. While the program has featured the gay male pair, Kurt and Blaine, a great deal of the Twitter activity around the program has centered on the relationship between cheerleaders Brittany and Santana (Marwick, Gray, & Ananny, 2013). While their relationship was primarily hinted at, the fan base was important to convincing the writers to put the pair in an open romantic relationship. At the same time, the relationship between these fans and the program's creator has been contentious. When the pair

FIGURE 5.6 Connotation 2.0?: A quick look between Kirk and Spock is exchanged before they embark on their next voyage
Source: Star Trek (2009).

broke up in 2012, in an episode that featured four of the major couples breaking up, "Brittana" fans were especially upset that the program included dialogue hostile to them. In explaining to male character Sam why she cannot kiss him, the non-labeled Brittany responds,

> No, it's not just Santana. It's like, all the lesbians of the nation. And I don't know how they found out about Santana and I dating, but once they did, they started sending me like Tweets and Facebook messages on Lord Tubbington's [her cat's] wall.
>
> (Douglas, 2012)

A recap on the website Wetpaint.com used the hashtag BringBackBrittana to further cite Brittany saying,

> I think it means a lot to them to see two super-hot popular girls in love. And I worry if they find out about you and I dating that they'll turn on you and get really violent and hurt your beautiful face and mouth.
>
> (ibid.)

While this example shows that relationships between fans and producers are not always easy, it nonetheless demonstrates the ways that contemporary fan culture moves beyond the reading of texts to both producing and circulating their own fiction, and increasingly to interacting with and pushing for more queer content in their favorite shows.

Whether it is audiences or producers who initiate these particular understandings, contemporary popular culture is still full of examples of camp, subtext, and the pleasures of resisting heteronormativity. The visibility of GLBTQ characters or situations does not in and of itself guarantee necessary resistance to dominant cultural norms. At the same time, despite a rise in visibility, for certain groups, there is still enough of an absence of representation in mainstream media to lead audiences to make their own meanings. However, a quick Google search of the term "queerbaiting" makes clear that while some audiences find pleasure in these practices, others are frustrated by programs like *Rizzoli and Isles* (2010–) which acknowledges the pleasures that lesbian fans take in the friendship between the two title character women, but refuses to actually represent lesbians. Some audience members believe the program merely perpetuates homophobia by teasing GLBTQ audiences with enough content to earn their viewership, while working to not dissuade broader audiences from tuning in. Is this more acknowledged subtext an even more insidious form of the homophobic connotations of the past? In many ways, this is much like the discussion of gay-window advertising in Chapter 4. There can be no doubt that in a world where homophobia creates a situation where mainstream media producers understand that their financial success relies on not alienating mainstream audiences, subtext will continue to exist. At the same time, as the history of GLBTQ audiences has shown, people have found both meaning and pleasure in a range of media texts.

▶ CONCLUSION

This chapter has been framed around the concepts of resistance and appropriation. Historically, both producing media by and for GLBTQ audiences and engaging with mainstream culture required creativity and unique modes of engagement. The act of producing media about GLBTQ issues for GLBTQ-identified audiences was an act of resistance in an age when media largely was made by and for the majority. At the same time, the overall cultural hostility to the GLBTQ population meant that media audiences had to learn ways of reading that allowed for the pleasure of media consumption without fully accepting all of the meanings contained in the texts. Of course, not all GLBTQ individuals engaged in camp, decoded subtext, or even saw content specifically aimed at them. Reading subtextual cues and camping are learned, communal practices, and not everyone had access to the subcultural spaces within which such practices flourished. At the same time, there were undoubtedly heterosexual-identified viewers who learned to make sense of what they saw on the screen or who delighted in the witty humor and skewering of social norms of camp.

In our current media environment, GLBTQ content is more available to lots of different audiences. What used to be subcultural practices meant to sustain and build self-esteem and community in the face of intense homophobia have today become recognizable to more and more media consumers. Today, lots of audiences routinely notice homoerotic subtext in music, films, and television shows. Indeed, media producers happily play up such elements in order to deliver the kind of hip, sophisticated audiences that advertisers desire. Is this now the appropriation of communicative forms from the gay and lesbian subcultures for the mainstream consumption? Are these practices resistant? At the same time, the continued narrow lens brought to bear on GLBTQ communities means that GLBTQ producers and audiences still find ways to resist mainstream meanings and media.

▶ REFERENCES

Akhavan, D. & Jungerman, I. (Writer, Director, & Producers). (2010, September 5). Episode 5: It Gets Better [web series]. *The Slope.* Retrieved from http://theslopeshow.com/episodes/page/2.

Babuscio, J. (1999). The cinema of camp aka camp and the gay sensibility. In F. Cleto (Ed.), *Camp: Queer aesthetics and the performing subject: A reader* (pp. 117–135). Ann Arbor, MI: University of Michigan Press.

Benshoff, H.M. & Griffin, S. (2005). *Queer images: A history of gay and lesbian film in America.* Lanham, MD: Rowman & Littlefield Publishers.

Butler, J. (1990). *Gender trouble: Feminism and the subversion of identity.* New York, NY: Routledge.

Doty, A. (2000). *Flaming classics: Queering the film canon.* New York, NY: Psychology Press.

Douglas, B. (2012, December 7). Brittany and Sam: Top quotes of *Glee* season 4, episode 9: "Swan Song." *Wetpaint.* Retrieved from http://www.wetpaint.com/glee/articles/brittany-and-sam-top-quotes-of-glee-season-4-episode-9-swan-song.

Driver, S. (2007). *Queer girls and popular culture: Reading, resisting and creating media.* New York, NY: Peter Lang.

Dyer, R. (1999). It's being so camp as keeps us going. In F. Cleto (Ed.), *Camp: Queer aesthetics and the performing subject: A reader* (pp. 110–116). Ann Arbor, MI: University of Michigan Press.

Farmer, B. (2005). The fabulous sublimity of gay diva worship. *Camera Obscura, 20*(2), 165–195.

Farrugia, R. & Hay, K. (2013). Queering hip hop. (Unpublished manuscript). Department of Communication and Journalism, Oakland University, Rochester, MI.

Fradley, M. (2012). Why doesn't your compass work? *Pirates of the Caribbean*, fantasy blockbusters, and contemporary queer theory. In K. Ross (Ed.), *The handbook of gender, sex, and media*. New York, NY: John Wiley & Sons, Ltd.

Gregg, R. (2010). Queering Brad Pitt: The struggle between gay fans and the Hollywood machine to control star discourse and image on the web. In C. Pullen & M. Cooper (Eds.), *LGBT identity and online new media* (pp.139–146). New York, NY: Routledge.

Gross, L. (2001). *Up from invisibility: Lesbians, gay men, and the media in America*. New York, NY: Columbia University Press.

Halberstam, J. (2003). What's that smell? Queer temporalities and subcultural lives. *International Journal of Cultural Studies, 6*(3), 313–333.

Hall, S. (1980). Encoding/decoding. In S. Hall, D. Hobson, A. Lowe, & P. Willis (Eds.), *Culture, media, language* (pp. 128–138). London: Hutchinson.

Halperin, D.M. (2012). *How to be gay*. Cambridge, MA: Belknap Press.

Hammer, R. (2010). Internet fandom, queer discourse, and identities. In C. Pullen & M. Cooper (Eds.), *LGBT identity and online new media* (pp. 147–158). New York, NY: Routledge.

Jenkins, H. (1988). *Star Trek* rerun, reread, rewritten: Fan writing as textual poaching. *Critical Studies in Mass Communication*, 85–107.

Jenkins, H. (2008). *Convergence culture: Where old and new media collide*. New York, NY: New York University Press.

Jenkins, H. (2012). *Textual poachers: Television fans and participatory culture*. New York, NY: Routledge.

Kohnen, M.E.S. (2008). The adventures of a repressed farm boy and the billionaire who loves him: Queer spectatorship in *Smallville* fandom. In L. Stein (Ed.). *Teen television: Essays on programming and fandom* (pp. 207–223). Jefferson, NC: McFarland & Company.

Lambe, S. (2012, December 13). The year hip-hop went queer. *BuzzFeed Community*. Retrieved from http://www.buzzfeed.com/stacylambe/the-year-hip-hop-went-queer.

Marwick, A., Gray, M., & Ananny, M. (2013). Dolphins are just gay sharks: *Glee* and the queer case of transmedia as text and object. *Television and New Media*, published on-line, February 26, pp. 1–21.

Miller, D.A. (1991). Anal rope. In D. Fuss (Ed.), *Inside/out: Lesbian theories, gay theories (after the law)* (pp. 119–141). New York, NY: Routledge.

Moore, C. (2009). Liminal places and spaces: Public/private considerations. In V. Mayer & M. Banks (Eds.), *Production studies: Cultural studies of media industries* (pp. 125–139). New York, NY: Routledge.

Newton, E. (1979). *Mother camp: Female impersonators in America*. Chicago, IL: University of Chicago Press.

Newton, E. (1999). Role models. In F. Cleto (Ed.), *Camp: Queer aesthetics and the performing subject: A reader* (pp. 96–109). Ann Arbor, MI: University of Michigan Press.

Ng, E. (2008). Reading the romance of fan cultural production: Music videos of a television lesbian couple. *Popular Communication, 6*(2), 103–121.

Ott, B.L. & Mack, R.L. (2010). *Critical media studies*. New York, NY: John Wiley & Sons.

Rich, A. (1980). Compulsory heterosexuality and lesbian existence. *Signs, 5*(4), 631–660.

Russo, V. (1987). *The celluloid closet: Homosexuality in the movies.* New York, NY: HarperCollins.

Sender, K. (2012). No hard feelings: Reflexivity and queer affect in the new media landscape. In K. Ross (Ed.), *The handbook of gender, sex and media* (pp. 207–225). Hoboken, NJ: Wiley & Sons, Ltd.

Sontag, S. (1964). Notes on "camp." *Partisan Review, 31*, 515–530.

Taylor, J. (2008). The queerest of the queer: Sexuality, politics and music on the Brisbane scene. *Continuum: Journal of Media and Cultural Studies, 22*(5), 651–665.

Thomas, A. (1989). The house that kids built: The gay black imprint on American dance music. *Out/Look, 1*(2), 34–42.

The Closet

On October 11 each year, GLBTQ people around the country celebrate National Coming Out Day, a day to celebrate their own choices to publicly proclaim their sexualities. This annual celebration, begun in 1988 to mark the anniversary of the National March on Washington for Lesbian and Gay Rights, holds up what has become for many in the GLBTQ community a rite of passage. Coming out is equated with being true to one's identity, being honest with others, finding connection and support within the GLBTQ community, and ultimately liberating oneself from the oppression of the closet. In fact, the metaphor of the closet and related coming-out narratives have been central to Western culture's understanding of homosexuality for the past half-century. Media have played an important role in upholding the closet as a structuring device that frames the way people—gay and straight, transgender and cisgender—think about the social and political oppression of sexual minorities. However, some scholars question the logic of the closet, suggesting that, at best, it is an outdated concept that no longer reflects the lived realities of GLBTQ people and, at worst, reinforces a heteronormative worldview.

This chapter will explore the role of traditional and new media in reinforcing and challenging the metaphor of the closet as a framework for making sense of GLBTQ sexuality. First, we will explore how the metaphor of the closet emerged and how "coming out" has become both a personal narrative for understanding one's minority sexual status and an assumed necessary act for self-acceptance. In this discussion, we will consider how the coming-out narrative has been reinforced and extended by media. Then, we will consider a shift in GLBTQ media narratives beginning in the late 1990s that presumes a post-gay world in which closeted sexuality is no longer necessary due to widespread social acceptance. In this ostensible post-closet era, media narratives continually position closeted gay men as tragic characters who bring harm to those around them. Finally, we will consider queer critiques of the closet that suggest its associated logic relies on heteronormative assumptions that privilege a white, heterosexual worldview.

▶ THE METAPHOR OF THE CLOSET

Stonewall-era gay rights activists were the first to use the closet metaphor to frame the gay experience as one of oppression. When gay rights organizations associated with the homophile movement began organizing in the 1950s, many framed their missions in terms of resisting an oppressive system. This oppression was conceptualized as a matter of spatial confinement. For instance, the initial goal of the Mattachine Society was to educate homosexuals that they comprised "a social minority imprisoned within a dominant culture" (D'Emilio, 1998, p. 65). On at least a limited scope, some writers used similar spatial metaphors for homosexual oppression, like James Baldwin in his 1956 novel, *Giovanni's Room*. Chauncey (1994) speculates that the first use of the "closet" metaphor may have referenced gay men who were covert about their sexuality, likening it to "skeletons in the closet." By its very definition, the closet is a non-social, less legitimate space than the world outside it. As Kushnik (2010) writes, "All this paints a picture of what it's like to conceal one's sexual identity: difficult, unnatural, dark, precarious, isolating, and probably doomed to failure" (p. 679).

By the 1970s, as the gay rights movement shifted to an identity politics model that likened sexual oppression to racial oppression, the ultimate goal became to escape the oppressive secrecy of the closet by publicly revealing one's sexuality. In the major gay liberationist anthology *Out of the Closets*, editor Karla Jay (1992) proclaimed her great hope "that one day all gay people will be out of the closet" (p. lxii). D'Emilio (1992) has suggested that positioning "coming out" as a supreme political act was "a tactical stroke of great genius" (p. 244). This personally meaningful act also is a political act available to all people, which then leaves them exposed and invested in the gay rights movement. The general idea of these arguments is that as more gays and lesbians "come out," their greater visibility will lead to greater equality. (Textbox 6.1 considers the ethics of "outing" gay people without their permission).

BOX 6.1   The Ethics of Outing

Until the 1980s, gay and lesbian celebrities largely were able to circulate in gay circles without media attention to their sexuality because of an unspoken code within the gay community and among many journalists not to reveal the sexual orientation of gays and lesbians. Among the first people to break this code were gay writer-activists like Michelangelo Signorile and Armistead Maupin, who saw it as their political mission to "out" closeted politicians and staff members who supported anti-gay causes and closeted celebrities and businessmen who benefited by keeping secret their sexual orientation. The political strategy of outing continues today, with Michael Rogers' blogACTIVE.com, which includes "The List" with names of politicians or staff members of conservative politicians whom Rogers suggests are privately gay, yet publicly supportive of anti-gay legislation. Visitors to the blog can donate money to an "investigation fund" to support "breaking stories on hypocrites." Rogers also appears in *Outrage*, a 2009 documentary by filmmaker Kirby Dick that indicts closeted conservative politicians.

Publicly outing gay people has been controversial. Opponents of outing suggest a person's sexual orientation should fall under their moral right of privacy, and depriving someone of that right is analogous to theft—of their ability to control that personal information. For instance, Mayo and Gunderson (1994) argue that gay people need control over that private information to maintain autonomy over their sexual identities, a necessity for gay people to work through their sexuality. Additionally, they suggest that people should not be robbed of the ability to come out in their own time. They write, "Coming out is important not simply because one *is out* at the end of the process but also—and perhaps primarily—because one has been the primary agent of this self-affirming development" (p. 54, emphasis in original). Yet, others (see, for instance, Mohr, 1992) support a "radical" position of outing, suggesting that all gay people who are not open about their sexuality should be outed because their secrecy upholds the oppressive structure of the closet, and the only way to put an end to homophobia is for all gays and lesbians to become visible as such.

Today's changing cultural and media landscapes have altered the playing field of outing. Being an out gay man or lesbian does not necessarily carry the same social stigma it once did. (Although, we should remember that, at the time of this writing, gay people can be fired from their jobs or denied housing because of their sexual orientation in 29 states.) Today's 24/7 media also have made it increasingly difficult for people to keep their private lives out of public view. Nonetheless, the ethics of

(Continued)

outing have not been fully resolved. As Gross (1993) notes, "The real question, therefore, is *where* in the middle one draws the line, and *who* has the right to decide on which side of the line any particular instance falls?" (p. 3, emphasis in original). Where is *your* line? Consider the following cases and discuss the underlying values/ethics that inform your position:

1. Do you support the outing of closeted politicians who support anti-gay legislation? What about closeted politicians who support pro-gay legislation?
2. The obituary of Sally Ride, the first U.S. woman in space, stated that she was "survived by Tam O'Shaughnessy, her partner of 27 years." Ride's family members reported that she was an intensely private person and, although out with close friends, did not publicly discuss her sexuality while alive. Should Ride have been public about her sexual orientation before her death? Did the fact that her sexual orientation dominated headlines after her death overshadow her professional accomplishments?
3. If you have a friend who is gay or lesbian, what factors would you consider in determining whether to share photos or information that might disclose their sexual orientation on social media sites? How has the Internet changed boundaries between private and public?

Coming-Out Narratives

Almost a half-century since the Stonewall Riots, coming out remains an important part of GLBTQ identity construction, as sexual minorities reveal their identities to themselves, their family and friends, and/or the broader public. In fact, the ubiquity of coming-out narratives can make it difficult for all people to conceptualize of the experiences of sexual minorities as *not* involving some coming-out process. In social science and psychology, coming out usually is described as involving a series of stages, beginning with early feelings that lead to the questioning of one's gender or sexual identity, self-recognition, and naming. Most models point to these early stages as often confusing, anxiety-provoking, and as a point where people remain closeted. An important next step for people is admitting to others, including friends and family, that they are GLBTQ. Models aimed at children and those specific to transgender people often emphasize telling parents about one's identity as a key moment. A number of models also stress the importance of finding connection with the GLBTQ community as another step. Most models offer an end point that refers to achieving a sense of self-acceptance and openness about one's identity in day-to-day life. Transgender models of development further deal with questions of transitioning and the complexities of finding, funding, and managing healthcare needs during that time, especially given the fact that transgender identity is less understood or accepted in broader society. As Barnhurst (2007) argues, these stories all tend to feature a before state of being closeted, a liminal state of translating self-recognition into recognition by others, and, finally, the after state of being "out."

The closet metaphor is so central to our notions of sexual difference that most people who claim the GLBT, and even Q identities, will at some point tell a story about "coming out." Psychological models of GLBTQ identity center on coming out and being out as crucial to happiness. Yet, just as the closet can be understood in different ways, so can coming-out stories. While models of development treat the closet as a fact, other theorists work to understand coming-out narratives as stories we tell ourselves and others, suggesting that the speech act itself constitutes sexuality as a source of identity. Ken Plummer (1994) argued that, while we typically think of "coming out" as *revealing* a truth about our identity, it rather *creates* an identity rooted in sexuality. Plummer notes that, like all stories, the coming-out story can be understood as a genre. The coming-out genre has its roots in the post-Stonewall moment and the feminist movement of the 1970s, which focused on turning the personal into the political and the importance of women telling their sexual stories of rape and survival. What Plummer makes clear is that these stories are not individual. Identities always are mediated by cultural stories and are built through our interactions with others.

Mediating the Closet: Coming-Out Stories

Media have played a key role in circulating coming-out stories, offering up models through which GLBTQ people make sense of their own feelings and experiences. Sometimes this can be in very prescriptive ways, like *BuzzFeed*'s "24 Awesomely Creative Ways to Come Out of the Closet" (Nigatu & Karlan, 2013), but, more typically, media narratives ascribe to and reinforce common themes of the coming-out story and the underlying logic of the closet. As discussed in Chapters 2 and 3, pre-Stonewall mainstream media rarely presented homosexuality in direct ways. Instead, it was hinted at, and largely as a form of pathological deviance. As the metaphors of the closet and coming-out narratives became the central organizing discourses for GLBTQ identity, they likewise became key features of media representations.

Coming-out storylines have been particularly prevalent since the 1970s, especially on television. The first major fictional coming out occurred in 1971 on the barrier-pushing Norman Lear comedy *All in the Family* (1971–1979), in which a friend of the main character, Archie Bunker—a staunch conservative clinging often unsuccessfully to white patriarchal ideals—comes out to him. The first unscripted coming out was on the PBS documentary *An American Family* (1973), which documented seven months in the life of a "typical" American family. In an unexpected turn, a son in the family grapples with his sexuality, coming out to himself, his family, and all of America. Later in the 1970s came the character of Jodie in the sitcom *Soap* (1977–1981), who although generally criticized by the GLBTQ community for his stereotypical effeminate qualities, comes out on screen to his big brother in a loving exchange that challenged the demonization of gay men. Twenty years later, viewers of the critically acclaimed, but short-lived, *My So-Called Life* (1994–1995) watched the first coming-out storyline involving a person of color, as character Rickie Vasquez (played by gay actor Wilson Cruz) suffers abuse from his father and schoolmates for his gender nonconformity, but eventually reaches self-acceptance and adopts the label "gay" to identify himself.

Since the new era of GLBTQ visibility in the 1990s, coming-out storylines have become so prevalent that GLBTQ media studies scholar Larry Gross described them as "almost a cliché of television stories" (Friedlander, 2011). This new era was ushered in by the simultaneous on-screen and off-screen coming out of Ellen DeGeneres, then the star of the sitcom *Ellen* (1994–1998). Entire reality programs for the Logo channel, like *Coming Out Stories* (2006) and *Out on the Job* (2008), continue to solidify the logic of the closet and naturalize the coming-out process as a necessary step to self-acceptance and happiness for GLBTQ people.

The coming-out stories that circulate in media and culture more broadly follow a similar pattern. As Plummer (1994) describes them,

> It tells initially of a frustrated, thwarted and stigmatized desire for someone of one's own sex—of a love that dares not speak its name; it stumbles around childhood longings and youthful secrets, it interrogates itself, seeking "causes" and "histories" that might bring "motives" and "memories" into focus: it finds a crisis, a turning point, an epiphany: and then it enters a new world—a new identity, born again, metamorphosis, coming out.
>
> (p. 52)

In the process, coming-out stories are confessional in nature, presenting coming out as an issue of honesty and as a linear process that largely assumes a happy ending. These stories offer a model for GLBTQ viewers as they make sense of their own feelings and work to construct their own sexual identities. (Textbox 6.2 considers media coverage of professional athletes' coming-out stories). Gay and lesbian rights groups like GLAAD applaud these seemingly positive post-Stonewall representations that reinforce social acceptance of gayness; however, as we will discuss later in the chapter, queer theorists are more critical of these common coming-out narratives.

BOX 6.2   Out in Sports

Outsports.com hailed 2013 as the year of the gay athlete. The website, founded in 1999, covers issues related to gay athletes and sports, introducing readers to professional and amateur GLBTQ athletes, sports writers, and leaders in the sports industry. For evidence of its claim, *Outsports* pointed to 77 people who came out in sports during the 2013 calendar year (Outsports, 2013). Some of these were headline-grabbing announcements, like NBA player Jason Collins, who after becoming a free agent and signing with the Brooklyn Nets became the first openly gay player in any of the four major North American pro sports leagues. His announcement earned him a spot on *Time Magazine*'s "100 Most Influential People in the World" list in April 2014 (Time, Inc., 2014). The November 2013 wedding of Puerto Rican professional boxer Orlando Cruz to his boyfriend José Manuel Colón in New York's Central Park also made headlines, as had his coming-out announcement the year before. Also in 2013, former NFL tackle Kwame Harris was publicly outed by ESPN.com after facing domestic abuse charges against a former boyfriend. Harris confirmed that he was gay and would eventually talk to media outlets about his time as a closeted player, saying that he did not think being gay was "compatible" with a career in professional football (Huffington Post, 2013). In 2014, as a seventh-round pick for the St. Louis Rams, Michael Sam became the first openly gay football player selected in the NFL draft. Seconds after his selection, Sam shared a televised kiss with his longtime boyfriend Vito Cammisano that earned media descriptions like "Kiss Seen Round the World" (Brydum, 2014) and "the most famous gay kiss of all time" (Glazek, 2014).

Although these athletes certainly are not the first gay athletes to come out about their sexuality, their sexuality gained widespread media attention because they are men playing in what are considered to be some of the most masculine sports. Research into sexuality and sports historically has found that organized sports teams in Western cultures are highly homophobic, particularly with contact sports teams reproducing and reinforcing traditional hegemonic masculinity. As Kwame Harris noted, for many, contact sports and homosexuality seem incompatible. More recently, though, researchers are finding sports teams increasingly accepting of a broader range of sexuality (Anderson, 2011). To encourage you to think more fully about this recent "gay sports movement" and the role of media, consider the following:

(Continued)

1. Read some of the athlete profiles found on Outsports.com. Do they follow the same narrative trajectory described by Plummer (1995)—"suffering, surviving and surpassing?"
2. R.W. Connell (2005) argues that in Western culture masculinity *is* homophobia. That is, boys socialize each other into cultural norms of masculinity by calling out any traditionally feminine characteristics in boys or men as a sign of homosexuality. How do coming-out stories of male athletes attempt to reconcile this association?
3. Compare stories about gay male athletes in contact sports (boxing, football, basketball) and non-contact sports (e.g., swimming, skating, gymnastics). How are they similar or different?
4. Analyze media stories about lesbian athletes (e.g., U.S. Olympic soccer player Megan Rapinoe, WNBA player Sheryl Swoopes, or pro golfer Rosie Jones). How do the stories compare to those about male athletes? How do stereotypes about female athletes differ from those of male athletes, and how might they affect the way lesbian athletes' comings out are covered?
5. Compare stories across different media outlets about a gay athlete coming out. Is the story covered differently in mainstream media, by sports writers, by gay press, etc.?

Coming Out Online: Community, Connection, and Learning

There can be no doubt that the Internet has altered the contours of the closet, itself part of the broader changes that have transformed GLBTQ coming-out stories over the last 20 years. For a great number of people making sense of their sexual identity, the Internet has become a vital resource. Even in our age of increasing visibility, many young people experience their earliest non-heterosexual or non-gender-normative desires in a situation of confusion and even isolation. The ability to use the Internet to learn about, connect with, discuss, and work out identity issues has been crucial to the lives of many people in the United States and globally for negotiating and making sense of their sexual identities. The Internet also has gone beyond traditional media's modeling of coming-out narratives to allowing users to actively construct their own coming-out stories and share advice about coming out with others.

The Internet particularly has been a resource for people whose identities may not align with sexual minorities most visible in traditional media, allowing them to find the information and language necessary for crafting their own coming-out stories. For example, transgender people turn to the Internet for health information at a much higher rate than non-GLBTQ-identified individuals (GLSEN, CIPHR, & CCRC, 2013). Heinz (2012) argues that the "institutional erasure" of trans identity makes it difficult for transgender people to find reliable information, and, thus, it is up to individuals to both find and create resources. In a study of blogs written by female-to-male transgender bloggers, he examines how individuals and communities maintain these sites over the course of many years, frequently detailing the complexities of the coming-out and transition process. Similarly, Cooper (2010) found that a chat room for lesbians married to men operates as a key site for identity negotiation and support. The space offers a risk-free environment for questioning identity and offers advice, education, and resources. In the process, the women collectively make sense of their shared experiences and construct a coming-out narrative that acknowledges the uniqueness of their married status. For these participants, the forum becomes a space to creatively build what eventually becomes a standardized coming-out narrative available to other lesbians married to men.

Vlogging has become another space in which out GLBTQ people share their coming-out experiences in an effort to support others. These videos have become a distinct genre that applies the confessional, amateur style of YouTube vlogging to the standard coming-out genre discussed above, while also offering variations that complicate standard coming-out narratives (Alexander & Losh, 2010). Vloggers often share advice, for example, telling young GLBTQ youth about appropriate times and ways to come out. As a distinct and recognized genre, the videos, as a group, are very popular, even if individual videos rarely are seen. So popular is the genre that the mainstream gay press will cover them, like when *Huffington Post* published blogger Davey Wavey's list of top five coming-out videos for Pride 2013 (Lazar, 2013).

The videos, including a number made by transgender people, demonstrate the ways that people use this digital platform both to tell their own stories and to offer connection and advice to their viewers. For example, an early video from the proudly androgynous Gigi Gorgeous, a regular vlogger who has become a star of the YouTube MTV-styled reality series *The Avenue* (2011–2013), tells the story of *not* coming out, because it was clear to everyone that he was gay. While he repeats some of the central parts of the coming-out genre, such as feeling different from a young age and struggling with self-hatred, he goes farther, claiming that he is telling his story as a service to the people who watch his videos and then message and email him with their own stories. In fact, as central as individual coming-out stories are to the vloggers, so are appeals to community, as bloggers frequently discuss support for their viewers as a key motivation for telling their stories.

FIGURE 6.1 "It Gets Better" project dedicated to the acceptance of LGBT youth
Source: http://www.itgetsbetter.org.

The same is true in the most recent iteration of the coming-out genre, the "It Gets Better" campaign discussed in earlier chapters. Initiated by Dan Savage, who made a video in September 2010 in the wake of a rash of publicized suicides by young gay men, this video campaign features a range of confessional videos telling young people to basically hang in there because life for gays and lesbians improves as they get older. A great number of these videos are self-made. These videos extend the existing logic of the coming-out video genre, with its emphasis on telling stories not merely as personal expressions, but as expressions of support. They directly appeal to GLBTQ youth struggling with bullying, hostility, rejection, and isolation, offering the promise of a better future. In this genre the emphasis is less on the moment of coming out, and more on how to survive and thrive as an out GLBTQ person. (Textbox 6.3 considers criticisms of the "It Gets Better" campaign as reflecting and reinforcing inequalities of the offline world.) Although digital media have complicated the coming-out genre, the underlying logic of the closet is still upheld. The presumption is that GLBTQ people cannot reach full self-realization, acceptance, and happiness until they have made a public pronouncement of their sexuality to others.

BOX 6.3   What Is "Better"?

Developed as a response to a seeming crisis point in suicides by teenagers struggling with their sexual and gender identities, Dan Savage's "It Gets Better" campaign featured short videos by GLBTQ-identified adults telling their own stories of
struggle and how adult life has offered far more than they might have imagined
when they were young. "It Gets Better" has become the mantra meant to offer
hope, support, and the sense that there *is* a viable future to teens driven to desperation by their current situations. The project began with everyday people, but
quickly expanded to include celebrities, and, eventually, even employee groups
from different corporations produced their own versions. Many of these emotionally raw videos include stories of suicidal feelings or suicide attempts by the storytellers, including celebrities, such as *Project Runway* (2004–) star, Tim Gunn.

However Jasbir Puar (2010) invites us to think about the possible limitations of
the campaign. She notes that the discourse mimics a "pull yourself up from your
bootstraps" mentality that puts the onus of survival on teens themselves. Pointing to the overwhelming number of videos by white gay men, she points out that
"queer people of colour, trans, genderqueer and gender noncomforming youth,
and lesbians have not been inspirationally hailed by IGB in the same way as white
gay male liberals." She suggests this is because "getting better" is linked to class
mobility, an upper-middle-class lifestyle, and monogamous coupling.

Still, as Puar (2010) points out, there also are videos that suggest things do not
get better. For example, transgender activist Kate Bornstein shares her honest perspective that "it" does not necessarily always get better, but viewers have a right
to make themselves feel better. Rather than telling teens to "grin and bear it" for a
more happy future, contributors like Bornstein suggest that they have the right to
make their now better for themselves.

For this exercise, watch some of the "It Gets Better" videos, available at
www.itgetsbetter.org, or the organization's YouTube channel, http://www.
youtube.com/user/itgetsbetterproject. Look for a variety of videos by celebrities, corporate employees, and individuals. As you watch, consider the following questions:

1. How does each of the storytellers define "better"? What does a "better"
    future look like in the videos? What evidence do the video makers offer of a
    "better" life?

(Continued)

2. As you look for videos, consider the makers of the videos in terms of race, class, and gender. Who makes most of the videos? From the perspective of struggling GLBTQ youth, who is offered the most hope of a better life ahead?
3. What are the different production values of the videos? Do professionally made videos offer better advice than amateur videos? Is there a link between the kinds of better futures offered and those aesthetics? Do the aesthetics reinforce a certain version of a better future?
4. Based on your own viewing, what do you think about the criticisms of the campaign?
5. Taking into consideration the critiques raised here, what might *you* say to struggling GLBTQ youth in your own "It Gets Better" video?

▶ THE PERILS OF SECRECY

Increasingly, many of today's gay and lesbian characters no longer need to navigate the metaphorical closet, as their sexuality is made apparent from their first on-screen appearance. This is true in television programs like *Will & Grace* (1998–2006), *Modern Family* (2009–), *The New Normal* (2012–2013), *Sean Saves the World* (2013–2014), and *Brooklyn Nine-Nine* (2013–). Gay characters in these programs make no secret of their sexuality and rarely, if ever, face negative consequences for being out in their professional and personal lives. Becker (2009) contends that, beginning in the late 1990s, television representations of gayness have "support[ed] a liberal assumption that we have entered a 'post-gay' civil-rights era" (p. 126). These representations suggest that GLBTQ people no longer have anything to fear by coming out, positioning the closet as an unnecessary and archaic space. Becker suggests that the post-gay world of television offers a clear line between gayness and straightness by portraying gay characters as out and open about their sexuality. In this presumed post-closet world, closeted sexuality is a problem because it disrupts liberal assumptions that full GLBTQ equality has been reached and makes the line between heterosexuality and homosexuality more difficult to identify. Therefore, closeted characters must be contained, so as not to pose a risk to television's ostensibly post-gay world. Not unlike media representations of gay men prior to the 1990s that portrayed them largely as victims or villains, contemporary depictions of closeted gay men present an equally tragic image. The difference, though, is that their deviance comes not from their status as gay men, but as a consequence of keeping secret their sexual identity.

If we take a look at recent representations of closeted gay characters, none of them are pretty. We have those who appear to be frozen in time, subscribing to a logic of gayness that demarcates the closeted character from an identity-politics understanding of the promises of liberated out gayness. Other closeted gay characters meet their ends through tragic means, and closeted gay men, especially, are presented as homophobic and desperate to keep their secret. This includes black gay men, who are portrayed as putting their secret sex lives with other men ahead of the health and safety of their "innocent" wives and girlfriends. The underlying assumption of such representations is that secrecy about one's sexuality almost inevitably leads to tragedy.

Tragedy of the Post-Gay Closet

The 2005 blockbuster film *Brokeback Mountain* offers an example of the tragedy of the closet. Described by Osterweil (2007) as "a strange fusion between a Douglas Sirk melodrama and a John Ford Western" (p. 38), the film is set in 1963 Wyoming and follows the love story of cowboys Ennis Del Mar (Heath Ledger) and Jack Twist (Jake Gyllenhaal). After meeting and developing a sexual (and seemingly romantic) relationship while shepherding on fictional Brokeback Mountain, the men return to their own lives and traditional expectations of family. The men continue their sexual relationship mostly in secret by meeting for infrequent fishing trips, until Ennis discovers from returned mail that Jack is deceased. Ennis's imagination leads him to believe Jack has met a violent death, and the audience is left with an intentionally ambiguous ending.

While *Brokeback Mountain* offers a sympathetic portrayal of closeted gay men, which, as Ron Becker (2009) argues, has the effect of situating the closet as a sad relic of the past, contemporary stories treat characters who do not come out of the closet as troubled or as sources of trouble. The popular television program *Glee* (2009–), which has been heralded for its progressive representations of gay characters like Kurt Hummel and Blaine Anderson, presents very different characterizations of the show's closeted gay characters. The first two seasons of *Glee* include the character Sanford Ryerson, who goes by the nickname Sandy. Sandy appears to have walked straight out of a Hays-Code-era movie. Even before his gayness is confirmed, his appearance and behaviors are clearly designed to code his sexuality. He is a middle-aged man with a receding hairline and a penchant for pastels. Like Hays-Code-era characters, Sandy's unspoken homosexuality is represented through deviance. Just in case viewers somehow miss Sandy's "creepiness," his fellow character Sue Sylvester makes them explicit after visiting his apartment: "The only thing missing from this place is a couple dozen bodies lying in shallow graves and rotting under the floor boards" (Falchuk, Brennan, & Murphy, 2009). The quip is a reference to real-life serial killer John Wayne Gacy, who in the 1970s sexually assaulted and murdered more than 30 teenage boys and young men, hiding most of their bodies in the crawl space of his home. Sandy's deviance and presumed perversion as a closeted gay man is striking in an otherwise gay-friendly program. Sandy clearly represents an "old" version of gayness, one that is closeted and creepy by comparison to the new generation of out-and-proud gay men represented by other characters in the program. The closet is no longer imagined as a confined space of social oppression, but as an archaic past where sexual deviance festers.

In an alternative model of closeted gayness, *Glee* (2009–) presents the character of David Karofsky, a football player who initially targets Kurt for bullying. In season two, viewers (and Kurt) learn the real reason for Karofsky's aggression toward Kurt is his own desire for him. In a moment of hazing in which Kurt confronts Karofsky, the hulking football player responds by planting an aggressive kiss on Kurt. Karofsky begins the journey toward self-acceptance; however, when his gayness is revealed at the new school where he transfers, he unsuccessfully attempts suicide by hanging himself and is briefly hospitalized (Aguirre-Sacasa, Brennan, Falchuk, Hodgson, & Murphy, 2012). Although there are clear differences between Karofsky and Sandy, they have one thing in common—their closeted sexuality. Although the character Kurt endures bullying for being out, the narrative positions him as being in a better place than his closeted counterparts. The underlying message is that the closet does terrible things to people; the inability to openly express one's sexuality turns gay men into perverts, bullies, or tragic victims.

This same theme of the deviancy of the closet particularly can be seen in crime dramas, in which the secrecy of the closet leads to villainous behavior. If in the past a character's possible non-heterosexuality was treated as the source of deviant behavior that could lead to murderous consequences, in a world of increasing acceptance of GLBTQ individuals, and the subsequent imperative to come out, it is the secrecy of the closet rather than homosexuality itself that is treated as a problem. For example, a 2008 episode of *Law and Order: SVU* (1999–), titled "Closet," centers on the tragic consequences of a football player's decision to remain in the closet (Wolf, Storer, & Leto, 2008). The program opens with the murder of a middle-aged professional, discovered in a compromising position by his young assistant. The detectives' suspicion turns to a late-career football player, whom they accidentally "out." The suspect himself then becomes victim of an apparent anti-gay hate crime. In the end, it becomes clear that the football player's publicist is responsible for these crimes, angry that the football player's success will be thrown away if he comes out of the closet. In this episode, the closet is experienced as a tragedy for the football player, who has lost the love of his life and his football career, and as a source of trauma and anxiety for heterosexuals, including the investigating detectives.

Similarly, in *Law and Order: Criminal Intent* (2001–2011), a firefighter's closeted sexuality leads to tragedy for himself and everyone around him (Wolf, Balcer, Reingold, &

McKay, 2006). The 9/11 hero and activist for survivors stumbles into the fire station stabbed 22 times, leading police to begin an investigation into his murder. Detectives quickly determine that the dead firefighter had been having an affair, and that his wife knew about the infidelity, and, finding herself pregnant, demanded he stop it. What detectives find is that the firefighter's affair was with a gay serial killer, who once before had murdered a closeted lover after he had tried to break it off because his wife was pregnant. In this case, again, the closet leads to tragic consequences, including the death of a hero, a pregnant widow, a broken relationship between urban police and firefighters, and a detective under investigation. These narratives hinge on the terrible consequences of the secrecy of the closet, not only on the closeted individuals, but on those around them. While the stories suggest that societal pressure causes the need for people to be in the closet, they also work to figure secrecy itself as the source of the criminal activity that unfolds.

Media narratives about transgender characters complicate the tragedy of the closet with the possible perils of passing. While gay and lesbian coming-out narratives follow a fairly linear path, the transgender coming-out process involves a more complex process in which they must first come to terms with their gender identity and then make the decision about how to present their gender in daily life. Transgender self-representation may vary significantly from person to person, with some individuals desiring to pass undetected as their preferred gender, while others may insist on the continued importance of specifically identifying as transgender or gender queer. From *Paris Is Burning* (1990) to *Boys Don't Cry* (1999), the gap between an individual's biological and "true" gender identity is shown as leading to the threat of violence and death. Both films share real stories of transgender experience that exemplify the horrifying statistics of violence and murder against transgender individuals. Still, as in the post-closet stories about gays and lesbians, media stories of transgender individuals increasingly emphasize the costs of secrecy.

For example, *Degrassi: The Next Generation* (2001–) depicts the complexity of the closet and coming out for transgender youth. The drama, which originated in Canada but is rebroadcast in the United States and other countries, is the latest production in the *Degrassi* franchise, which dates back to 1979. This most recent iteration featured a storyline involving FtM transgender teen Adam Torres. In the two-part episode "My Body is My Cage" (Grassi, Hood, Moore, & Schuyler, 2010), Adam weighs the possible perils of passing with the self-hatred he experiences when closeting his transgender identity. Shortly after Adam reveals his transgender status to his two best friends, he is exposed publically as transgender by another classmate. After his secret is revealed, Adam is assaulted in the men's restroom—the quintessential space of danger for transgender people—and his stepbrother is beaten up trying to stick up for him. Adam's return to the closet for the sake of others, including his mother and grandmother, comes with a price: he begins burning himself, a form of self-injury he had begun before he transitioned into living as a boy. Viewers never witness Adam's original coming out; however, they learn that the closet was and is a tragic place for Adam, one that involves despair and self-injury. He would rather face the potential dangers of passing than return to the "cage" of the closet. What we see again and again in this presumed post-gay television world of GLBTQ representations is that keeping secret one's sexual or gender identity always has tragic consequences. Such narratives uphold liberal assumptions that being "out" always is the better, if not only, choice. (Textbox 6.4 looks at how even children's characters are encouraged to come out of the closet.)

BOX 6.4   Closeted Children's Characters

When *How to Train Your Dragon 2* (2014) debuted, a supporting character in the film, Gobber the Belch (voiced by Craig Ferguson), grabbed headlines with one off-handed remark. As the main character's mother and father are arguing, Gobber mutters "This is why I never married. This and one other reason." After Ferguson ad-libbed the latter sentence, the film's director, Dean DeBlois, opted to keep it in and interprets the line as a confirmation of Gobber's sexuality (although, likely one that would fly over the heads of most kids, and possibly their parents). While Gobber may be one of the first "out" characters in a children's animated film or television program, the sexual orientation of other children's characters long has been fodder for conversation.

Websites like the *Guardian*, *Daily Beast*, and *Cracked* all have published stories on closeted children's characters. On most lists are *Teletubbies'* (1997–2001) Tinky Winky, *SpongeBob SquarePants'* (1999–) title character and his best friend Patrick, *Sesame Street's* (1969–) Bert and Ernie, *Peanuts'* (1950–2000) Peppermint Patty, *Scooby-Doo's* (1969–1972) Velma, any number of the Smurfs, and 1980s classic He-Man. Framing this discussion of characters' sexuality in language of the closet implies that viewers have put together visible clues to detect that which goes unspoken. Draper's (2012) concept of the "lens of detection" is one way to help make sense of people's attention to something as seemingly silly as animated characters as sexual subjects. In critiquing media coverage of 2009 *American Idol* (2002–) contestant Adam Lambert, Draper offers examples of how viewers were encouraged to use elements of Lambert's non-normative gender performance to confirm his gayness. Similarly, online lists of closeted children's characters offer evidence that draws on the characters' qualities that do not adhere to hegemonic masculinity or femininity. Part of Cracked.com's description of Kermit the Frog offers an example:

> Unlike many of the characters on this list, we're not even sure this lonely bastard knows he's gay. One of his first gigs was on *The Muppet Show* where he was the show-tune singing head of a theatre troop. After suppressing his enthusiasm for musical theater, he went on to a long film career comprised mostly of being propositioned by a sexually aggressive female pig and turning her down.
>
> (Methven, 2007)

FIGURE 6.2 Kermit the Frog singing in his natural habitat
Source: *The Muppet Movie* (1979).

Draper (2012) contends that the "lens of detection reinforces the illusion that the line between gay and straight can be confidently known" (pp. 212–213). Take a look at some of the online "Closeted Characters" lists found through a Google search and discuss the following questions:

1. Are you surprised by any of the characters on the lists? Why or why not? What does your answer say about your own assumptions about gays and lesbians?
2. What clues are offered as evidence of characters' gayness? What do the "clues" say about cultural assumptions about appropriate gender and sexuality performances?

(Continued)

3. Search for stories on conservative religious leaders who have criticized "gay characters" in children's programs (e.g., Jerry Falwell's claims about Tinky Winky). What fears about children and sexuality inform such thinking?
4. Search for stories about the "lesbian subtext" some viewers saw in the Disney film *Frozen* (2013), including Elsa's performance of "Let It Go" as her coming-out moment. Such claims came under attack by people in both conservative and liberal camps. Why?
5. Read the work of academics who do "queer readings" (see Chapter 5) of children's or family films (e.g., Doty's [2000] read of *The Wizard of Oz* [1939] as lesbian fantasy or Griffin's [2005] interpretation of *The Lion King*'s [1994] Timon and Pumbaa as a gay couple). Why do they turn their attention to children's programs, rather than limit such readings to adult programming?

Racing the Closet: The Down Low

All of the examples above of the tragedy of the closet involve white characters. The secrecy of black male homosexuality or bisexuality is framed almost exclusively as a case of the "down low." However, similar to closeted white men, black men on the down low often are associated with deviance and tragedy. In the past decade, newspapers, magazines, and talk shows have popularized the tale of the "down low," African-American men in relationships with women who have sex with other men. The term originated in R&B/hip-hop music in the 1990s, beginning with R. Kelly's song "Down Low (Nobody Has to Know)" (1995). In the song, Kelly assures his lover that their relationship can be kept "on the down low." Eventually, public health scholars and workers began using the term to describe behaviors within a community of men who engaged in same-sex sexual activity but did not identify as gay (Robinson, 2009). By 2001, the term was becoming part of popular discourse, as media ranging from the *New York Times* to *Village Voice* and *Oprah* (1986–2011) turned their focus to this "new" phenomenon.

The down low descriptor was applied almost exclusively to men. The invisibility of women in down low (DL) discourses is not because similar behavior does not occur among straight-identified women. In fact, recent studies have found that women are at least as likely as men to engage in bisexual behaviors, and African-American women are more likely than African-American men to engage in sexual behaviors that do not align with their sexual identity. Yet, black men have been the primary focus of DL discourses, likely because male homoeroticism seemingly contradicts accepted codes of masculinity, particularly black masculinity. Additionally, cultural acceptance of close female relationships may allow sexual encounters between women to go unnoticed. Many scholars argue that the media attention to men on the down low in black communities reinforces racist assumptions about black male sexuality.

One of the themes that emerged in DL discourses is the association between the down low and HIV cases in African-American women. A common narrative is that men have exposed their innocent female partners to sexually transmitted diseases, including HIV, by not revealing their unprotected sexual encounters with other men. Phillips (2005) suggests this narrative was "cemented with the publication of J. L. King's (2004) controversial exposé and personal narrative, *On the Down Low: A Journey into the Lives of "Straight" Black Men Who Sleep with Men* (p. 6). King appeared on an *Oprah* episode (2004, April 16) about the down low, speaking out to "warn other women about men like me." Other guests on the episode included the director of the Black AIDS Institute and a woman who was infected with HIV by her husband, who was on the down low and aware of his HIV-positive status. Phillips (2005) believes that this connection between the down low and AIDS that has been popularized by the media is problematic. He writes,

The popular version of bridge theory allows the assertion that bisexual Black men *cause* HIV/AIDS in Black heterosexual women, when in actuality, HIV/

FIGURE 6.3 J.L. King's appearance on *Oprah* in 2004 explaining his life "on the down low"
Source: American Broadcasting Company.

>AIDS in Black heterosexual women is caused by the entrance of the HIV/
>AIDS virus into their bodies when no barriers are present.
>
>(p. 8, emphasis in original)

Researchers actually are unable to pinpoint a single cause for the high rate of AIDS in the black community, but point to a range of factors, including multiple sex partners, sex trade in impoverished black communities, and also a possible genetic factor that may increase African-Americans' susceptibility to HIV (Robinson, 2009). Phillips (2005) argues that focusing on partners' sexual orientation is "false and dangerous" (p. 8).

The popular DL narrative also suggests deception on the part of the male partner that puts the unsuspecting female partner at risk. However, statistics from the Centers for Disease Control and Prevention paint a more complicated picture. In reality "12% of young men who disclose their sexual orientation (i.e., out gay or bisexual men) reported having one or more female sex partners within the last six months" (Robinson, 2009, pp. 1478–1479), meaning that the male partners are open about their sexual "status" with their female partners. Other studies of self-identified DL men found that few of the DL-identified men had a primary female partner, yet heterosexual relations that fall outside the boundaries of a committed relationship are not discussed in popular DL discourses.

These DL relations also are routinely depicted as being a matter of animal lust and sexual desire, rather than as potential romantic relationships. As Pitt (2006) describes it, "instead of being drawn to extramarital encounters with men because of the more respectable emotion of love, black men are presumed drawn to them by a more base emotion: lust" (p. 257). The coverage of down low on *Oprah* (1986–2011) perpetuated stereotypes of the hypersexualized black man. In discussing his own DL experiences on the talk show, J.L. King told Oprah that he is not interested in a relationship with any of the men with whom he has been involved, saying, "when you're on the D.L., all you want is to have sex. It's about gratification, not orientation" (2004, April 16).

If we compare discourses about black men engaged in DL behaviors with those of white men, the differences are striking. Pitt (2006) compared caricatures of black men on the DL with coverage of the film *Brokeback Mountain* (2005). Although the film was released in the midst of the DL discourse, not one of the 170 newspaper articles Pitt reviewed referred to the relationship between Ennis and Jack in this way, even though it seemingly would fit the description. Additionally, Ennis and Jack's relationship is represented as being an all-encompassing and inescapable love, not just one of sexual desire, as DL discourses about black men typically are. Another point of comparison is an *Oprah* episode with the estranged wife of former New Jersey governor Jim McGreevey (2006, September 19). Despite the fact that the governor, a white man, was engaged in a sexual relationship with his male aide, the term "down low" was never used to describe his situation. A separate interview with Governor McGreevey focused on his fears and self-hatred as a closeted gay man and his ability to find "true love" with his new male partner.

The differences in these representations are revealing. Some argue that they demonstrate residual anxiety about black male sexuality. Black men in DL discourses promoted in popular media are dangerous, deceptive, and hypersexual. Unlike some of the earliest media narratives about black men that presented them as a danger to white women, DL discourses present them as dangers to innocent black women, infecting them with HIV, despite the women's attempts to do everything right in order to have a committed relationship with one of the few available, acceptable black men. Robinson (2009) argues that DL men also need to be contained because they threaten the gender/sexuality binary. Part of DL culture is hypermasculinity, subscribing to an R&B/hip-hop performance of masculinity. Robinson writes,

> Stories on the down low frequently stress how shocked women are that the men featured in these stories do not appear feminine or otherwise stereotypically gay. The DL man alarms people not simply because of his behaviour but because of a widespread belief that gender identity and sexual orientation correlate in men.
>
> (pp. 1476–1477)

Therefore, the DL man transgresses social norms in performing masculinity persuasively and failing to affiliate with gay culture. In doing so, he upsets the expectation that gay men should be identifiable, which makes it easy for society to relegate them to the margins.

A common theme across representations of men on the down low and closeted GLBTQ characters is that they challenge the liberal assumption that people with non-normative sexual and gender identities have no reason to keep secret their differences. In an assumed post-gay, post-closet world, they presumably would be greeted with, if not acceptance, at least tolerance. Therefore, those who reject the promises of this ostensible world of equality must be contained before they disrupt the clear lines between normative and non-normative gender and sexual identities made visible in a world of "out" sexuality.

▶ CRITIQUING THE CLOSET

Because the logic of the closet has framed Western perspectives on sexuality for the past 50 years, it can be difficult to step back and recognize the metaphor for what it is—a discourse. You may recall that a discourse is a set of meanings and practices that circulate around a particular bounded area of social experience, like sexuality and gender, making those social experiences appear to be "natural" and beyond questioning. Discourses about the closet have shaped the way we make sense of sexuality in ways that have produced "truths" not just about homosexuality, but also about heterosexuality and the people for whom those identity labels matter. On the one hand, GLBTQ rights advocates, often working within the logics of identity politics, see the closet as a repressive structure from which GLBTQ people need to escape in order to achieve self-liberation and eventual equality. Their goal is to fight against the closet by the insistence that everyone come out. This perspective has been advanced in media depictions of coming-out stories, as well as more recent media depictions of closeted gay characters that present the secrecy of the closet as being inherently problematic. On the other hand, queer theorists and others critical of identity politics have critiqued the closet as a discourse that ultimately reinforces heteronormativity.

For theorists such as Eve Sedgwick (1990) and Diana Fuss (1991), the closet itself is tied to a range of binary oppositions that structure the hetero/homosexual splitting. Linked to ideas of public/private, inside/outside, normal/abnormal, openness/secrecy, the continued use of the metaphor continually replays these binaries as a shaping presence for everyone. They contend that the common call to come out of the closet has the effect of maintaining the presumption of heterosexuality as the norm by continually reinforcing the idea that homosexuality is always secondary to this norm. (The heterosexual questionnaire in Chapter 1 (Textbox 1.2) draws attention to cultural assumptions of heterosexuality as the presumed norm that does not need to be named or defended.) Coming out does not weaken the closet, but rather it reinforces the metaphor as a central organizing principle for understanding sexuality.

The closet also creates an expectation that sexual minorities must announce their sexuality by coming out. However, the presumed coming-out ritual does not match the realities faced by GLBTQ people. For example, closet discourses treat coming out as a single moment in one's life, ignoring the ways that GLBTQ people must continually negotiate the closet's boundaries. As Halperin (1995) notes, people who are in the closet will still wonder who knows about the truth of their identity, and think that if they are out of the closet, straight people might still treat them as if they know a secret about them that others do not. Additionally, there never is a right time for GLBTQ people to come out of the closet. They either come out too early, when their heterosexual audience is not yet prepared for their sexual proclamation, or they come out too late after those in their life already know about their sexuality (Sedgwick, 1990). Ultimately, GLBTQ people are left in an impossible situation. Below, we will apply some of these critiques of the closet to mediated experiences of coming out before taking up alternative conceptualizations of minority sexual identity that largely have been ignored because of the powerful force of the dominant closet narrative.

Complicating the Coming-Out Narrative

Although coming-out narratives in traditional media increasingly end at a point of social acceptance, queer theorists critique them for ritualizing and even fetishizing the coming-out moment. Evan Brody (2011) offers as an example the coming out of the character Kurt Hummel on *Glee* (2009–2015). Although most of Kurt's friends take for granted his unspoken sexuality, the program insists upon him verbalizing and confessing his sexuality to his friends and to his father. The uncertainty of how straight people will react to news of a person's sexuality heightens the drama of the moment. In the case of Kurt, viewers know little about his father beyond the fact that he is a widowed mechanic who seemingly disapproves of his son's flamboyant style choices. Kurt's coming-out moment is a moment of confession in which his father holds the ultimate judgment. The reality program *Coming Out Stories* (2006) follows this same coming-out formula, with the gay or lesbian subject spending most of each episode expressing fears about the impending confession to close family or friends. Editing conventions heighten the tension, as key sound bites emphasizing the potential rejection that characters face are replayed for dramatic effect. Although these fears may ring authentic to many GLBTQ viewers, Brody (2011) reminds readers that straight people "are never obliged to make this same type of sexual truth production" (p. 39). The coming-out storylines reinforce a worldview of assumed heterosexuality, which need not be spoken. By comparison, homosexuality is relegated to its devalued binary and can only be made "real" through verbal confession to heterosexuals, who hold the ultimate power of judgment.

Online discussions of celebrities coming out heighten the idea of the coming-out moment as a one-time public event. In fact, websites have made a sport of keeping track of the "best" celebrity coming-out moments. However, if we look more closely, we will see that the point at which celebrities are defined as officially "out" is generally arbitrary, raising questions about to whom or to how many people a GLBTQ person must share his or her sexuality before the coming out is deemed official. For example, CNN anchor Anderson Cooper made a 2012 celebrity coming-out list after his "long awaited announcement . . . finally putting to rest all that speculation" (The Dish, 2012). In his much-publicized email to friend and blogger Andrew Sullivan, Cooper wrote,

> I have given some the mistaken impression that I am trying to hide something—something that makes me uncomfortable, ashamed or even afraid. This is distressing because it is simply not true . . . The fact is, I'm gay, always have been, always will be, and I couldn't be any more happy, comfortable with myself, and proud . . . I have always been very open and honest about this part of my life with my friends, my family, and my colleagues.
>
> (The Dish, 2012)

FIGURE 6.4 Kurt Hummel gratefully receives a hug of acceptance from his father after coming out
Source: *Glee*, Season 1, Episode 15, "Preggers," 2009, FOX Broadcasting Company.

Despite Cooper's openness with people in his life, which likely involved many coming-out experiences, only by publicly claiming the label was he credited with finally "coming out."

These mediated representations also generally present coming out as a linear experience, which fails to acknowledge the continual coming-out process that GLBTQ people face. Because our heteronormative world assumes people to be straight unless they mark themselves otherwise, GLBTQ people are put in situations every day in which others are learning about and perhaps surprised by their sexual or gender identity. This might happen in their college classrooms as they mention their same-sex partner or in a car dealership when jointly purchasing a new car or on the job interview when they ask if a company offers partner health benefits. These are the daily negotiations masked by the logic of a linear coming-out narrative.

Digital media, in particular, challenge the idea of coming out as a linear process, as online websites and social media sites allow viewers to negotiate the boundaries of their identity in more complex ways than being simply "in" or "out" of the closet. When it comes to the Internet, especially the use of social networking services, the negotiations of public and private associated with the closet intermingle with the ways that these sites complicate issues of privacy. While many GLBTQ individuals use social networking sites, from more general ones like Facebook to gay-specific apps like Grindr, they also work to negotiate being out within the complexities of privacy and publicness on the Internet. As much as many GLBTQ individuals turn to the Internet for support and community, their relationship with social media is more complex, with 4 in 10 reporting to have revealed their orientation on a social networking site (Pew Research Center, 2013). While GLBTQ-specific sites, blogs, and chat rooms offer anonymity, the rapid spread of social media means that people are often negotiating their relationships in both online and offline contexts.

Widely used social networking sites such as Facebook present certain challenges to GLBTQ users in negotiating the closet in their daily lives. Cooper and Dzara (2010) name a number of scenarios reported in their study of Facebook, including people out to their friends offline, but who keep their identity closeted on Facebook because their families or employers do not know. One person reported that he had a Facebook account, but slightly altered his last name in order that family members, including his sister, would not find his account (Gudelunas, 2012). Interactions with the extended friendship networks mean that users who do not want to be fully public about their sexuality must work to actively manage privacy settings or to avoid any hint of their sexual identity on Facebook,

In fact, use of specifically gay-oriented social networking sites or apps further indicates the complicated nature of the digital closet. For example, during the era of Don't Ask Don't Tell (DADT) military men got involved in the site RealJock.com, a dating site (Tsika, 2010). On the one hand, being involved in a dating site risked the possibility of being identified as gay, on the other, as DADT was aimed at *behavior* rather than *identity*, gay servicemen participated on the basis of fitness and diet, emphasizing those aspects as the reason they turned to the site. Even though civilian users respond in passionate, sexualized ways to the presence of military men, the military men themselves claimed to be celibate. Even users of online hook-up apps, like Grindr and Manhunt, negotiate the line between being out and being closeted, with some users blurring out their faces in their online picture postings. One user blurred his face when he was at home, but did not when traveling (Gudelunas, 2012). Although this process may seem cumbersome or confusing, Gudelunas (2012) argues that the men in his study actually enjoyed the ability to manage their identities across a range of sites. In addition, they enjoyed the freedom offered by gay hookup sites because they felt that they could express more there than they could on more general sites like Facebook.

Whiteness and the Closet

As increasing attention has been paid to the intersections of race, class, gender, and sexuality, queer studies scholars of color have suggested that the closet largely is a white imagining. For instance, Marlon Ross (2005) coined the term "claustrophilia" to describe what he saw as "a fixation on the closet function as the grounding principle for sexual experience, knowledge, and politics" (p. 162). According to Ross, this fixation overlooks the lived experiences of many gay black people. He offers as evidence anthropologist William G. Hawkeswood's ethnographic study of gay men in Harlem in the 1990s. Hawkeswood found that many of these men never felt the need to "come out" to their friends and family because their sexuality always had been assumed. As Ross writes,

> [T]o announce one's attraction by "coming out" would not necessarily indicate a progress in sexual identity, and it would not necessarily change one's identity from closeted to liberated as conceptualized in the dominant closet narrative. When the question of telling loved ones what they already know does become an issue, it can be judged a superfluous or perhaps even a distracting act, one subsidiary to the more important identifications of family, community, and race within which one's sexual attractions are already interwoven and understood.
>
> (p. 180)

Such an experience deviates from dominant cultural narratives of gayness that require and even fetishize the ritual coming-out moment as necessary for full liberation, even when gayness is an "open secret" to which all are privy.

Others have critiqued the white imagining of the closet on the basis that it is understood primarily as a repressive space. As described at the beginning of this chapter, a closet has negative connotations—hidden, dark, and isolated. However, a closet could also be understood as a space of protection or play outside of everyone's view. For example, anthropologist Jeffrey McCune (2008) critiques the metaphor of the closet as a descriptor for black men who engage in "Down Low" activities and even rejects the idea that being "out" is the ultimate space of liberation. Based on his ethnographic study at The Gate, a gay black club in Chicago, McCune suggests that secrecy allows the DL men he writes about to build a queer black world in which to work through their sexuality. McCune (2008) suggests that a "gate" provides a better metaphor for understanding their experiences:

> In actuality, most men at The Gate are not "coming out," but participating in a sort of "comin' in." They have arrived in a queer space that welcomes them, but does not require them to become official members. The Gate is a black home they can come into, where the relatives understand the fullness of diversity, liberalness, and transgressiveness, and are honest about different forms of desire. The discursive demand that one must be "out" to participate

in gay activities ignores the fact that all gay activity does not take place in the public domain.

(p. 310)

Coincidentally, McCune's reimagining of the sanctity of the closet actually echoes pre-gay liberation conceptions of gay community. As Chauncey (1994) points out, in the early 20th Century, the term "coming out" actually referred to galas in which gay men would come out to the gay world, not dissimilar to a debutante ball in which upper-class families officially introduce their daughter who has reached the age of maturity to society. The focus was on recognizing and celebrating one's gayness within the gay community, rather than on announcing it to the heterosexual world.

Because early enclaves of gay men, like those living in New York in the late 1800s until pre-World War II, largely existed as a pocket separate from straight society, many gay men who moved between these worlds actively kept separate their personas between their jobs and/or families, living what they referred to as "a double life, or wearing a mask and taking it off" (Chauncey, 1994, p. 6). Yet, even though their identities were kept hidden, they did not use the language of the closet to describe this experience. As Chauncey (1994) writes,

> For some, the personal cost of "passing" was great, but for others it was minimal, and many men positively enjoyed having a "secret life" more complex and extensive than outsiders could imagine. Indeed, the gay life of many men was so full and wide-ranging that by the 1930s they used another—but more expansive—spatial metaphor to describe it: not the gay closet, but the *gay world*.
>
> (p. 7, emphasis in original)

These examples are not meant to suggest that we return to a period when people with non-normative sexualities maintained secrecy out of fear for the social and legal consequences of their identities. However, they demonstrate alternative imaginings of the relationship between sexuality and privacy that largely have been foreclosed by the dominance of closet discourses.

▶ CONCLUSION

This chapter encouraged you to think critically about the metaphor of the closet and the significant role it has played in shaping people's understandings of the oppression of sexual minorities. The rallying cry, "Out of the closets, into the streets," which was made famous by the gay rights movement, sets up the coming-out process as a significant personal and political act for GLBTQ people. However, as Plummer (1994) notes, coming-out stories do not just help people talk about their sexual identities, but they help construct an identity rooted in sexuality. Media have played a significant role in circulating coming-out stories in culture, and digital media have allowed GLBTQ people to construct coming-out messages designed to support other GLBTQ people. In this seemingly post-gay world of tolerance and acceptance, representations of closeted gay men have linked secrecy about one's sexuality with tragedy. Finally, this chapter critiqued the very idea of the closet as a structuring device for GLBTQ experiences, recognizing how it can uphold heternonormative ideals. Examples from media demonstrated how closet and coming-out narratives assume a linear coming-out process that culminates in a verbal confession to heterosexuals. Such a necessary public proclamation by heterosexuals is almost unimaginable. In critiquing the closet as largely a white construction, we introduced alternative imaginings of sexuality that rejected spatial metaphors of oppression.

▶ REFERENCES

Aguirre-Sacasa, R., Brennan, I., Falchuk, B., Hodgson, M., Murphy, R., Maxwell, R. (Writers) & Buecker, B. (Director). (2012, February 21). On my way [Television series episode]. In I. Brennan, D. DiLoreto, B. Falchuk, & R. Murphy (Executive Producers), *Glee*. New York, NY: Fox Network.

Alexander, J. & Losh, E. (2010). "A YouTube of one's own?": "Coming out" videos as rhetorical action. In C. Pullen & M. Cooper (Eds.), *LGBT identity and online new media* (pp. 37–50). New York, NY: Routledge.

Anderson, E. (2011). Masculinities and sexualities in sport and physical cultures: Three decades of evolving research. *Journal of Homosexuality*, *58*, 565–578.

Baldwin, J. (1956). *Giovanni's room*. New York: Dell Publishing Company.

Barnhurst, K.G. (2007). Visibility as paradox: Representation and simultaneous contrast. In K.G. Barnhurst (Ed.), *Media/queered: Visibility and its discontents* (pp. 1–21). New York, NY: Peter Lang Publishing.

Becker, B. (2009). Guy love: A queer straight masculinity for a post-closet era? In G. Davis, & G. Needham, (Eds.), *Queer TV: Theories, histories, politics* (pp. 120–140). New York, NY: Routledge.

Brody, E. (2011). Categorizing coming out: The modern televisual medium of queer youth identification. *Spectator*, *31*(2), 35–44.

Brydum, S. (2014, May 11). The kiss seen round the world. *Out*. Retrieved from http://www.out.com/entertainment/sports/2014/05/11/how-world-reacted-michael-sam-joining-rams-nfl-gay.

Chauncey, G. (1994). *Gay New York: Gender, urban culture and the making of the gay male world, 1890–1940*. New York, NY: Basic Books.

Connell, R.W. (2005). *Masculinities* (2nd ed.). Berkeley, CA: University of California Press.

Cooper, M. (2010). Lesbians who are married to men: Identity, collective stories, and the Internet online community. In C. Pullen & M. Cooper (Eds.), *LGBT identity and online new media* (pp. 75–86). New York, NY: Routledge.

Cooper, M. & Dzara, K. (2010). The Facebook revolution: LGBT identity and activism. In C. Pullen & M. Cooper (Eds.), *LGBT identity and online new media* (pp. 100–112). New York, NY: Routledge.

D'Emilio, J. (1992). *Making trouble: Essays on gay history, politics and the university*. New York, NY: Routledge.

D'Emilio, J. (1998). *Sexual politics, sexual communities: The making of a homosexual minority in the United States, 1940–1970*. Chicago, IL: University of Chicago Press.

Doty, A. (1993). *Making things perfectly queer: Interpreting mass culture*. Minneapolis, MN: University of Minnesota Press.

Doty, A. (2000). *Flaming classics: Queering the film canon*. New York, NY: Routledge.

Draper, J. (2012). Idol speculation: Queer identity and a media-imposed lens of detection. *Popular Communication, 10*, 201–216.

Falchuk, B., Brennan, I., Murphy, R. (Writers) & Buecker, B. (Director). (2010, November 9). Never been kissed [Television series episode]. In I. Brennan, D. DiLoreto, B. Falchuk, & R. Murphy (Executive Producers), *Glee*. New York, NY: Fox Network.

Falchuk, B., Brennan, I. (Writers) & Murphy, R. (Director). (2009, September 23). Preggers [Television series episode]. In I. Brennan, D. DiLoreto, B. Falchuk, & R. Murphy (Executive Producers), *Glee*. New York, NY: Fox Network.

Friedlander, W. (2011, January 3). Gay and lesbian characters are popping up on shows for young people: "Gossip girl," "90210," "glee" and others incorporate story lines of youths coming out. *Los Angeles Times*. Retrieved from http://articles.latimes.com/2011/jan/03/entertainment/la-et-gay-characters-20110103.

Fuss, D. (1991). *Inside/Out: Lesbian theories, gay theories*. New York, NY: Routledge.

Glazek, C. (2014, July 9). Michael Sam and the draw that changed American sports forever. *Out*. Retrieved from http://www.out.com/entertainment/sports/2014/07/09/michael-sam-and-draw-changed-american-sports-forever.

GLSEN, CIPHR, & CCRC. (2013). *Out online: The experience of lesbian, gay and transgender youth on the Internet*. New York, NY: GLSEN.

Gorgeous, G. (2010, May 11). My coming out story [YouTube video]. Retrieved from https://www.youtube.com/watch?v=bO9Y-UkQ02o.

Grassi, M., Hood, K., Moore, Y. (Writers), & Schuyler, L. (Director). (2010, August 11). My body is a cage: Part 1 [Television series episode]. In D. Lowe & S. Brogen (Producers), *Degrassi: The next generation*. Ontario, CA: DHX Television.

Griffin, S. (2004). Pronoun trouble: The queerness of animation. In H. Benshoff & S. Griffin (Eds.), *Queer cinema: The film reader* (pp. 105–118). New York, NY: Routledge.

Gross, L. (1993). *Contested closets: The politics and ethics of outing*. Minneapolis, MN: University of Minnesota Press.

Gudelunas, D. (2012). There's an app for that: The uses and gratifications of online social networks for gay men. *Sexuality & Culture, 16* (4), 347–365.

Halperin, D. (1995). *Saint Foucault: Towards a gay hagiography.* New York, NY: Oxford University Press.

Hawkeswood, W. (1996). *One of the children: Gay black men in Harlem.* Berkeley, CA: University of California Press.

Heinz, M. (2012). Transmen on the web: Inscribing multiple discourses. In K. Ross (Ed.), *The handbook of gender, sex and media* (pp. 226–240). Hoboken, NJ: Wiley & Sons, Ltd.

Huffington Post. (2013, March 29). Kwame Harris, former 49ers, Raiders player, talks about being gay in the NFL. *Huffington Post.* Retrieved from http://www.huffingtonpost.com/2013/03/29/kwame-harris-gay-interview-nfl_n_2981538.html.

Jay, K. (1992). Introduction to the first edition. In K. Jay & A. Young (Eds.), *Out of the closet* (pp. xii–xii). New York, NY: New York University Press.

King, J.L. (2004). *On the down low: A journey into the lives of "straight" black men who sleep with men.* New York: Broadway Books.

Kushnick, H.L. (2010). In the closet: A close read of the metaphor. *Virtual Mentor, 12* (8), 678–680.

Lazar, S. (2013, June 28). Top 5 coming out videos on YouTube (WATCH). *Huffington Post.* Retrieved from http://www.huffingtonpost.com/shira-lazar/top-5-coming-out-videos-o_b_3517354.html.

Mayo, D. & Gunderson, M. (1994). Privacy and the ethics of outing. *Journal of Homosexuality, 27,* 47–65.

McCune, J.Q. (2008). "Out" in the club: The down low, hip-hop and the architecture of black masculinity. *Text and Performance Quarterly, 28*(3), 298–314.

Methven, J. (2007, November 9). The next 9 children's characters that should come out of the closet. *Cracked.com.* Retrieved from http://www.cracked.com/article_15668_the-next-9-childrens-characters-that-should-come-out-closet.html.

Mohr, R. (1992). *Gay ideas: Outing and other controversies.* Boston, MA: Beacon Press.

Murphy, R., Brennan, I., Falchuk, B. (Writers), & Scott, J. (Director). (2009, September 16). Acafellas [Television series episode]. In Brad Falchuk (Producer), *Glee.* New York, NY: Fox Network.

n.a. (2006, March 3). The identical twin (Van) [Television series episode]. In Simon, K. & Goodman, K. (Producer), *Coming out stories.* Boise, ID: Logo Television Series.

Nigatu, H. & Karlan, S. (2013, March 14). 24 awesomely creative ways to come out of the closet. *Buzzfeed.* Retrieved from http://www.buzzfeed.com/hnigatu/24-awesomely-creative-ways-to-come-out-of-the-closet#2o1wh3l.

Osterweil, A. (2007). Ang Lee's lonesome cowboys. *Film Quarterly, 60*(3), 38–42.

Outsports. (2013, December 17). 77 people who came out publicly in sports in 2013. *Outsports.* Retrieved from http://www.outsports.com/2013/12/17/5204920/come-out-gay-lgbt-sports-athletes-coaches-2013.

Pew Research Center. (2013, June 13). A survey of GLBTQ Americans: Attitudes, experiences and values in changing times. *Pew Research: Social & Demographic Trends.* Retrieved from http://www.pewsocialtrends.org/2013/06/13/a-survey-of-lgbt-americans.

Phillips, L. (2005). Deconstructing "down low" discourse: The politics of sexuality, gender, race, AIDS and anxiety. *Journal of African American Studies, 9*(2), 3–15.

Pitt, R.N. (2006). Downlow mountain? De/stigmatizing bisexuality through pitying and pejorative discourse in media. *Journal of Men's Studies, 14*(2), 254–258.

Plummer, K. (1995). *Telling sexual stories: Power, change and social worlds.* Philadelphia, PA: Routledge.

Puar, J.K. (2010). In the wake of It Gets Better. *theguardian.com.* Retrieved from http://www.theguardian.com/commentisfree/cifamerica/2010/nov/16/wake-it-gets-better-campaign.

Robinson, R.K. (2009). Racing the closet. *Berkeley Law, 61,* 1463–1533. Retrieved from http://scholarship.law.berkeley.edu/facpubs/1290.

Ross, M. (2005). Beyond the closet as raceless paradigm. In E. Johnson & M. Henderson (Eds.), *Black queer studies.* Durham, NC: Duke University Press.

Savage, D. (2010, September 21). It Gets Better: Dan and Terry [YouTube Video]. *It Gets Better Project.* Retrieved from https://www.youtube.com/watch?v=7IcVyvg2Qlo.

Sedgwick, E. (1990). *Epistemology of the closet.* Berkeley, CA: University of California Press.

The Dish (2012, July 2). Anderson Cooper: "The fact is, I'm gay." *The Dish.* Retrieved from http://dish.andrewsullivan.com/2012/07/02/anderson-cooper-the-fact-is-im-gay.

Time, Inc. (2014, April 23). 100 most influential people in the world. *Time Magazine.* Retrieved from http://time.com/time100–2014.

Tsika, N. (2010). "Compartmentalize your life": Advising army men on RealJock.com. In C. Pullen & M. Cooper (Eds.), *LGBT identity and online new media* (pp. 230–244). New York, NY: Taylor & Francis.

Wolf, D., Balcer, R., Reingold, J. (Writers), & McKay, J. (Director). (2006, October 10). Maltese cross [Television series episode]. In D. Wolf (Producer), *Law and order: Criminal intent.* New York, NY: Wolf Films.

Wolf, D., Storer, K. (Writers), & Leto, P. (Director). (2008, April 22). Closet [Television series episode]. In D. Wolf (Producer), *Law and order: Special victims unit.* New York, NY: Wolf Films.

Comedy

David Letterman: George H.W. Bush and Bill Clinton have been spending more and more time together. Doesn't that seem like an unusual couple to you, honestly? Earlier today they went to go see that gay cowboy movie.

Conan O'Brien: President Bush was asked by someone in the audience if he'd seen Brokeback Mountain. The president said he hadn't seen it, but he'd be happy to talk about ranching. Then he added, Ranching still means gay sex, right?

Jay Leno: The Golden Globes were last night. It was the biggest gathering of Hollywood celebrities that wasn't an anti-Bush rally. . . . The big winners were "Brokeback Mountain," "Capote" and "Transamerica." All movies with gay themes. I think this is God's way of punishing Pat Robertson.

(Kurtzman, n.d.)

When *Brokeback Mountain*, a film about two cowboys who meet and fall in love, was released in 2005, it set off a wave of jokes throughout the media, particularly on late-night comedy programs. Even a decade after the film's release, the Internet is filled with parodied versions of the movie poster, and one of the film's oft-quoted lines, "I wish I knew how to quit you," has been played for adult laughs in animated children's movies like *Smurfs* (2011) and *Gnomeo and Juliet* (2011). The very number of jokes raises the question of why so many people would find cause for humor in a dramatic film about a tragic love story. As we consider this question, we quickly discover some of the broader issues related to the complex relationship between comedy, media, and GLBTQ identity.

Comedy has tremendous power to both challenge and reinforce social norms. Comedy has been described as a "subversive form of rhetoric" (Duncan, 1962, quoted in Manning, 2010, pp. 3–4) because it can allow people to challenge social hierarchies and political authorities in ways that could potentially precipitate social and political change. For instance, Jay Leno's joke above about Pat Robertson, who, as we discussed in Chapter 2, had made the claim that AIDS was God's punishment for the evils of homosexuality, mocks the idea that gay people are subject to God's wrath and may call into question Christian conservatives' beliefs that homosexuality is a sin. Yet, comedy is not always transgressive. In many cases, comedic content may reinforce norms that assume non-normative sexualities are inherently inferior to heterosexuality. Comedy may just as easily reinforce heteronormativity through homophobia.

This chapter attempts to complicate the way you think about media comedy to better equip you to recognize its complexity the next time you watch late-night comedians, film comedies, sitcoms, and web series or even read comic strips with GLBTQ content. Below, we will wrestle more fully with the complexities related to the polysemic quality of humor, in which context as much as content is key to deciphering why something is funny, and when laughter can challenge or reconfirm social norms. The chapter will then consider the relationship between gender and sexuality that is central to both comedy *about* GLBTQ communities and comedy *by* GLBTQ communities. Finally, we will consider how genre conventions specific to situation comedy further complicate considerations of media, comedy, and GLBTQ identities.

▶ WHAT'S SO FUNNY? COMEDY AND CULTURAL NORMS

During the 2011 Country Music Awards, hosts Blake Shelton and Reba McEntire shared in their own *Brokeback Mountain* joke. The two were discussing the breakup of actor Jake Gyllenhaal and, at that time, America's country music sweetheart, singer Taylor Swift.

McEntire: She writes songs about guys who break up with her, which I don't understand in the first place. She's beautiful, she's talented, she's sweet. What in the world was Jake Gyllenhaal thinking?

Shelton: Wait a minute. . . . He *was* in *Brokeback Mountain*. (*US Weekly* Staff, 2011)

The "wink wink" joke left the live audience roaring with laughter. But what were they laughing at? Were they laughing at the idea that actor Jake Gyllenhaal might be secretly gay, suggesting that could be the only reason anyone would break up with Swift? If so, did this small bit of comedic banter reinforce cultural assumptions about the deviance of homosexuality, making gayness an "accusation" to be made and laughed at by hetero-sexuals? Or did people laugh because the joke poked fun at the presumption that every-one was heterosexual or, if gay, out of the closet? Does the humor lie in people's desire for Jake Gyllenhaal to *be* gay? Was it a progressive joke that at least acknowledged the existence of non-normative sexualities? Or, was it "just a joke," a throwaway line with no particular meaning at all? No harm intended, no foul results.

A great deal of contemporary comedy rests on playing with cultural and social norms around unstable categories such as gender, race, and sexuality. Comedy has the poten-tial to point out and challenge sexism, racism, and homophobia, but it is just as likely to do the opposite; it might just as easily *be* racist, sexist, or homophobic. On the surface it might appear easy to tell the difference between comedy that mocks homophobia or transphobia and humor based on reinforcing those beliefs, but it actually can be quite complicated. Determining the meaning of a joke requires a great deal of interpretive work from joke tellers and audiences.

Like the "wink wink" joke above, one of the key rhetorical devices used to create humor is irony. Irony suffuses popular culture today. In common parlance, irony refers to something that means the opposite of what it directly states. Usually, there is something in the performance that lets the audience know that a state-ment is meant ironically. This might be a vocal expression, body language, the use of sarcasm, or even a wink that signals that the person means the opposite of what they have said. In some cases, the comedy format or the joke's content may mark its ironic intention. One of the key things to understand about irony is that it oper-ates as a double discourse (Banet-Weiser, 2007; Griffin, 2008; Hutcheon, 1994; 2000; Tasker, 2011). There is a surface meaning that points to a different underly-ing meaning. For an audience to understand a joke *as* ironic, they must recognize and understand *both* meanings.

For example, in the Conan O'Brien joke that opened this chapter, he is being ironic when he suggests President Bush said that "Ranching still means gay sex" (Kurtzman, n.d.). The late-night comedy format and seemingly outlandish claim of the joke makes it clear O'Brien is using irony. After all, Bush was a conservative president, whose public persona involved being not only an experienced Texas rancher, but also a family man who campaigned on a family values platform, including strong support of the Defense of Marriage Act (DOMA), which defined marriage as being between a man and a woman. The irony is in the idea that President Bush would somehow have intimate knowledge about something so contradictory to his political persona as gay sex. Viewers need to understand both the conventions of the comedy show and the discourse surrounding President Bush in order to get the humor of the joke.

The content of a joke alone, however, cannot fully determine whether its humor is critiquing homophobia or is homophobic. As we discussed in Chapter 1, media texts are polysemic, meaning they allow for multiple meanings to be made by audience members who bring to bear their own lived experiences when interpreting the texts. Historically, comedy has relied upon a rather narrow context: a close relationship between joke tellers and their audiences (Mills, 2009). For example, jokes shared among friends are told within the same "in-group," increasing the likelihood that the humor of a joke will be "gotten" in the way that it was intended. Many of us tell jokes among our friends and family that we would not dare to say outside of those contexts. Media complicates this teller-receiver relationship of comedy by greatly expanding the context. First, it may be difficult to know for certain the meaning of jokes with intended political or social content because it can be unclear who the originator of the joke even is. Is it the actor? The writer? The producer? Although audiences may feel a connection to situation comedy characters, particularly for long-running series, they may know little to nothing about the program's creators, producers, and writers. Additionally, because most media texts need to be enjoyed by a fairly broad audience base to be considered successful, the jokes need to be ambiguous enough that people from a range of backgrounds can find humor in them. For these reasons, media scholar John Fiske (1989) suggests that audience members will never experience a universally uniform response to comedy texts.

Comic discourses, then, rely on both the joke teller and receiver sharing and understanding a set of cultural codes and meanings that provide the context in which the comedy gains meaning *as* funny for audiences (Hutcheon, 1994). Let us take the joking exchange between McEntire and Shelton as an example. The setting was the Country Music Awards. While country music is extremely popular and has a broad fan base, it is traditionally associated with "Middle America" and an attendant set of conservative, family values that historically have been hostile to GLBTQ communities (though, many country music fans—including ones who are GLBTQ—do not share this view!). Country music tends to be associated with a kind of rough-and-tumble, pull-yourself-up-by-your-bootstraps masculinity that stands in stark contrast to the kinds of masculinity stereotypically associated with gayness. The joke was delivered by a normatively masculine country star, though we cannot be sure if he was the joke writer. Within this context, the joke mostly can be understood as casting aspersions on Gyllenhaal's masculinity. The joke implies that any "normal," red-blooded American man would not dare break the heart of America's country music sweetheart. Therefore, the only explanation left is the sexual deviance of Gyllenhaal. The context clearly narrows down the possible meanings of the joke.

While context strongly shapes both the content and kinds of jokes told, it also can shape why people laugh at what they see. Traditionally, theorists have considered three possible reasons for people's laughter: superiority theory, incongruity theory, and relief theory (Mills, 2009). Superiority theory suggests that we laugh at others as a way to feel superior to them. That is we laugh "<u>at</u> others, at their failings, misdeeds, and accidents, in an effort to feel superior to them" (Goldstein, 1993, p. 246, emphasis in original). The theory originally considered how oppressed groups can use laughter to critique and feel superior to those *more* powerful; however, as Mills (2009) points out, comedy in media has historically made fun of marginalized groups, including women, racial/ethnic minorities, and GLBTQ people. A classic example of this is the laughter that has been directed at the sissy character, as discussed in Chapter 3. The character allows some men to feel more masculine and, thus, superior to men who seemingly fail at masculinity. In the case of Blake Shelton's *Brokeback Mountain* (2005) joke, the content combined with the context suggests that the audience's feeling of superiority to GLBTQ people was a key source of humor.

The central idea of incongruity theory is that people laugh when their expectations are confounded by two competing ideas brought together in juxtaposition. Context is key to understanding when incongruity is taken to be humorous, and many media texts work to exaggerate such juxtapositions to make sure audiences get the humor. For example, the 1995 classic *To Wong Foo, Thanks for Everything! Julie Newmar* operates on the premise of incongruity humor by casting Wesley Snipes and Patrick Swayze as drag queens. Both leading men actors were known for their roles in action films and were strongly associated with traditional notions of masculinity. The juxtaposition of these men's past roles and masculine, muscular bodies with feminine markers of makeup, long locks, bling, and gowns creates an unexpected, and, thus, humorous image.

Relief theory of laughter has its roots in psychoanalysis. "Freud (1905) popularized the view that laughter could be symptomatic of conflict, repressed sexuality, and anger" (Goldstein, 1993, p. 247). Comedy dealing with traditionally taboo cultural topics, including sexuality, allows for a momentary release from culturally ascribed repression surrounding these topics. For example, the tremendous number of *Brokeback Mountain* jokes might be understood as allowing for relief from the anxiety created in some viewers by a gay love story. Superiority, incongruity, and relief are not mutually exclusive. Laughter at a single joke might be accounted for by all three of these theories at the same time and points to the fact that people may find humor in jokes related to GLBTQ people and issues for a range of reasons (see Textbox 7.1).

BOX 7.1   Why Do We Laugh?

FIGURE 7.1 The shower scene in *I Now Pronounce You Chuck & Larry* (2007)

In considering why we laugh, we begin to consider to what extent humor reinforces or challenges homophobia. The content of jokes alone cannot answer that question. It is also important to consider the context within which they appear and the possible reasons why people laugh. To consider the ways *why* we laugh is important, we will explore how a single scene in a film comedy may draw on all three theories of laughter.

The 2007 film *I Now Pronounce You Chuck & Larry* (Bernardi, Gallow, Kavanaugh, & Dugan) stars Hollywood funnymen Adam Sandler and Kevin James. The premise of the movie is that two straight firefighters pretend to be gay so that they can legally enter a civil union to guarantee insurance benefits for the children of one of the characters—a widower. Their farce results in homophobic reactions from their co-workers, which are played for laughs with a seeming broader message of tolerance. One popular scene of the movie (as evidenced by the number of times it appears in YouTube clips) is a locker room shower scene in which their fellow firefighters, believing Chuck and Larry's relationship to be authentic, cower (hiding behind towels, etc.) when the two enter the showers. The tension is heightened as not just one, but two, firefighters accidentally "drop the soap" and are too afraid to pick it up. Enter Fred Duncan (Ving Rhames), a character who visibly connotes African-American hypermasculinity, complete with giant muscles and tattoos. In a previous scene, Fred has confided to Chuck that he is gay. Without reservation, he bends over to pick up the soap (revealing a "bad ass" tattoo on his backside), winks at Chuck, and then commences singing Whitney Houston's, "I'm Every Woman" while lathering up.

If we consider why people find this scene so funny, we can think in terms of relief theory, juxtaposition, and superiority. From a relief theory perspective, people may laugh because the shower scene gets at the heart of cultural fears/taboos about masculinity—the possibility of anal sex, even rape. The "bad ass" character offers a juxtaposition between dominant hypermasculinity and effeminate behavior, thus reinforcing the link between effeminacy and gay masculinity. Finally, someone may laugh at this scene from a position of superiority because of the firefighters' over-the-top homophobic reactions to Chuck and Larry. They may feel superior to them, thinking their behavior is unwarranted (but still funny).

We encourage you to watch *I Now Pronounce You Chuck & Larry* (even if you have seen it before) and make a note of every time you laugh.

1. What's the cause of the laughter? Superiority? Incongruity? Relief?
2. What/Who exactly do you feel superior to?
3. What incongruities cause you to laugh? Do those incongruities play with the boundaries between homo- and heterosexual identities?
4. What kinds of relief does your laughter offer? What kinds of content create discomfort that needs relief?
5. Look over the reasons that you and your classmates gave for laughing. Consider if your class is laughing at homosexuality or laughing at the ridiculous way it is portrayed in the movie.

Feelings of superiority, incongruity, and relief are strongly shaped by the dominant norms. Who or what we feel superior to, what incongruities cause us to laugh, and what taboos are so anxiety-provoking that they require release are socially and culturally situated. In fact, the same joke could cause laughter by two people, but depending on the context, who they feel superior to, what they see as incongruous, and what they need relief from could be entirely different. For example, what if the same joke about *Brokeback Mountain* that was delivered at the Country Music Awards had been said in a gay bar or another gay-friendly context? Told between two men, the joke might be read as camp. In this situation, the joke teller would aim his or her humor at the presumed heterosexuality of stars or the gender norms surrounding Taylor Swift. Likely, the reference to *Brokeback Mountain* would not be filled with anxieties over gay male sex, as were many jokes about the film (see Chapter 8 for a further discussion of this topic).

The idea that humor might be read differently in different contexts especially is true when irony is used. The double discourse of irony can create a disconnection between creators' intentions and audiences' interpretations, especially given the fact that audiences have different reasons for laughing (Griffin, 2008; Hutcheon, 1994). Creators and audiences often are working in different contexts. Take, for example, *The Colbert Report* on Comedy Central. It began as a parody of the conservative talk shows on Fox News Channel. The show has a strong liberal sensibility, often expressed through irony. A 2009 study showed that while liberal and conservative college students both thought the show was funny, they did so for different reasons. Conservative viewers found surface level content sincere and funny. By contrast, liberals understood the program as satire, thus recognizing the double discourse of irony (LaMarre, Landreville, & Beam, 2009). While the creators presumed the context of parody would cue viewers to see that its surface meaning was meant ironically, viewers interpreted the meaning of the program's jokes in different ways depending on their prior political beliefs.

Similar results were found in a well-known study of viewers of the 1970s sitcom *All in the Family* (1971–1979) (Vidmar & Rokeach, 1974). The Norman-Lear-created show was meant as a satire of racist and sexist attitudes by placing those attitudes in the mouth of Archie Bunker, a middle-aged, lower-middle-class cab driver dealing with the civil rights, feminist, and counterculture movements of the late 1960s and 1970s. Satire is a form of irony that uses comedy to critique some aspect of our social world, often through irony. Using the laugh track and reactions of other characters, and making Archie's statements so clearly racist, the show's creator meant for viewers to understand the show to be making fun *of* Archie's outdated attitudes. That is, the show's producers assumed that viewers would understand the show as satire, and further understand his comments as ironic—meaning the opposite of what was directly stated by Archie. Instead, viewers who shared Archie's perspective enjoyed the show precisely because they felt Archie expressed their view of the world. A risk of irony is that viewers might buy into the surface meaning without either understanding or engaging with the secondary discourse it points to.

This becomes especially tricky when dealing with majority and minority groups. While humor shared between members of a dominant group about a minority group has the power to reinforce racism, sexism, and/or homophobia, there is a long tradition of minority groups using humor as a source of support, community-building, and transgression of dominant norms. A key example of this is camp humor, primarily associated with gay men, as introduced in Chapter 5. Camp humor historically involves witty jokes that play with the performativity of gender roles and the reviled status of both femininity and homosexuality in a homophobic culture. As gay visibility has increased over the past 20 years, camp has become more mainstream. Like much ethnic humor, a lot of camp humor involves comic put-downs of each other. Comic insults between members of the same group are a way of gentle teasing, and often a way of bonding together. Within a minority group, insults can be delivered and understood *as* ironic. The surface discourse points to a critical discourse underneath aimed at turning criticism away from the minority group and toward the majority group (see Textbox 7.2 for a discussion of minority humor as a "reverse comic discourse"). At the very least, even if not fully critical, the humor nonetheless confronts the pain of being in the minority. Minority groups often use humor that might seem racist, sexist, or homophobic on the surface, but often use that humor to point out how ridiculous or harmful those discourses are.

BOX 7.2 Reverse Comic Discourses

As we have discussed in this chapter, comedy has the ability to challenge dominant ideologies, including those about sexuality. However, the risk in using humor is its polysemic quality. That is, the creator of a message is unable to completely control the meaning that an audience takes from it. As minority sexualities have become more prominent in the media, particularly in comedy genres, scholars have begun to wrestle with the pros and cons of comedy's ambiguity. It is difficult to know whether audience members are inclined to laugh "with" or "at" satirical representations meant to challenge heteronormative assumptions.

Drawing from writings about race and comedy, we can think about whether there are ways to limit the likelihood of unintended readings/interpretations by audience members. Weaver (2010) introduces the idea of reverse comic discourse to consider this dilemma. He rejects a laughing "at" or "with" dichotomy, suggesting instead that reverse comedy requires "consideration of how the images of humour both *simultaneously* 'play on' and 'play off' the long-established stereotypes" and how one can remove/reduce the polysemic potential in the discourse (p. 33, emphasis in original).

We can apply Weaver's concept to discourses about sexuality to consider the potential effectiveness of limiting their messages. The comic strip below is from a web comic called *A Softer World*. The comic, created by Canadians Joey Comeau and Emily Horne, has gained a significant following since it came on-line in 2003, often appearing in the *Guardian*. The comics, which typically are three panels long,

(Continued)

FIGURE 7.2 *A Softer World*: **Comic Strip #766: especially gay marriage in video games, created by Emily Horne and Joey Comeau.**
Source: **Reprinted with permission.**

contain an additional layer of commentary based on each strip's title, which is visible to viewers when they hover their cursor over the comic. The title of the strip above is "especially gay marriage in videogames." Let us consider the humor of this strip and how it requires "sign slippage" but simultaneously limits its polysemic potential. We all know the ending to the popular moniker "Guns don't kill people" is generally "People kill people." It is a phrase popularized by gun control opponents. Yet, in this strip, the end of this saying initially about guns is replaced with "gay marriage does." Of course, the resulting statement, that gay marriage kills people, would (hopefully) be found a ridiculous assertion by readers. Given the weightiness of the beginning of the "joke," the end of it is unexpected and seemingly absurd. The humor in this joke lies in prominent anti-gay marriage discourses, which have stressed the slippery slope that gay marriage will lead down—loss of the sanctity of marriage, polygamy, even bestiality. However, in positioning gay marriage as leading to the death of people, through its absurdity the joke calls into question other claims about the evils of gay marriage. This critique leaves little room for alternative meaning making.

Using the searchable archive available on-line (http://www.asofterworld.com), take a look at other on-line *A Softer World* comics that reference GLBTQ issues. For each, consider how the comics work to either open up or constrain the possible meanings that audiences will make (be sure to include the comics' titles in your critiques). Below are the titles of five *A Softer World* comics to get you started:

1. He got his hopes up once they started letting the gays marry.
2. I'm gay married to the sea.
3. I make sure to show him all my teeth.
4. Don't get me wrong. My vagina is awesome.
5. The school for girls who like schools for girls.

As the GLBTQ population gains more political, social, and cultural recognition, public understanding has shifted from acknowledging that GLBTQ individuals are deviant to considering them oppressed by a system of homophobia. At the same time, the majority group has embraced camp humor, incorporating it into mainstream texts. This situation makes determining the line between humor that calls into question heteronormativity or is homophobic increasingly complicated. In recent years, feminist scholars, in particular, have noted the rise of ironic humor as a way to tell jokes that replay sexist or racist ideas, but allow the joke teller and even audiences to claim that they did not mean the joke *as* sexist or racist. The use of irony comes to act as a shield, where one can claim one made the joke but meant the opposite of it. The additional layer is that when people *do* attempt to point out that a particular joke is racist or sexist, the ironic nature of the joking allows the jokester to dismiss the critic as "not getting it," or as not having a sense of humor (Douglas 2010; Gill, 2007).

Blogger Carmen Van Kerckhove has attacked such humor related to race as "hipster racism" (Lim, 2012). She offers examples like a series of hip-hop parties organized by wealthy, white hipsters in Williamsburg, named "Kill Whitey," or the white man dubbed "Blackface Jesus" who received repeated exposure on Gawker.com for showing up in locations around New York wearing an American flag as a dress, accessorized with a crown of thorns and blackface makeup. Feminist scholars identify this kind of ironic humor as key to contemporary articulations of post-feminism and post-racism, the rise of a certain cultural discourse that assumes that gender and racial equality have been achieved, and, thus, goals for equality are no longer necessary. This irony plays on the ability of the joke teller to say I know it's wrong and because I know its wrong I can say it ironically.

▶ THE INTERSECTION OF GENDER AND SEXUALITY

While jokes directed *at* gay people may have become less popular in the media, jokes *about* sexuality and gender abound and are often treated as a key source of humor. A key question, then, is: To what extent does this humor express homophobic attitudes, tied to the maintenance of heteronormativity, or to what extent does such humor challenge heteronormativity by operating as a "reverse discourse"? As discussed in Chapter 1, a lot of this humor occurs around areas of instability over the meanings of and intersections between masculinity, femininity, gender identity, and sexual identities. As the discussion above indicates, in an age when irony reigns as the dominant comic discourse, recognizing when humor challenges or reinforces homophobia is not always clear.

"That's So Gay"

Hegemonic masculinity, a concept first explored by sociologist R.W. Connell (1995), considers the building of an ideal form of masculinity as key to maintaining the patriarchal status of men and women. Hegemonic masculinity does not consider masculinity as an essential or innate state of being a man, but rather as a historically variable and changing set of ideas and definitions of how men should act and be in the world. For a number of years, especially after World War II, a key tenet of hegemonic masculinity was the rejection of homosexuality as central to the assertion of proper, heterosexual masculinity. This gave rise to the concept of the gay panic, the belief that unwanted advances from another man could make a man go temporarily insane, and was central to the maintenance of a strong boundary between gay and straight masculinity (Becker, 2006). However, the rise of gay visibility and the gay rights movement, along with challenges to hegemonic masculinity by the feminist movement, has created a far blurrier line between gay and straight masculinity (Becker, 2006; 2009). When this is combined with the increasing emphasis on homosocial bonding as a popular pastime for men, as evidenced in things like bromance films, video-game playing, sports, and gambling as widespread activities enjoyed by groups of men together, we can see that humor about gayness becomes central to the experience of masculinity (Kimmell, 2009).

It is not surprising, then, that jokes about gayness are a key part of media aimed at young men, many of whom have grown up in a culture where words like "faggot," "sissy," "queer," "gay," "fag," and "homo" are used as taunts between boys. From comic kisses between men in movies like *Talladega Nights* (2006) to viral video parodies like James Franco and Seth Rogen's *Bound 3* (2013), gay jokes are a perpetual device used to evoke laughter in audiences. In many of these texts homophobic humor is so pervasive that it is impossible to imagine what else the characters might joke about (Hansen-Miller & Gill, 2011; San Filippo, 2013). In a famous scene from *The 40-Year-Old Virgin* (Apatow, Robertson, Townsend, & Apatow, 2005), friends Cal (Seth Rogen) and David (Paul Rudd) exchange a series of barbs while playing video games. When David tells Cal he is not sleeping with anyone, Cal's retort is, "You're gay now?" David responds that he is "just celibate," and the conversation takes off as each tries to one-up the other with "do you know how I know you're gay" jokes. The reasons include liking the band Coldplay, making macramé jean shorts, liking *Maid in Manhattan* (2002), making spinach dip in a sourdough bread loaf, and having a "rainbow bumper sticker on your car that says, 'I love it when balls are in my face.'"

Of course, this humor is ironic, indicating to the audience that they are not to take such jokes seriously. The humor is not necessarily directed *at* gay men, and the good-humored nature with which the two men rib each other indicates that they are not even seriously making fun of each other. They are not *exactly* homophobic. Earlier in the film they tell their friend Andy (Steve Carell), the titular virgin, that they thought he was gay, but quickly qualify that they do not see anything wrong with that. As Ron Becker (2006) argued, this became a common refrain on television shows throughout the 1990s. Examining the use of politically incorrect humor on the FX show *Rescue Me* (2004–2011), Maria San Filippo (2013) considers that the ways that

> the slurs and provocations that pepper *Rescue Me's* dialogue and plot turns both flatter the knowing liberal spectator and please the homophobic, while encouraging everyone to laugh it off. This ironic syntax, present throughout *Rescue Me*, enables the show's teasing evasion of attempts to pin it down as certifiably sexist, homophobic, or ideologically skewed in any clear unilateral direction.
>
> (p. 228–9)

The reliance on irony can make it hard to pin down where the line between regressive homophobia or transgressive play with heteronormativity lies. That is to say, these jokes express a continued ambivalence. However, it is clear that, while this joking expresses ambivalence about heterosexual masculinity, it continues to play on both the persistent belief in the deviance of sexual desire between men and the failed masculinity of gay men. Hansen-Miller and Gill (2011) point out that the bromances, or what they call "lad flicks," use irony to indicate that they know that they are being offensive, but they are not serious, thus no one should take offense. They see this humor *as* homophobic because it "serves consistently to disavow and deflect the homoerotic potential among the characters or between male audiences and those on screen" (Hansen-Miller & Gill, 2011, p. 44). While the disavowal line—"I'm not gay . . . not that there's anything wrong with that"—could be seen as a positive advance in attitudes toward gay men, it also could be seen as a "modernized, more knowing, and pernicious form of heterosexism, a new way of doing homophobia that parallels shifts in the ways in which racism and sexism are practiced" (p. 45). Aimed at policing the line between the homosocial—that is, male-only spaces of comradery and juvenile pursuits—and homosexuality, "that's so gay" jokes reinforce the denigrated status of male homosexuality. While the humor can be seen as ambivalent about the current status of masculinity, it also can be seen as perpetuating homophobia as a key element of heterosexual masculinity.

Sexism and GLBTQ Humor

If jokes about homosexuality are a common occurrence in entertainment aimed at young men, another pattern found in media comedy involving GLBTQ characters is humor that pokes fun at lesbians or makes gay men the butt of jokes by comparing them to women. Although such humor could be understood as attempting to draw attention and disarm stereotypes about lesbians and gay men, some media critics suggest these representations reflect misogynistic views found in homosexual communities, as well as American culture more broadly. Here we confront different levels of privilege within the GLBTQ community, as well as the different ways that homophobia works when it intersects with misogyny (Textbox 7.3 examines comedy at the intersection of race, gender, and sexuality).

BOX 7.3   "Snap Queens" and the Intersection of Race, Gender, and Sexuality

Although non-white GLBTQ characters historically have been absent in media representations, when black gay men have appeared in film and television, it has typically been in very narrow roles. The effeminate, black gay queen became popularized in the 1970s in films like *Carwash* (1976), in which the character Lindy was an effeminate cross-dresser with memorable lines like "Honey, I am more man than you'll ever be, and more women than you'll ever get." In the 1990s, the effeminate, black gay queen character attained a whole new level of visibility in the FOX television program *In Living Color* (1990–1994) in which Damon Wayans and David Alan Grier popularized the dynamic duo of Antoine and Blaine in the skits "Men on Films," which eventually grew to include other "Men on . . . " skits like "Men on Vacation" and "Men on Football." Although the men's gayness never was stated overtly, it was marked by their flamboyant dress and mannerisms, their overt desire for men and anything connoting male sexual organs (e.g., *Lethal Weapon* [1987, 1989, 1992, 1998] and *Great Balls of Fire* [1989]), and their misogynistic rejection of all things female. The men employed a rating of finger snaps to rate films in the same way that popular movie reviewers of the time, Siskel and Ebert, used a thumbs-up/down rating system. More recently, effeminate, black gay hairstylists Miss Lawrence and Derek J have appeared in the Bravo programs *The Real Housewives of Atlanta* (2008–) and *Fashion Queens* (2013–).

As we have discussed in this chapter, effeminate, gay male characters long have been played for laughs in the media. Because of the ambiguity of comedy and the diverse audiences that media comedies reach, such roles may be interpreted as a form of camp, subverting dominant hegemonic heterosexual masculinity, or as reinforcing narrow stereotypes about male gayness and effeminacy. Yet, media, sexuality, and race scholars have drawn attention to how black queen characters lie at the intersection of race, gender, and sexuality. For instance, such characters draw upon devices associated with black and gay/drag cultures, like "reading"— insulting someone (oftentimes based on their physical appearance)—and "snapping"—the punctuation of an insult with a finger snap. Writers like Gray (1995)

FIGURE 7.3 Miss Lawrence and Derek J on their Bravo reality-television show *Fashion Queens*
Source: "Take It or Weave It," April 3, 2013, Bravo TV.

and E. Patrick Johnson (1995), and filmmaker Marlon Riggs (1991) suggest snap queens have been understood as the disavowal of gayness and femininity reflective of a homophobic and misogynistic black male culture. *Madame Noir* writer Charing Ball (2012) has suggested "the gay black man [in reality programs] has become the new housemaid 'Mammy' to these women's Scarlett O'Haras" (p. 1).

Consider how race complicates representations of gayness and effeminacy by viewing and discussing the following media texts:

1. Watch the spoken performance "Institute of Snap!thology" in Marlon Riggs' documentary *Tongues Untied* (1989) performed by black gay men. Why do you think Riggs thought it was important to include this in his documentary on black male sexuality? How has "snap culture" been appropriated for laughs by mainstream media culture?
2. Watch several "Men on. . . " skits from *In Living Color* (1990–1994). How does the fact that the actors are heterosexual complicate their representations as "queens"? Why do you think the objects of their attraction are mostly white men?
3. Compare representations of Miss Lawrence and Derek J in *The Real Housewives of Atlanta* (2008–) or *Fashion Queens* (2013–) with those of effeminate, white gay fashion experts like the men of *Queer Eye for the Straight Guy* (2003–2007). How does race (blackness *and* whiteness) factor into these portrayals?

One place that gender and sexuality intersect is in the stereotype of the masculinized, unattractive, and angry lesbian, which persists in media comedy. One of the more over-the-top representations appeared in an episode of a 1990s cartoon short called *Cow and Chicken* on Cartoon Network. The cartoon, known for its outlandish humor and use of double-entendres, sometimes crossed the line even for Cartoon Network executives. One such episode, called "Buffalo Gals" (Burnett, Feiss, Alvarez, Feiss, & Reed, 1998), featured a gang of masculine female bikers wearing saggy blue jeans and white undershirts who burst into people's homes to eat their carpet. The episode never referenced the women as lesbians; however, the innuendos were apparent as the literal "carpet munchers" made pitcher and catcher jokes and expressed their hatred of chickens, easily taken as a stand-in for men. Even if the jokes would fly over the heads of children watching the show, they were not missed by executives, who initially banned the episode, nor by adults who continue to point to its veiled references to lesbian stereotypes in on-line posts. The difficulty of attacking such negative representations is the claim they are merely jokes meant to be ironic, poking fun at such stereotypes, not reinforcing them.

Although such over-the-top depictions of lesbians (even in animated form) might seem unlikely to be tolerated today, some of the most egregious cases are in sitcoms with leading gay male characters. Television producer Ryan Murphy came under attack for making lesbian jokes in FOX's *Glee* (2009–) and NBC's *The New Normal* (2012–2013) (Rosenberg, 2012). In the pilot of *The New Normal*, an often politically incorrect, middle-aged mom in the program insists that a lesbian couple, with their child, are really two "ugly men" (Murphy, Adler, & Murphy, 2012, September 10). In the following episode, Bryan (Andrew Rannells) and his partner David (Justin Bartha) make plans for a night out on the town "before we fully morph into an old lesbian couple, minus the frowns and the gingerbread man bodies" (Murphy, Adler, & Murphy, 2012, September 11). The program also pokes fun at female body parts, like in Bryan's comment, "I faint at the sight of vagina. They're like tarantula faces." Gay men mocking lesbians and women more generally is not new. In *Will & Grace*, the effeminate Jack McFarland (Sean Hayes) made no attempt to hide his disdain for lesbians. In one episode in which Jack and Will are rehearsing a skit on GLBT tolerance for the police department, Jack quips, "Before we begin, I ask that you refrain from the use of flash photography as the lesbians may attack you" (Kohan, Mutchnick, & Burrows, 2000, October 26).

Such jokes might not be tolerated if spoken by a straight man or woman, but they are part of the common repertoire of jokes by gay men in media. People disagree about the intentions behind such jokes and the effect they might have. One perspective argues that gay men and lesbians are part of the same oppressed in-group, and, therefore, when gay men mock lesbians it is meant to be ironic, poking fun at stereotypes in the same way that they might draw attention to effeminate stereotypes of gay men. However, others argue that such jokes reflect the fact that gay men are not immune to the misogynistic culture in which they were raised just because of their oppressed status as gay men (Geoghegan, 2009). Also, such jokes might reflect historic tensions between gay men and lesbians who have faced different forms of oppressions. Nick Maxwell works on behalf of older GLBT people and raises this as one possibility:

> The animosity . . . could also come from a sense that gay men have fought different battles—like being criminalised by the law and dealing with HIV—that lesbians have not faced, although lesbians have long been at the forefront of the successful campaign to change the law.
> (Geoghegan, 2009)

Another way some people see women devalued in gay male comedies is humor created by feminizing gay men. Linneman (2008) draws a distinction between effeminacy, which speaks to the way a gay man may choose to perform his identity, and feminization, in which "gender may be *done to him* by others" (p. 584, emphasis in original). Regardless of how masculine or feminine a gay character may appear, other characters often mark the character as different from straight men by associating his gayness with femininity. Linneman conducted a quantitative content analysis of the first seven seasons of *Will & Grace* (1998–2006) and found that the lead gay characters Will and Jack were consistently feminized in what he viewed as potentially harmful ways. Feminization might happen when one of the characters is referred to as a girl, woman, or lady, hailed by a feminine name like Nancy or Mary, or called a female-associated derogatory term like "bitch." Although Linneman found that gay characters were feminized an average of 3.5 times per episode, what he found more problematic was the context in which this feminization was happening. Almost a third of the feminine references to gay characters made by other characters (gay or straight) were during conflict or as a way to express disdain for them. Linneman explains, "This shows that such references are a common way to make the gay characters feel bad: I am currently mad at you, so I am going to put you down by calling you a woman" (p. 593). One example that Linneman offers is from the episode involving police sensitivity training mentioned earlier in this chapter:

> Will: I just asked you to abandon that queer voice.
> Jack: Queer? Who you callin' queer, you blouse-wearin' fairy?
> Will: This from the homo who minces around the gym in a Lycra onesie!
> Jack: Grace wears one!
> Will: She's a woman, you girl!

Jack: Don't call me a girl! Eyebrow-plucker!
Will: Leg-waxer!
Jack: Lady!
Will: Tramp!

(ibid.)

Linneman (2008) suggests that using feminization as a put-down reinforces misogynistic cultural assumptions that women are inferior to men. Similar to the childhood taunt "You run like a *girl*!" the use of feminization as a put-down for gay men simultaneously devalues their status as gay men, as opposed to their straight counterpoints, and does so at the expense of women. Surprisingly, Linneman found that a third of the put-downs using feminization were uttered by the women in the program. That is, even the female characters made associations between gay men and women as a way to insult the men.

▶ SITUATION COMEDY CONVENTIONS

In considering whether media comedy operates in ways that might challenge or reinforce traditional understandings of sexuality and the associated gender binary, it can be instructive to examine the generic conventions in which they appear. Media formulas are a key element in shaping content, and situation comedy is one of the most popular television genres, ranking second only to movies (Scarborough, 2013, June 7). Sitcoms also are a familiar place to find GLBTQ characters. In the 1970s, the first recurring character on television appeared on the sitcom *Soap* (1977–1981). Fast-forward 20 years, and sitcoms like *Ellen* (1994–1998) and *Will & Grace* (1998–2006) featured the first lesbian and gay leads on television. By 2013, 10 comedic series on broadcast television featured leading and/or supporting GLBTQ characters (GLAAD, 2013). Toss in cable network programs like FX's short-lived animated program *Chozen* (2013) about a white gay rapper and PBS's airing of the British sitcom *Vicious* (2014–), about an older gay couple, and GLBTQ representations in sitcoms are easy to find. In addition, sitcom classics like *Will & Grace* have a long afterlife in syndication. Since going into off-network syndication, *Will & Grace* has aired on WGN America, Lifetime, WE, and LOGO networks. *Modern Family* (2009–) entered off-network syndication in 2013, when its rights were sold to USA and 10 FOX affiliates. In a single week in November 2013, USA Network aired 25 hours of a *Modern Family* marathon.

In this chapter, we already have discussed the complicated ambiguity of comedy, and that discussion includes comedy found in situation comedies. However, genres are important contexts for both setting up comic situations and shaping how we understand jokes. While mixing genres has become common in contemporary television, there is, nonetheless, a typical formula to which most sitcoms ascribe. Mintz (1985) offers the following description:

> A sitcom is a half-hour series focused on episodes involving recurring characters within the same premise. That is, each week we encounter the same people in essentially the same setting. The episodes are finite; what happens in a given episode is generally closed off, explained, reconciled, solved at the end of the half hour (the exceptions, again, might be significant individually, but they have not altered the formula in any substantial or permanent way).
>
> (p. 115)

These genre characteristics point to four specific qualities of sitcoms that have implications for considering how GLBTQ characters are represented in them: emphasis on the domestic, circular narrative structure, reliance on stock characters, and laughter-cueing devices like laugh track and editing conventions.

At its most literal, the focus on the domestic indicates that sitcoms often are centered around families, including workplace "families," and the misunderstandings that stem from family or work life. However, the domesticity of sitcoms also speaks more broadly to the ways that the genre focuses on the personal lives of the recurring characters, whom we rarely see outside of the central series setting of either the family space or a work space. The result is that sitcoms almost always focus on the personal rather than political concerns of characters. We rarely see the effects of homophobia on the lives of gay and lesbian characters in sitcoms. This was especially true of 1990s sitcoms such as *Ellen* (1994–1998) or *Will & Grace* (1998–2006). More recently, the literal and broader meanings of domestic both shape portrayals of gay and lesbian characters, as we see an increasing focus on gay and lesbian families. Examples include ABC's *Modern Family* (2009–), in which Mitch, Cam, and their adopted daughter are positioned alongside two heterosexual couples. In NBC's *The New Normal* (2012–2013), partners Bryan and David hire a surrogate to help them fulfill their paternal longings. Even the flamboyant Jack McFarland from *Will & Grace* becomes domesticated in the short-lived NBC sitcom *Sean Saves the World* (2013–2014), where the actor who played McFarland (Sean Hayes) plays a gay man who moves from part-time parent to full-time father after his ex-wife moves away to pursue a career and his daughter decides to stay in order to finish school with her friends.

This focus on the domestic can have ideological implications because of the limited range of representations. Mills (2009) writes, "For the majority of the sitcoms the home is equated with the family, and the kinds of family which are represented can be critiqued as disturbingly traditional" (p. 21). While all three sitcoms mentioned above certainly emphasize the changing face of American families, they simultaneously privilege traditional notions of family.

FIGURE 7.4 Soon-to-be husbands, David Sawyer and Bryan Collins embracing their newborn child
Source: *The New Normal*, 2013, National Broadcasting Company.

This is perhaps best exemplified in *The New Normal* (2012–2013) when the two fathers decide it is important for them to marry before their son is born. In a typical sitcom twist, their surrogate goes into labor at their wedding ceremony, interrupting their plans. However, before the episode is over, they find themselves in a position to be able to throw themselves an impromptu wedding on a beach with their closest friends. The traditional ceremony is even officiated by a priest who privileges his relationship with the men over his church's ban on same-sex marriage. The final shot of the finale episode of the first (and last) season is of the married men jointly hugging their infant son (Adler, Murphy, & Winkler, 2013, April 2).

In many ways, the sitcoms mentioned above are incredibly progressive given the visibility they afford gay people, validating their abilities to be loving partners and parents. Of course, these representations are limited in that they are exclusively upper-class, white, male characters. Yet, queer media scholars would go even farther in their critique of these programs and the sitcom genre more broadly because of the way they reinforce heteronormative logics that exclude people who do not organize their lives around traditional notions of family.

Although there may be disruptions to the traditional family unit in sitcoms featuring GLBTQ people, such disruptions generally are limited by a second sitcom formula, their narrative structure. The typical narrative structure for a sitcom has been described as "confusion, disruption, and reconciliation" or "confusion-dilemma-untangling" (Mintz, 1985; Zillman & Bryant, quoted in Goldstein, 1993). While dramas generally follow a linear story narrative, with characters and plot developing over a season or the entire series, sitcoms follow a more circular plotline each episode. Roger Rollin critiques this return to the status quo as going against comedy's traditional function of advancing social change (Mintz, 1985). In particular, traditional values of the nuclear family are returned to in the end, including an emphasis on monogamous coupled home life as the key source of comfort and support in our lives.

Similar examples of how threats to family values are contained through the circular narrative of the sitcom can be found in NBC's *The New Normal* and BBC's *Vicious* (2014–) (aired by PBS in the United States). Both include episodes in which the couples long for a return of their younger days of clubbing and carefree ways. In *The New Normal*, Bryan and David's night out on the town results in a younger man propositioning the two of them. However, the couple chide the young man for suggesting such a thing and emphasize the age difference between them. By 9:45 p.m., they grow tired and decide to return to their domestic space (Adler, Murphy, & Winkler, 2013, April 2). Similarly, an episode of *Vicious* follows one of the characters as he tries to keep up with significantly younger men at a gay club. When one of the younger companions asks where they should go next, he has difficulty continuing his façade of youth and vitality, uttering, "Next? You mean after *THIS*?" After telling the men he will meet up with them later, he puts his head down on the table and is quickly sound asleep (Janetti & Bye, 2013, July 20). The humor from both of these episodes lies in the fact that the men have matured to the point that the swinging ways of their youth are beyond recapturing. While both storylines have an element of ageism to them, the storylines also contain any risk to the family unit, whether laughing off a ménage à trois or making unimaginable the potential of an intergenerational one-night stand. In the end, the gay men are relieved to be returned to the comfort and safety of their domestic space.

Another aspect of sitcoms that may limit their transgressive potential is their reliance on "stock characters," or what some might refer to as "stereotypes." Oversimplified characters may be more prevalent in sitcoms than other genres because of the limited time available in a sitcom. After allowing time for commercials, a typical episode only has 22 minutes to set up a situation, disrupt it, and resolve it, leaving little time for deep character development. In writing about the stereotype of "working-class buffoons" in sitcoms (think Homer Simpson), Richard Butsch (1995) suggests stereotypical character traits provide shorthand for audience members to understand characters quickly. We can see this in sitcoms featuring GLBTQ characters, as well. For example, in the first minutes of the pilot episode of *Sean Saves the World* (2013–2014), Sean's daughter asks him how he and her mom conceived her if he is gay. Between his daughter's questions and Sean's physical mannerisms, viewers are quickly able to "make sense" of Sean as a gay, somewhat flamboyant man wrestling with his new role as a full-time father (Fresco & Burrows, 2013, October 3).

As we discussed in Chapter 3, there are limitations to examining media representations in the context of stereotypes because it assumes some singular reality of social groups against which media characters should be compared. However, using the same stock characters (e.g., the flamboyant gay man or the husky, athletic lesbian) limits the range of portrayals and denies characters the chance to develop complexity or depth. This does not mean, however, that stereotypes cannot be used to challenge hegemonic assumptions. Yet, the success of this strategy is complicated by its reliance on irony.

A common stock character in sitcoms and comedy more generally is the role of the "fool." This character warrants its own discussion in GLBTQ sitcoms because the fool sometimes has the greatest potential to make outlandish comments that challenge traditional norms. Across literature, fool and clown characters are often able to speak truths that fundamentally challenge dominant ideological power structures or dominant norms. Take the case of *Will & Grace's* ultimate fool characters, Karen and Jack (Battles & Hilton-Morrow, 2002). A number of media critics have argued that Karen was the queerest member of the cast because she resists attempts to fix her sexuality and deconstructs the sanctity of marriage by describing it in transactional terms (e.g., her husband gets sex; she gets jewelry). While Jack might be dismissed as a mere stereotype, he also is a character who has no investment in heteronormative values of domesticity and family life. Happy to date without settling down, refusing adult responsibilities, and ignoring many social conventions, Jack, like Karen, challenges us to rethink the centrality of heteronormative values. Yet, because these characters fulfill the stock character type of the fool, audience members can more easily dismiss their pointed critiques of heteronormative institutions. More than that, as we discussed above in the case of laughter, we can never be sure if audiences are laughing *with* the characters, taking pleasure in their oppositional humor, or laughing *at* characters, seeing them as mere fools.

In other instances, fool characters espouse the most offensive positions, intended by program creators to be dismissed as backward views. Archie Bunker of *All in the Family* (1971–1979) offers such an example; however, as discussed above, audiences did not always interpret the intended irony of his comments. Contemporary fool characters in GLBTQ comedies also run a similar risk. One such character is Jane Forrest, the mother of Bryan and David's surrogate on *The New Normal* (2012–2013). One blogger described her as "an unlikeable and unsuccessful attempt at creating a modern day Archie Bunker" (Lips, 2012, September 3). Forrest's bigoted remarks primarily target racial and sexual minorities. She unapologetically uses the term "gay" as a negative descriptor, as in "That's the gayest thing I've ever heard," and spews the most offensive of epithets, even referring to gay men as "fudge packers." Forrest's position as the clear fool of the series allows her to verbalize homophobic attitudes that likely would not be tolerated by other characters seemingly for the purpose of ridiculing such beliefs. Yet, again, though in the reverse, the danger of irony remains that audience members may laugh *with*, rather than *at* the regressive fool.

The final convention of situation comedies worth exploring is editing. Editing conventions are used to cue audiences that what they are watching is meant to be funny. Mills (2009) suggested that sitcoms' signaling of "their intention to be funny" is what makes them distinctive from other genres (p. 93). The humor that sitcoms are meant to invoke is made obvious through the use of laugh tracks. Sitcoms are the one genre that does not show an audience on screen, yet inserts the intended audience's reaction into the program itself. Although we have discussed the polysemic quality of comedy and the differing interpretations that ambiguity allows for, the laugh track and other editing conventions contribute to what Umberto Eco (1984) would describe as an "open text," one that limits the possible audience interpretations of the text. Laugh tracks may not signal to audiences exactly *why* something is supposed to be funny, but they certainly make clear *what* is meant to be funny, and not even just in the hypothetical. This shared laughter speaks to the communal experience of comedy and a shared reaction. It leaves little space for alternative reactions—you are either with us (those laughing) or against us (those not). As Mills (2009) wrote,

> The existence of the laugh track has been seen as evidence of the hegemonic ways in which television comedy works. . . . The laugh track presents the audience as a mass, whose responses are unambiguous and who signal a collective understanding of what is and isn't funny. . . there is a pleasure to be had in going along with the rest of the crowd.
>
> (p. 103)

This is not to say that laugh tracks and other editing devices entirely rob audiences of the ability to decide whether a sitcom or jokes in it are funny or offensive. In fact, Bore (2011) found that a laugh track points audience attention to moments when their own reactions do not align with those intended meanings of producers. However, the laugh track can invite viewers to "feel at one with the few dozen people s/he can hear laughing, and by extension with millions of others across the country" (Medhurst & Tuck, 1982, p. 45).

Another important function of the laugh track is that it allows a space in which it is acceptable to laugh *at* other people. Goldstein (1993) suggested that laugh tracks give audiences permission to laugh at taboo topics by defining situations as ones that warrant laughter. The sitcom *Two and a Half Men* (2003–) offers many examples of sexist humor, including remarks channeling male fantasy about lesbian sexual relations that take place on the show. The laugh track gives permission, if not encouragement, to find such remarks humorous rather than offensive.

Of course, increasingly sitcoms omit the laugh track. However, we should not confuse this lack of a laugh track as encouraging alternative interpretations. Audience research by Bore (2011) found that audiences watching the 1970s sitcom *M*A*S*H** (1972–1983) laughed in similar places regardless of the inclusion of a laugh track (Mills, 2009). This is, of course, because jokes are generally recognizable; however, the laugh track is only one of the "cues" audiences are given that they are to interpret the text as funny. In the absence of laugh tracks, comedies can use reaction shots, or mockumentary style "confessionals" to indicate what should be laughed at (Textbox 7.4 considers the ways that the changing nature of the sitcom genre might encourage different understandings of GLBTQ life).

BOX 7.4   Opening Up the Sitcom Structure?

Historically, the narrative structure of the situation comedy has been remarkably consistent. As we have argued here, the sitcom structure often can contain transgressive humor by safely situating it within the conventions of domesticity, circular narratives, fool characters, and editing. However, over the past decades, sitcoms have incorporated elements of drama and seriality—continuing storylines—into the formula. The question becomes: to what extent do these changes open up the possibility for the more transgressive qualities of humor to serve as a critique of dominant norms? Two recent situation comedies, *Brooklyn Nine Nine* (2013–), about police detectives, and *Sirens* (2014–), about an ambulance rescue team, play more with the genre formula. Both also prominently feature African-American gay characters as central cast members. Because they focus on fighting crime or rescuing people, both sitcoms also include interactions between the main characters and people outside of their immediate workplace families. The question is whether these sitcoms, in both their casting choices and play with the traditional sitcom formula, open up space for comedy that challenges rather than reinforces hetero- and homonormativity.

Watch at least one episode of one or both of these programs. As you watch the programs, pay particular attention to the *structure* of the program, focusing on domesticity, the narrative structure, fool characters, and editing.

1.   How faithful is the program to the *domestic* structure of the sitcom? How does that domesticity open up or close down possibilities for transgressive humor?

2. Does the program engage with the typical circular narrative structure of the sitcom? Does the program offer continuing storylines or introduce a conflict that is not resolved by the end?
3. Does the program have a "fool" character? What kinds of jokes does the "fool" tell? How do other characters react to the fool? Are viewers meant to laugh *with* or *at* the fool?
4. How does editing work to tell us when to laugh?
5. Do these shows significantly challenge the sitcom format? Do they shape the ways that the gay characters are represented in the comedy format?

Situation comedies are only one genre within which GLBTQ characters appear on television, but they have been and remain an important one. The genre conventions work to reduce the polysemic quality of humor by attempting to close down the more transgresssive aspects of humor. Because they tend to keep characters inside a usually hermetically sealed world where they mostly explore their personal lives, sitcoms largely keep their characters contained in domestic spaces of either home or work spaces. Narratives offer brief moments of conflict or misunderstanding that can be resolved easily, and even use editing conventions to suggest at the very least when something funny has happened. At the same time, however, the polysemic nature of comedy means that sitcoms cannot fully determine why audiences laugh. A fool character provides the potential to challenge social norms, even while audiences are able to dismiss his or her worldview.

▶ CONCLUSION

There can be no doubt that comedy has served an important role in both reinforcing and challenging heteronormativity. Pejorative jokes about GLBTQ individuals and communities have generated laughter through superiority, incongruity, and relief, allowing heterosexual men, especially, to maintain the line between gay and straight masculinity. At the same time, like many other minority groups, GLBTQ communities have developed their own comic discourses in which they have used humor and laughter as a way to find sustenance in the face of a homophobic society. However, the rise of gay visibility, combined with the generalized use of irony as a key comic discourse across the media landscape, has led to a growing ambiguity and even ambivalence in comedy, especially dominant group comedy about minority sexualities.

In this chapter we asked you to examine the polysemic quality of comedy. When it comes to questions of irony, jokes cannot be understood by content alone; they need an understanding of the context. Who creates the joke, their intentions, the setting within which a joke is delivered, the intended and actual audiences, and the competencies of both the joke teller and audience to manipulate the double discourses of irony must all be taken into account to consider the cultural work of a joke. In many ways, it is the context that helps us better understand if a joke challenges or reinforces heteronormativity. As we examined in the case of "gay" jokes in entertainment aimed at young heterosexual men, even if ambivalent and not directly about gay people, jokes still have the power to reinforce a sense of male homosexuality as deviant. At the same time, when jokes about sexuality intersect with gender, even in-group humor among gay males can be seen as devaluing the feminine. Finally, we considered the ways that the situation comedy, as the genre that has been most open to GLBTQ characters, can contain threats to heteronormativity through genre conventions.

Comedy has been central to both the maintenance of and challenges to homophobia and heteronormativity. As the relationship between sexual minorities and the sexual majority begins to change, there can be not doubt that there will be points of friction for both groups. As these relationships change, interpretations of what is and why something is funny also begin to change. Still as joke tellers and audiences for comedy, it is important to be aware of precisely *what* makes something funny to us. Recognizing that is an important step in preventing comic discourses from perpetuating the idea that minority sexual identities are deviant and abnormal, and, thus, available to be laughed at, diminishing the humanity of GLBTQ individuals and communities.

▶ REFERENCES

Adler, A., Murphy, R. (Writers), & Winkler, M. (Director). (2013, April 2). The big day [Televison series episode]. In D. Di Loreto, A. Adler, & R. Murphy (Producers), *The new normal*. Studio City, CA: 20th Century Fox.

Apatow, J., Robertson, S., Townsend, C. (Producers), & Apatow, J. (Director). (2005). *The-40-year-old virgin*. Universal City, CA: Universal Pictures.

Ball, C. (2012, June 27). Are gay men the new "mammies" of reality television? *Madame Noire*. Retrieved from http://madamenoire.com/191818/are-gay-men-the-new-mammies-of-reality-television/2.

Banet-Weiser, S. (2007). *Kids rule!: Nickelodeon and consumer citizenship*. Durham, NC: Duke University Press.

Battles, K. & Hilton-Morrow, W. (2002). Gay characters in conventional spaces: *Will & Grace* and the situation comedy genre. *Critical Studies in Media Communication, 19*(1), 87–105.

Becker, R. (2006). *Gay TV and straight America*. New Brunswick, NJ: Rutgers University Press.

Becker, R. (2009). Guy love: A queer straight masculinity for a post-closet era? In G. Davis & G. Needham (Eds.), *Queer TV: Theories, histories, politics* (pp. 120–140). New York, NY: Routledge.

Bernardi, B., Gallow, L., Kavanaugh, R. (Producers), & Dugan, D. (Director). (2007). *I now pronounce you Chuck & Larry*. Universal City, CA: Paramount.

Bore, I. K. (2011). Laughing together? TV comedy audiences and the laugh track. *The Velvet Light Trap, 68*, 24–34.

Burnett, B. & Feiss, D. (Writers), Alvarez, R., Feiss, D., & Reed, B. (Directors). (1998). Buffalo gals [Televison series episode]. In Vincent Davis (Producer), *Cow and chicken*. Burbank, CA: Cartoon Network Studios.

Butsch, R. (1995). Ralph, Fred, Archie, and Homer: Why television keeps recreating the white male working-class buffoon. In G. Dines & J. Humez (Eds.), *Gender, race, and class in media* (pp. 403–412). Thousand Oaks, CA: Sage.

Connell, R.W. (1995). *Masculinities*. Oakland, CA: University of California Press.

Douglas, S. (2010). *Enlightened sexism: The seductive message that feminism's work is done*. New York, NY: Times Books.

Eco, U. (1984). *The role of the reader: Explorations in the semiotics of texts*. Bloomington, IN: University of Indiana Press.

Fiske, J. (1989). *Television culture*. New York, NY: Routledge.

Fresco, V. (Writer) & Burrows, J. (Director). (2013, October 3). Pilot [Televison series episode]. In M. Solakian (Producer), *Sean saves the world*. Studio City, CA: Universal TV.

Geoghegan, T. (2009, September 28). Why lesbians are the butt of gay men's jokes. *BBC News Magazine*. Retrieved from http://news.bbc.co.uk/2/hi/uk_news/magazine/8278398.stm.

Gill, R. (2007). *Gender and the media*. Cambridge, MA: Polity Press.

GLAAD. (2013). *Where we are on TV report: 2013*. Retrieved from glaad.org/whereweare ontv13.

Goldstein, J. (1993). Humor and comedy in mass media. *Zeitschrift für Medienpsychologie, 54*, 246–256.

Gray, H. (1995). *Watching race*. Minnesota, MN: University of Minnesota Press.

Griffin, H. (2008). Queerness, the quality audience and Comedy Central's *Reno 911*. *Television and New Media, 9*(5), 355 n370.

Hansen-Miller, D. & Gill, R. (2011). "Lad flicks": Discursive reconstructions of masculinity in film. In H. Radner & R. Stringer (Eds.), *Feminism at the movies* (pp. 36–50). New York: Routledge.

Hutcheon, L. (1994). *Irony's edge: The theory and politics of irony*. New York, NY: Routledge.

Hutcheon, L. (2000). *A theory of parody: The teachings of twentieth century art forms*. Chicago, IL: University of Illinois Press.

Janetti, G. (Writer) & Bye, E. (Director). (2014, July 20). Episode 1.4 [Televison series episode]. In G. Reich & J. Featherstone (Producers), *Vicious*. London, UK: Brown-Eyed Boy.

Johnson, E.P. (1995). SNAP! Culture: A different kind of "reading." *Text and Performance Quarterly, 15*, 122–142.

Kerchkhove, C.V. (2007, January 15). The 10 biggest race and pop culture trends of 2006: Part 1 of 3. *Racialicious: The intersection of race and pop culture*. Retrieved from http://www.raciali cious.com/2007/01/15/the-10-biggest-race-and-pop-culture-trends-of- 2006-part-1-of-3.

Kimmel, M. (2009). *Guyland: The perilous world where boys become men*. New York, NY: Harper Perennial.

Kohan, D. & Mutchnick, M. (Writers) & Burrows, J. (Director). (2000, October 26). Girl trouble. In D. Kohan & M. Mutchnick (Producers), *Will & Grace*. Studio City, CA: National Broadcasting Company.

Kurtzman, D. (n.d.). *Brokeback Mountain* jokes: Late-night jokes about *Brokeback Mountain*. *Political humor: About.com*. Retrieved from http://politicalhumor.about.com/od/brokebackmountain/a/brokebackjokes.htm.

LaMarre, H., Landreville, Kl, & Beam, M. (2009). The irony of satire: Political ideology and the motivation to see what you want to see in *The Colbert report*. *International Journal of Press/Politics, 14*(2), 212–231.

Lim, T. (2012). A historical guide to hipster racism. *Racialicious*. Retrieved from http://www.racialicious.com/2012/05/02/a-historical-guide-to-hipster-racism.

Linneman, T.J. (2008). How do you solve a problem like Will Truman? The feminization of gay masculinities on *Will & Grace. Men and Masculinities, 10*(5), 583–603.

Lips, A. (2012, September 3). "The new normal embraces stereotypes". *Waitwhatsadial*? Retrieved from http://waitwhatsadial.com/2012/09/03/the-new-normal-makes-everything-a-stereotype.

Manning, J. (2010, June). *The humor of coming out: A critical analysis of acceptance in coming out narratives*. Paper presented at the International Communication Association Suntec, Singapore International Convention & Exhibition Centre, Suntec City, Singapore.

Medhurst, A., & Tuck, L. (1982). The gender game. In J. Cook (Ed.), *BFI dossier 17: Television sitcom* (pp. 43–55). London: BFI.

Mills, B. (2009). *The sitcom*. Edinburgh, UK: Edinburgh University Press.

Mintz, L. (1985). Situation comedy. In B. Rose (Ed.), *TV genres* (pp. 105–129). Westport, CT: Greenwood.

Murphy, R., Adler, A. (Writers), & Murphy, R. (Director). (2012, September 10). Pilot [Televison series episode]. In D. Di Loreto, A. Adler, & R. Murphy (Producers), *The new normal*. Studio City, CA: 20th Century Fox.

Murphy, R., Adler, A. (Writers), & Murphy, R. (Director). (2012, September 11). Sofa's choice [Televison series episode]. In D. Di Loreto, A. Adler, & R. Murphy (Producers), *The new normal*, Studio City, CA: 20th Century Fox.

Riggs, M. (1991). Black macho revisited: Reflections of a Snap! Queen. *Black American Literature Forum, 25*(2), 389–394.

Rosenberg, A. (2012). *The new normal*: Why can't Ryan Murphy stop making lame lesbian jokes? *Slate.com*. Retrieved from http://www.slate.com/blogs/xx_factor/2012/09/12/the_new_normal_why_can_t_ryan_murphy_stop_making_lame_lesbian_jokes_.html.

San Filippo, M. (2013). *The b word: Bisexuality in contemporary film and television*. Bloomington, IN: Indiana University Press.

Scarborough. (2013, June 7). Comedy is a favorite of the top TV genres. *Nielson Local*. Retrieved from http://dialog.scarborough.com/index.php/comedy-is-a-favorite-of-the-top-tv-genres.

Tasker, Y. (2011). *Enchanted* (2007) by postfeminism: Gender, irony, and the new romantic comedy. In H. Radner & R. Stringer (Eds.), *Feminism at the movies* (pp. 67–79). New York: Routledge.

US Weekly Staff. (2011, April 4). Blake Shelton makes gay joke about Jake Gyllenhaal. *US Weekly*. Retrieved from http://www.usmagazine.com/entertainment/news/jakegyllenhaal-taylor-swift-leann-rimes-mocked-at-acms-201144.

Vidmar, N. & Rokeach, M. (1974). Archie Bunker's bigotry: A study in selective perception and exposure. *Journal of Communication, 24*(1), 36–47.

Weaver, S. (2010). The 'other' laughs back: Humour and resistance in anti-racist comedy. *Sociology, 44*(1), 31–48.

Bodies

By this point of reading this book, you certainly realize that increased GLBTQ visibility does not signal full sexual equality. In fact, oftentimes heteronormative cultural ideals inform the way we see GLBTQ representations on screen. One particular place we see this is in the treatment of bodies that do not conform to norms of gender and sexuality. For example, an episode of the ABC Family romantic sitcom *Melissa and Joey* (2010–) illustrates the discomfort many on-screen and off-screen audiences still have with same-sex physical intimacy. The basis of the episode is that the title characters decide to enter a local version of *Dancing with the Stars*. However, through typical situation comedy missteps and mishaps, the character Joey (Joey Lawrence) ends up partnered with *Dancing with the Stars* (2005–) professional dancer Mark Ballas, which leads to the key comic moment of the episode, when Mark takes on the female role to Joey's male lead. As the two men dance closely, their body language, facial expressions, and the reaction shots of the crowd indicate that this is a strange and, for the men involved, uncomfortable experience. Ballas adopts highly feminine gestures—maintaining the appropriate gender division that grounds ballroom dancing. His over-the-top caressing of Joey is met with dismay by the character and audience laugh track. The discomfort that the men and the on-screen audience experience, verbalized by one young boy who remarks, "This is why I don't watch *Showtime*," signals the cultural taboos that continue to surround same-sex expressions of intimacy and GLBTQ bodies (Boran & Wass, 2010).

FIGURE 8.1 Joey is visibly uncomfortable with dance partner Mark Ballas
Source: Melissa & Joey, **Season 1, Episode 8, "Dancing with the Stars of Toledo," 2010, ABC Family.**

In previous chapters, we have explored a number of theoretical concepts and frameworks through which to consider the relationship between sexual *identities* and the media. This chapter will consider another site for thinking about media representations and GLBTQ sexuality, the *body*. How those bodies appear and how they express desire often are strongly shaped by heteronormative assumptions about the relationship between gendered bodies, sexual desires, and appropriate same-sex behaviors. In this chapter, we first will examine what it means to think about sexual identity and media through the category of the body. Second, we will examine how depictions of bodies engaged in same-sex intimacy reflect the heteronormative logics of our culture. Third, we will consider media's fascination with the transgender body as the key site for making sense of non-normative gender identities. Finally, we will consider how media representations of GLBTQ bodies also may challenge binary assumptions of gender and sexuality, thus, questioning the fundamental logic of heteronormativity.

▶ THINKING ABOUT BODIES

The physical body lies at the crux of many cultural assumptions about sexual and gender identities. Questions about the body bring us to questions of sexual desires and behaviors and the ways that heteronormativity shapes how same-sex desires and intimacy are represented. These assumptions also shape how we see gender. In our heteronormative culture, bodies are treated as guaranteeing the "truth" of our binary gender arrangement. This makes paramount the need for gender identification, some form of confirmation that the stripped-down body corresponds to its public display of gender characteristics. As a result, media depictions of transgender men and women often center upon examining and making sense of bodies that do not conform to sex/gender norms. However, questions about mediating the body do not end with the representations on the screen. We also need to consider viewers' bodies and the bodily response evoked by those depictions. For example, in the same way that you may experience an increased heart rate and physical anxiety while watching a scary movie, GLBTQ bodies may be depicted in ways designed to evoke visceral reactions in audience members. They appeal not to the logic of reason, but to deep-seated emotions tied to heteronormative expectations.

When we think about bodies on the screen, we begin to pay specific attention to the visual, to what we *see*. That is, we begin to think as much about the images themselves as we do about their narrative meaning. The idea that looking at images is a unique experience has been explored by a number of theorists. These theorists draw from psychoanalysis, which explores the relationship between the conscious and unconscious parts of our mind, suggesting that sometimes people's desires and bodily responses are not fully conscious. For example, Freud (1947/1905) argued that scopophilia, or the pleasure in looking, is one of the key drives in our unconscious search for pleasure. Scholars also draw on the work of Lacan (1978/1973), whose theory of the mirror stage of development posits that we have a deep-seated, unconscious relationship to screen images that trigger yearnings that go back to our infancies. These theories have relevance to media because they suggest that our reactions to screen images not only are determined by the story or narrative, but, in some cases, also by our unconscious bodily reactions to visual elements.

Informed by psychoanalytic thinking, the concept of spectacle sometimes is used in film and media studies to explain and make sense of both the highly visual aspects of media and of the sometimes unconscious, emotional, bodily reactions that media can elicit. At its most basic level, spectacle refers to something that attracts our visual attention because it stands out from what we consider normal. It might be a dramatic display, something that is unusual, something that is shocking, and in general, something that is over-the-top in its presentation. For example, we use the word "spectacular" to refer to something that is extraordinary because it exceeds our expectations. Spectacle also can refer to something that is disruptive, like when a parent tells a child misbehaving in public, "Don't make a spectacle of yourself." When applied to media, spectacle can refer to the "over-the-top" media coverage of an event. One example would be the 2014 murder trial of Oscar Pistorius, the South African runner nicknamed the "Blade Runner" because he competed in the Olympics as a double amputee. Spectacle also describes visual elements of media that are excessive and do not contribute anything to a story's narrative. For example, many action movies use computer-generated imagery and sound effects to create sequences that add excitement to the film but do not really change the basic plot. Instead, these effects cause intense reactions of excitement, fear, anticipation, and thrill in us as we watch.

In other cases, spectacle can elicit emotions like fear, disgust, desire, arousal, joy, pleasure, and even pain. For example, Linda Williams (1991) explored genres of movies that she called "body genres" because our engagement with them is based on our visceral reaction and emotional engagement. She considered horror, melodrama, and pornography as films that purposefully play with excesses of violence, emotion, or sex to create fear, tears, or arousal in audiences. There is an affective charge to spectacle in that we *feel* these things rather than *think* about or *interpret* them. The key here is that intense images of bodies on the screen—involving intimacy, emotions, or violence—can create intense responses in the viewer. It is important to realize that the spectacles are manipulated images specifically produced for reaction by playing with cultural norms surrounding appropriate bodily decorum and behavior and that our intense reactions, even while not entirely rational, are strongly shaped by those very same norms. The concept of spectacle provides us a framework for thinking about how media have dealt with GLBTQ bodies.

▶ MEDIATING SAME-SEX INTIMACY

Images of sexual intimacy are a pervasive facet of contemporary media. Issues around intimate acts always center around ideas of what is normal and what is deviant, what is private and what is public, and, more specifically, around the unstable intersections of race, gender, sexuality, class, and ability. The past 20 years have witnessed a sea change in the ways that sex and intimacy are presented in the media. A number of authors point out the ways that sex becomes a spectacle in contemporary culture (see, for instance, Kellner, 2003: Plummer, 2003). We are awash in images and talk of intimacy and sex. In part, this has been driven by changes in the media industries and technology and, in part, by the shifts in social attitudes toward sex and sexuality in the wake of the civil rights, feminist, and GLBT rights movements. The proliferation of channels, websites, and viewing technologies, leading to the end of large mass audiences, has created innumerable opportunities for the presentation of sexual content. Due to the adoption of hard-core porn aesthetics by Western art cinema producers, the graphic depictions of sex on cable channels, and the expansion of the pornography market on the Internet through sites like XTube, audiences today have increased access to more kinds of sexual content than at any time before (Krzywinska, 2005; Williams, 2008).

While varieties of sexual expression have increased, the fact remains that the vast majority of sexual activity we see across the mediated landscape is between people of the opposite sex. While we have witnessed a rise in the representation of GLBTQ individuals in the media, representations of same-sex affection continue to be quite limited. It is so limited, in fact, that their mere presence is bound to cause intense scrutiny and discussion. (Textbox 8.1 examines the uneven application of ratings and censorship for media representations of heterosexual and homosexual intimacy.) While heterosexuals routinely express forms of affection and intimacy in the media and in public spaces, even some supporters of gay rights suggest that displays of affection should be kept "private" behind closed doors. However, both the sentiments around same-sex intimacy and the conventions for representing it vary in important ways based on whether the intimacy involves the bodies of two women or two men.

BOX 8.1   The Ratings Game

Ratings are an important, but often overlooked, tool for regulating same-sex intimacy and sexuality, in general, in movies and television. The differing attitudes about gay and straight sex are on display in Kirby Dick's documentary, *This Film Is Not Yet Rated* (2006). In interviews with filmmakers, he points to the double standard of the Motion Picture Association of America (MPAA) when it comes to rating films containing gay content. For example, Jamie Babbit, director of the teen-oriented film *But I'm a Cheerleader* (1999), discusses how her film received an NC-17 rating for one scene involving a clothed gay teen attempting to masturbate, while another film aimed at teens, *American Pie* (1999), had far more explicit sexual content, but secured an R rating. This disparity extends to the depiction of a range of acts that sit outside normative ideas of heterosexual sex. For many critics, the question is not whether we need more or less sex in television or movies, but whether gay intimacy is treated differently in television and movies.

While the film industry long has used voluntary ratings systems to control access to films, and television more recently has joined the ratings bandwagon, a new area for censorship of GLBTQ content has been new media, particularly search engines and social media platforms. Over the past few years there have been a number of instances of social media sites taking down content based on gay or lesbian subject matter. For example, when Yahoo took over Tumblr, they blocked content tagged gay and lesbian, setting off a firestorm of debate on the social media site, which has a

(Continued)

FIGURE 8.2 The ratings game: *Boys Don't Cry* (1999) versus *American Pie* (2006).
Source: This Film Is Not Yet Rated, 2006

strong GLBTQ presence among its users. Explaining that it was trying to block explicit content, especially on its mobile platforms, Tumblr representatives said they were not trying to be anti-gay, but certain tags, like #gay or #lesbian often brought up pornographic content. However, critics pointed out that tags like #necrophilia were not censored (Manders, 2013). More recently, Facebook took down content from a page for the documentary *Girl on Girl: A Documentary Film* (2015). The photo pictured two women kissing in bed. The site's moderator found other pages with more graphic representations of women being sexual, but aimed at a male audience, to demonstrate how restrictions on sex are applied unevenly (Savitz, 2014).

For this activity, complete one of the following:

- Search for recent examples of social media censorship of images of gay and/or lesbian intimacy.

- Compare the ratings for television programs and movies that include sexual content between gays and/or lesbians with those that contain heterosexual sexual content.

Consider the following questions:

1. To what extent is same-sex and opposite-sex intimacy treated differently in the ratings system or by social media platforms? What kinds of same-sex

content are targeted with ratings or censorship? Is the same type of content involving heterosexual content treated similarly?

2. Thinking about the charmed circle (see Textbox 1.3), what kinds of sexual behavior is valued by society? What do the different treatments of same-sex and opposite-sex intimacy tell us about the extent to which we value or devalue non-heterosexual identities and intimacy?

3. How would you develop a ratings system or rules for sexual content on social media sites that treated same-sex and opposite-sex physical intimacy equally?

Between Women

When Darren Aronofsky's psychological thriller *Black Swan* (2010) was released, the marketing heavily promoted a short, fantasy-like love scene between the two lead actresses, Natalie Portman and Mila Kunis. The film, which focused on one ballerina's descent into madness, had an award-winning director, popular actresses, and enough rich content to draw in a range of viewers, yet the same-sex intimacy between the women was used as titillation for male viewers to draw them to what might otherwise be considered a "chick flick." Similar to lesbian-chic advertising (discussed in Chapter 4), many representations of women's same-sex intimacy are produced for the pleasure of male viewers. In fact, until quite recently, women's sexual pleasure had not received serious consideration.

Visual representations of intimacy between women builds upon film conventions that long have objectified female bodies. Film theorist Laura Mulvey (1975) developed the concept of the "male gaze" to describe the common camera perspectives used in classical Hollywood films. "Gaze" refers to a particular kind of looking, where one is given the power look, while another is presented as an object on display. Drawing from psychoanalysis, Mulvey argued that women's bodies were turned into a fetishized object, a spectacle to be gazed upon. Cameras would focus on the female form for no other reason than to allow audiences to stare at women as objects. Alternatively, women might be represented as a mystery needing investigation in order to be solved. In this case, the camera would follow the woman on the screen, often in order to uncover some deceit or trauma, a common tactic of many Hitchcock films. In either case, the male gaze had two important consequences. First, the male characters in the film were the primary actors and, thus, did the looking, while women were reduced to objects to be gazed upon. Second, through point-of-view shots that privilege what the male on the screen sees, film viewers were encouraged to identify with the male star and objectify the female star.

Mulvey's (1975) theory was criticized on a number of grounds. An important critique is of her assumption that all men and women are heterosexual and that identification and desire follow accordingly. Also important, though, is that Mulvey's theory does not account for audiences' ability to make their own meanings, identifications, and sense of what they see on the screen. As we explored in Chapters 1 and 5, meaning is never fully determined by a media text alone. Instead, meaning is negotiated by audience practices.

Regardless of these shortcomings of Mulvey's (1975) theory, she still draws attention to the ways that, in a patriarchal system, women often are objectified in the media and represented as objects of male pleasure, rather than as active agents interested in pleasure for themselves. In this vein, lesbian sexuality becomes one part of the broader cultural dynamic of the commodification and circulation of women's bodies in popular culture. As post-feminist media critics argue, today, women increasingly are compelled to put themselves on sexual display as a sign of their social success (Banet-Weiser, 2012; Gill, 2007).

Given this historical tradition of putting women's bodies on display, it is not a surprise that, in genres ranging from pornography to mainstream film and television, images of intimacy between women often are presented for the bodily pleasure of heterosexual men. An example can be found in the 2008 Katy Perry hit song and video "I Kissed a Girl." While the song lyrics tease listeners with Perry's potential pleasure in kissing a girl, the accompanying video is shot in typical video fashion, that is, through the male gaze. The video is set around a dream sequence, in which provocatively dressed Perry touches herself and teases viewers through the camera, but never kisses a girl. The sequence itself is set in a garden and features a group of women all dressed in lingerie. Through quick editing cuts, viewers are offered brief glimpses of scenes reminiscent of soft porn, including women engaged in a pillow fight, but never kissing. Both the song lyrics and video use same-sex kissing between women, not as a source of women's sexual pleasure, but ostensibly as a tease for heterosexual men (Hedahl & Besel, 2013).

A more recent example of representing sexual intimacy between women for the pleasure of men is found in the French art film *La Vie d'Adèle—Chapitre 1 & 2* (2012) (*Blue is the Warmest Color* [2013]). Based on a graphic novel, the film tells the story of Adèle (Adèle Exarchopoulos), a young, somewhat aimless high-school student who starts a relationship with college art student Emma (Léa Seydoux). The languid pacing and intensely intimate performances in the film earned a great deal of critical acclaim, including an unprecedented moment at the 2013 Cannes Film Festival, when the director and two stars were awarded with the Palme d'Or (Chang, 2013). Despite the critical acclaim, the film also received some criticism, especially for a 10-minute sex scene between the two leads. The long scene features the women completely nude, except for the prosthetics that cover their genitalia. The scene features extreme close-up shots of various body parts and frequent pans along both women's bodies, allowing viewers to gaze unabashedly at them as they perform a number of intimate sexual acts.

Although sex between women is not by its definition objectifying, this particular scene was criticized for the way it turned women's bodies and sex between them into a spectacle. Its extraordinary duration and the camera's voyeuristic perspective exceeded the narrative function of the sexual encounter in the storyline of the film. A number of commentators, especially lesbian and feminist film critics, point to the ways that the scene is not about female sexual pleasure, but instead emphasizes the pleasure of men looking. For example, Julia Maroh (2013), author of the graphic novel that served as the basis for the film, responded that the scene bore little relation to actual lesbian sex and evoked giggles rather than desire:

> The heteronormative laughed because they don't understand it and find
> the scene ridiculous. The gay and queer people laughed because it's not
> convincing at all, and found it ridiculous. And among the only people we
> didn't hear giggling were the potential guys too busy feasting their eyes on an
> incarnation of their fantasies on screen.
>
> (Jagernauth, 2013)

Similarly, a *New York Times* critic noted that the scene seemed out of place aesthetically, arguing that the "movie's carefully constructed realism is jettisoned along with bodily excesses and excretions in favor of tasteful, decorative poses" (Dargis, 2013). In fact, the actresses themselves both complained about the excessive nature of the scene (Stern, 2013).

Bisexuality, which, in mediated discourses, is most often found in female characters, also is framed through the male gaze. In particular, it often is treated as a source of titillation, a kind of difference that usually is resolved with a preference for heterosexuality. In movies like *Showgirls* (1995) and *Kissing Jessica Stein* (2001), and in TV shows like *Sex and the City* (1998–2004), women's same-sex sexuality either is treated as temporary lesbianism, which is abandoned in favor of sleeping with men, or as bisexuality, which, likewise, is treated as a side interest to the real male love interest (Kessler, 2011). In movies and TV shows, bisexuals seem to exist mainly as a form of exoticism framed for the pleasure of heterosexual audiences. Seen from the perspective of the male gaze, bisexual women's agency is further constructed as deceitful and duplicitous. Take bisexual character Kalinda Sharma (Archie Panjabi), from the CBS drama *The Good Wife* (2009–). Already rendered exotic because she is Indian, Kalinda's bisexuality is treated as a form of manipulation in the program, as she frequently uses sex to get information or favors. She generally is treated as incapable of forming any real long-term relationships. Maria San Filippo (2013) notes that bisexual women characters in television series offer a sense of mystery and erotic thrill. Bisexuals often are represented as promiscuous, because the only way to visually verify bisexual identity is by showing characters having sex with women and men.

The idea that women's sexuality might be for their own pleasure outside of reference to men rarely is allowed in media, especially mainstream media. Depictions of female intimacy that reject the male gaze typically portray sex between women as either dangerous or specifically non-erotic (Adkins, 2008; Beirne, 2008; Hidalgo, 2008). Such representations tend to frame lesbian relationships as an extension of female friendships (Adkins, 2008). For example, the successful 2010 independent film *The Kids Are Alright* tells the story of lesbian parents Jules (Julianne Moore) and Nic (Annette Benning), whose lives are upended after their children contact their sperm donor, Paul (Mark Ruffalo). From the beginning of the film, there simply is no passion between the lesbian characters. Instead, viewers see scenes of failed attempts at intimacy, including one in which the couple use gay male porn in an attempt to stimulate arousal. However, Jules finds plenty of sexual passion with Paul. Similarly, ABC Family's *The Fosters* (2013–), which mostly has been met with positive responses, has been criticized for the general lack of erotic relations between the lesbian couple. For example, a humorous review on the popular GLBTQ website Autostraddle featured a series of playfully tagged screen shots from the program's first season finale episode. A scene of the two women in bed facing each other and talking is tagged, "This is how lesbians have sex," while a shot of the pair kissing at their wedding is tagged, "They're resuscitating each other" (Vikki, 2013). The joke is that any sense of erotic desire between women is downplayed in favor of a kind of affection that seems little more than an extension of generic female bonding. The idea that women might find *sexual* satisfaction outside of sex with men or enact their sexual *agency* for their own pleasure rarely is seen in mainstream media.

Between Men

If intimacy between women is used specifically to titillate male viewers, sex between men still creates discomfort for many people. While Western countries continue to become more comfortable with gay *identity*, in the United States, gay male *intimacy* continues to remain outside of what Rubin (1984) called "the charmed circle," as discussed in Chapter 1. While monogamous, usually white, gay male couples, who keep their displays of affection private, have been increasingly included in the circle, more overt displays of intimacy, let alone sex, continue to be treated as a spectacle—that is, as unusual and potentially troubling. While displays of heterosexual affection abound in popular culture and in public, there still is a strong sense that affection between men should be kept *private*. Media targeting mainstream audiences typically do not include bodily displays of intimate affection between men, despite the ubiquity of heterosexual affection in media. For example, men and women hold hands, kiss, and touch each other in even mundane shows like HGTV's *House Hunters* (1999–), game shows like *Wheel of Fortune* (1983–), and even news reports featuring returning soldiers. In part, the erasure of gay intimacy can be traced to the work of gay activists who, in the wake of the AIDS crisis, worked to de-stigmatize gayness by disassociating it from sex and focusing on homosexuality as a cultural identity. The result has been, as a growing number of theorists argue, to erase eroticism from male homosexuality (Halperin, 2012). However, in the bigger picture, the reluctance to represent sex between men has a great deal to do with the relationship between homosexuality and masculinity.

While most representations of sex are meant to elicit some sort of bodily response, even if it is just attention or longing, many people still have a negative visceral reaction to erotic relations between men. The intensity of this reaction is tied to the ways that homosexuality is linked to hegemonic masculinity and homophobia. Representations of affection and sex between men are linked closely to constructions of masculinity and what it means to be a man. Sex between men is seen as a threat to hegemonic masculinity because one partner is considered to be in the feminine position as the partner being penetrated. In fact, it was not until 2003 that the Supreme Court finally overturned anti-sodomy laws in the United States, and, in general, anal sex is considered a taboo across cultures, even between men and women. Additionally, men's bodies are not objectified to the same extent as women's are across a range of media, further rendering our mediated experience of men's bodies as uncomfortable and strange (Coward, 1984; Dyer, 1993). This has had a tremendous impact on the representations of men and masculinity in the media. While women in the media often are represented as objects of the gaze, appearing primarily to be looked at, there has been a reluctance to present the male body *merely* as an object of display. This is partly because objectification of women historically has been linked to their passivity, whereas men's non-objectification was linked to action. As a result, media portrayals of men largely have discouraged possible erotic connections either between men in a film or television show, or between the men on the screen and male audience members. As Chapter 2 explained, for a number of years during and after World War II, gay panic served as the general cultural discourse regulating masculinity. Any hint of attraction or arousal between men was enough to threaten one's masculinity. While gay *identity* has received significant acceptance since that time, gay *sexuality* continues to be treated as deviant.

Because of cultural taboos on gay male sexuality, even simple affection that is commonplace between people of the opposite sex is treated differently when between two men (Morris & Sloop, 2006). For example, there is a long history of media treating kisses between men akin to an assault, a theme explored by the documentary *The Cel-luloid Closet* (1995). More recently, such outright prohibition has softened, but physical intimacy between men often is de-eroticized. Camera angles can serve as a key device to actually limit what viewers see when men kiss, for example, showing us the back of heads rather than lips locking (see Textbox 8.2). Kisses between men also might be treated comically, and thus stripped of any erotic potential. A *Saturday Night Live* (1975–) skit featuring guest star Andrew Garfield and his *Spider-Man* (2012) co-star and real-life girlfriend, Emma Stone, exemplify both of these approaches. In the skit, Garfield and Stone are presented as filming a scene from *Spider-Man* and are asked to kiss. After several attempts at very silly, very non-erotic kisses, Coldplay frontman, Chris Martin, enters the scene and offers to help. Martin dons a blond wig and spurns Stone in favor of Garfield, who offers exaggerated protestations when Garfield leans in for a "kiss." However, viewers actually do not see the men lock lips, because the implied kiss is obscured from view by Martin's head. These scenes use humor and the audience's secure knowledge that at least one of the kissing pair is heterosexual to downplay the idea that there can be erotic connections between men.

BOX 8.2   Is a Kiss Just a Kiss?

While representations of same-sex *affection* between men has become more com-monplace in the 2000s, same-sex *desire* rarely appears on broadcast television (i.e., ABC, CBS, CW, FOX, NBC). This is evident across a spate of recent sitcoms that have featured gay characters, including *Modern Family* (2009–) and the Ryan Murphy show, *The New Normal* (2013–2014). As Alfred Martin (2014) argues, narrative, camera angles, and shot composition often work to hide same-sex male affection. For example, while *Modern Family*, a popular U.S. sitcom, has received a great deal of praise for including a gay couple among the three intergenerational couples in the primary cast of the show, it has received less praise for is its handling of intimacy between the men. Martin discusses a Valentine's Day episode, in which the two heterosexual couples plan intimate dates, leaving the gay couple, Mitch (Jesse Tyler Ferguson) and Cam (Eric Stonestreet) to babysit and help their young nephew with his love life. While the straight couples share kisses, Mitch and Cam share only a hug.

In May 2010, fans launched a Facebook campaign asking producers to show the popular pair kissing. In the response episode, the first kiss between two men actu-ally occurs between Mitch and his father, Jay (Ed O'Neill). Martin (2014) argues that the kiss is an "OTS [over the shoulder] and is appropriately filled with the anxiety required when two men kiss on television" (p. 159). When Mitch and Cam finally kiss, it is in the background, and significantly, a kiss between Jay and his daughter is in the foreground. Martin further argues that, while *The New Normal* included more kisses between the main same-sex couple, those that occurred in the bedroom often were obscured through camera angles. He concludes,

> The inclusion of LGBT characters comes with conditions: while an argument can be made that gay relationships are treated similarly to their heterosexual counterparts in terms of storylines, when dealing with the same-sex intimate relations, the implicit heternormativity of televisual spaces becomes clear. Gay characters are allowed in these spaces, but implying sexual intimacy is not.
>
> (Martin, 2014, pp. 163–164)

For this activity, choose an episode of *Modern Family* (2009–) or any other sit-com featuring both heterosexual and GLBTQ characters. As you watch, carefully observe the ways that intimacy is represented in the program and answer the following questions:

1. How much intimacy is expressed between opposite-sex couples and same-sex couples?
2. What kinds of intimacy are expressed? Kisses, hand-holding, hugging, touching, caressing, etc.?
3. How erotic is the affection?
4. What do viewers actually see? Consider camera angles, shot composition, background/foreground, and other visual elements that may compete for viewers' attention.
5. Finally, drawing on these observations, compare and contrast the representation of intimacy between opposite-sex and same-sex couples. Are there differences? If so, what do these differences tell us about the ways we value different kinds of relationships?

If a kiss between men still can elicit a strong reaction, then media representations of sex between men continue to be sites of tremendous anxiety. There is no greater contemporary example of this anxiety than the responses to Ang Lee's film *Brokeback Mountain* (2005). The film became dubbed "the gay cowboy movie" and spawned intense public reaction, including in the form of jokes, as described in Chapter 7. Although art films, particularly the in-your-face films of New Queer Cinema described in Chapter 3, have depicted gay male sex since the late 1980s and 1990s, *Brokeback Mountain* broke new ground by bringing sodomy to the multiplex (Williams, 2008). Given the cultural frenzy surrounding the film, anyone who had not seen it might be surprised to discover how limited the representations of gay sex actually are. In fact, the film includes only one scene involving an explicit sexual encounter between the two lead characters. The scene begins with a visibly cold Ennis (Heath Ledger) entering the tent in which Jack (Jake Gyllenhaal) is sleeping. Jack takes Ennis's arm and wraps it around himself, and Ennis withdraws in fear and disgust. Jack keeps reaching for him, and eventually Ennis relents, unbuttons his pants and penetrates Jack from behind. This relatively short scene shows both men fully dressed. Viewers do, though, see Ennis spit into his hand, in a move that speaks more of gay pornography than romantic melodrama. This scene, marked by Ennis's struggle with his own desires of Jack, is more aggressive than intimate.

Although the scene is considerably chaste compared to more explicit heterosexual sex scenes common in many films, this on-screen visualization of gay sexuality resulted in a cultural reaction unparalleled by other films. Chapter 7 noted that the extent of jokes surrounding the film reflected deep-seated cultural anxieties about homosexuality. However, Rich (2007) draws attention to the reluctance of heterosexual men to actually go see the film because of their unease with seeing gay male sexuality onscreen. She describes one instance of what she terms "a new-fangled revival of the old-fashioned contagion theory":

> MSNBC contributor Dave White kept his tongue firmly in cheek with an advice column entitled: "The straight dude's guide to Brokeback." Posing as a queer-eye-for-the-straight-guy movie critic and acknowledging the discomfort that heterosexual male readers might be experiencing at the prospect of seeing the film . . . White offered reassurance. It's a Western, he advised, plus you get to see Anne Hathaway topless, there's only one minute of kissing, and so on. White even appealed to a sense of fair play: "It's your turn. Really, it is, and you know it. Imagine how many thousands of hetero love stories gay people sit through in their lives. So you kind of owe us. Now get out there and watch those cowboys make out."
>
> (p. 46).

Although meant to be taken as a joke, White's column treats visible displays of gay affection as something to be momentarily endured by straight men. It is worth noting that the original book upon which the *Brokeback Mountain* film is based devoted more time to Jack and Ennis's "outdoor idylls together" (Handley, 2011, p. 17). By contrast, the film version spent the bulk of its narrative exploring Jack and Ennis's domestic lives after they return to their respective homes and marry. This change limited the amount of on-screen intimacy between the men.

Although *Brokeback Mountain* was made more than a decade ago, anxiety over gay sex still continues to resonate, but in changing ways. As premium cable programs like *Queer as Folk* (2000–2005), *The Wire* (2002–2005), and *Six Feet Under* (2001–2005) pushed the envelope by showing more gay sex, more recent shows have come under fire for *not* pushing the envelope far enough. When HBO's half-hour series of three gay friends in San Francisco, *Looking*, premiered in 2014, bloggers called out the show for being too chaste, especially compared to other HBO series. While the show features scenes of intimacy between men, it rarely shows shots below the waist and features little nudity. The omission is noticeable when compared to other premium cable programs like HBO's *Girls* (2012–), which routinely features nude images of its star and head writer, Lena Dunham, and many graphic representations of sex.

Another way that gay male sexuality is disavowed is in interviews with straight actors playing gay roles that frequently stress how strange or difficult it must have been to be intimate with a man. Take, for example, Matt Damon's interview with *Entertainment Weekly* about his role as Liberace's young lover in the HBO film *Behind the Candelabra* (2013): "The scene where I'm behind him and going at him, we did that in one take," recalls Damon, laughing. "We do it. Cut. There's a long pause. And then you just hear Steven go, 'Well . . . I have no notes'" (*Entertainment Weeekly* Staff, 2013).

In interviews with the stars and directors, many questions focus on scenes depicting same-sex intimacy. By comparison, in films featuring heterosexual love scenes, interviewers rarely ask the stars how they felt about doing such scenes. Scenes of gay intimacy routinely become the object of intense scrutiny, including the bodily feelings of the actors involved. Male actors are compelled to dismiss any sense that the performance has impacted their own sexuality. Heterosexual stars who engage in same-sex intimacy on screen often go to great lengths, including through public declarations, interviews, appearances at awards shows, and paparazzi photographs, to assure audiences that they are, indeed, heterosexual.

▶ TRANSGENDER BODIES AS MEDIA SPECTACLE

As discussed above, despite increasing cultural acceptance of gay and lesbian identities, media depictions of same-sex intimacy and/or desire continue to reflect cultural anxieties about bodies that fall outside of the heteronormative binaries of gender, sex, and sexuality. Similarly, media treatment of transgender people often is informed by cultural anxieties about bodies that problematize those binaries. This section will explore the ways that transgender bodies have been spectacularized in ways that emphasize transgender individuals as deviant "others." As a number of theorists have argued, representations of the body play a key role in the objectification of other people. As in the example of the male gaze that you read about above, images often are involved in questions of power. Who does the looking (both the producer and viewer of the image) and how they look situate some groups as powerful and normal and other groups as objects to be inspected, used, and judged by those in power. That is to say, there are many kinds of gazes beyond the male gaze. For instance, we can consider the colonial gaze used by Western powers during the 18th and early 19th Century to portray people from Africa, Asia, and South America as exotic and unsophisticated. Prominent in mediated representations of transgender individuals is the visual examination of the body, particularly surveillance of the genitals, and the promise that attention to the body will offer some otherwise hidden "truth" about gender and sexuality.

Gay and lesbian activists largely have been successful at separating out identity from bodies and actions by upholding the boundary between public and private spaces. That is, what happens in the bedroom is nobody's business. Aside from their attraction to people of the same sex, gay bodies are indistinguishable from those of straight bodies. Yet, the very definition of "transgender" marks bodies as being different from those of cisgender people and, therefore, raises all sorts of questions, particularly for cisgender people. If individuals are transsexual, are they pre-op or post-op? In the case of transgender women, are breasts the result of falsies, hormone therapy, or breast augmentation? All of these questions focus on areas of the body generally considered private, but associated with deep-seated cultural assumptions of what it means to be a man or a woman. By the mere adoption of the identity of transgender, people find themselves under the powerful and disciplining cisgender gaze. In the process, the transgender body often is treated as a spectacle. (Textbox 8.3 describes trans actress Laverne Cox's response to deeply personal interview questions.)

BOX 8.3   Rejecting the Cisgender Gaze

When transgender model Carmen Carrera and transgender actress Laverne Cox appeared on the syndicated talk show program *Katie* in January 2014, they found themselves facing questions familiar to transgender people. Host Katie Couric steered the interview with Carrera to questions about her transition and then specifically asked about her "private parts." Carrera became visibly uncomfortable, responding,

> I don't want to talk about it. It's really personal. . . . That's been spoken about so many times, like in other interviews with trans people. They always focus on the transition or the genitalia, and I feel like there's more to trans people than just that.

When Cox joined Carrera on stage, Katie again brought up the issue, and Cox responded more fully:

I do feel there is a preoccupation with that. The preoccupation with transition and surgery objectifies trans people. And then we don't get to really deal with the real lived experiences. The reality of trans people's lives is that so often we are targets of violence. We experience discrimination disproportionately to the rest of the community. Our unemployment rate is twice the national average; if you are a trans person of color, that rate is four times the national average. The homicide rate is highest among trans women. If we focus on transition, we don't actually get to talk about those things.

The video of Cox's response to Couric went viral, and Couric received a lot of criticism for her questions and misuse of language, like using "transgenders" as a noun. As a result of the pushback, Couric invited Cox back to her program five months later for an episode devoted entirely to transgender issues. During the hour, Couric and Cox discussed the earlier "teachable moment" and talked about Cox's documentary about trans activist CeCe McDonald. They then brought on a Civil Liberties Union staff attorney and a GLAAD media strategist to focus on broader social issues affecting transgender people. During the episode, Cox argued that when people focus on transgender people's physical transition, including genitalia and surgeries, they turn them into objects, which dehumanizes them. When people are dehumanized, they are more likely to become the victims of violent crime.

How do other journalists and media personalities do when it comes to discussing transgender people? Using LexisNexis or another news archive, search for recent stories about transgender people. Also review GLAAD's reference for journalists covering transgender issues (available at http://www.glaad.org/reference/transgender), including their guidelines for reporting on transgender victims of crime (available at http://www.glaad.org/publications/transgendervictimsofcrime). Consider the following questions:

1. How do the stories describe transgender people? Do they include reference to their physical attributes?
2. Do the stories objectify or dehumanize transgender people in any way?
3. Do story topics and people involved make a difference in how transgender people are described? For instance, are transgender activists talked about differently than transgender crime victims? Does race matter? Are transgender people of color described differently than white transgender people? Do class or gender play any role?
4. Do GLAAD's guidelines address any of the issues raised by Carrera and Cox? Do the stories you found adhere to these guidelines?
5. Should GLAAD add or remove anything to their guidelines?

The Medical Gaze

Historically, medical discourses have played an important role in legitimizing trans-gender identity. Even the "tripartite conceptual framework of *somatic* [biological] sex, *social* gender role, and *psychological* gender" emerged from medical understandings of transsexual and intersex issues (Sullivan & Stryker, 2009, p. 55, emphasis in original). As discussed in Chapter 2, the medicalization of transgender identity was necessary for transsexual people seeking medical treatment and surgical procedures meant to help realign these three aspects of identity.

Early medical investigation of transgender (and intersex) bodies resulted in medi-cal images that can be interpreted as objectifying and even dehumanizing. Describing images of intersexed people commonly found in medical books between the 1930s and 1970s, Singer (2006) notes that in these nude images, the subjects' eyes are generally concealed, either by a graphic bar or hair. He suggests, "[the photographs] create anon-ymous character types and specimens of physical pathology, rather than of people with uncommon bodies" (p. 603). Singer found similar depictions of transgender bodies, noting the striking similarity of some of these images to police photographs:

> The collusion of the medical gaze with the criminological project is a residue
> of the way photography was used by police and medical professionals alike
> to establish visual evidence of physical pathology and criminal deviance. . . .
> The result encourages uncritical viewers to adopt a point of view that reduces
> the personhood of those with nonstandard bodies to a medical disorder or
> criminal character type, the "truth" of which . . . is located in the depicted
> body, rather than in the staging of the image.
>
> (p. 604)

The tradition of presenting non-gender-conforming bodies to be gazed upon by others informs contemporary media representations of transgender people.

A recent television series provides an example of how the medical gaze can render transgender bodies as objects of exploration and investigation. Discovery Channel's *Sex Change Hospital* (2007) fits within the popular medical reality genre of programs like *Trauma: Life in the E.R.* (1997), *Boston Med* (2010), and, more recently, *Sex Sent Me to the E.R.* (2013–). The "twist" of this program was that it focused on the stories of transgender men and women who were completing their transition by undergoing sex-reassignment surgeries. The series, set in the "Sex Change Capital," Trinidad, Colo-rado, features Dr. Marci Bowers, a post-op, male-to-female obstetrician/gynecologist. Each episode tells the stories of two different patients as they "struggle to become their true selves," in the words of the program's opening.

One could argue that the program goes a long way in humanizing transgender people by sharing their personal stories through moving self-narratives. All of the patients are presented as likable people who have wrestled deeply with making sense of their own identities. Surgery is presented as a final step in the process of self-realization and happiness. Although viewers get to know the personal stories of patients, a significant portion of each program is dedicated to the poking, prodding, cutting, slicing, and lying open of transgender bodies. The programs typically follow a standard formula, beginning with Dr. Bowers seeing each patient for the pre-op consultation. In this initial meeting, Dr. Bowers generally performs a physical exam, allowing viewers to see her poke and prod private areas to determine measurements of the perineum (located between the vagina or scrotum and anus) or to consider details about breast augmentation or mastectomy. Because of her identity as a doctor and a transsexual woman, Dr. Bowers is allowed to explore the transgender body for medical reasons. However, the camera often privileges Dr. Bowers' point of view, positioning viewers as voyeurs.

Each episode includes scenes of the surgeries, graphic in their visual attention to blood and body parts. The operating-room scenes can be viewed as an example of "spectacle," excessive within the broader narrative of the program and designed to evoke a visceral response from viewers. In these scenes, blood is ever present, sometimes spurting all over the doctors and nurses. The camera shows images of excess skin as it is harvested from the body and remolded into different parts. The focus on the body continues after surgery, when viewers see Dr. Bowers lifting sheets to check how

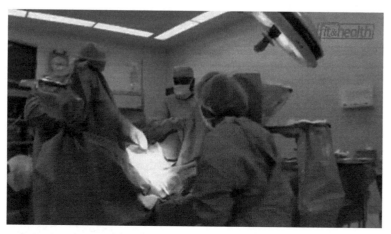

FIGURE 8.3 Dr. Marci Bowers and her medical team perform a sex-reassignment surgery
Source: Sex Change Hospital, **2007.**

the patients' bodies have healed. She often discusses the specifics of the surgery with patients and their family members, including details like the depth of a newly crafted vagina. While *Sex Change Hospital* (2007) can be credited for drawing increased attention to the struggles of transgender people, it simultaneously allows viewers to objectify transgender bodies through the medical gaze.

Monstrous Bodies

In 2008, Thomas Beatie became an international media spectacle after *The Advocate* published his personal account of being "a pregnant man." Beatie is a female-to-male (FtM) transsexual who has masculinized his appearance through hormones and a double mastectomy. When he and his then wife decided to start a family, Beatie elected to carry their child because his wife, Nancy, was unable to because of a prior hysterectomy. Beatie was by no means the first FtM transsexual to bear a child, but he was the first to put his story in the media spotlight. Quickly, Beatie's self-described status as *a* pregnant man became *the* pregnant man, and the image of his shirtless pregnant male body made headlines around the world. Soon afterwards, Beatie was discussion fodder for morning news programs to late-night comedy shows. He even appeared on *Oprah*, where the talkshow host fondled his baby bump. After the arrival of the Beaties' first daughter, ABC News' *20/20* aired a special Barbara Walters interview with Beatie and his wife.

Although the story itself became a media spectacle, it was the visual imagery of the pregnant male body that fueled the media frenzy. *The Advocate's* photograph of Beatie was beamed all over the world. The photo depicts a shirtless Beatie, with his arm raised overhead, making visible mastectomy scars on a flat chest and an enlarged pregnant belly. The image fits within what has become its own unique genre—the nude pregnancy photograph (Norwood, 2010). Such photographs first were popularized by the image of Demi Moore's nude pregnant body gracing the cover of *Vanity Fair* in 1991. Since then, the photograph of Moore and other pregnant celebrities, like Jessica Simpson, have spawned a plethora of similar ritualistic photographs of less famous mothers, all sharing the common pose with one arm covering breasts and the other cradling the pregnant belly. Beatie's image easily can be made sense of within these familiar pregnancy photographs; however, common markers of femininity are replaced by jarringly masculine markings like a square jaw and hair on his face and armpit. Instead of concealing female breasts, Beatie's raised muscular arm exposes his flat chest, complete with mastectomy scars. Not only is the image a collision of the feminine and the masculine, it has the marked signs of medical intervention.

Gender theorist J. Jack Halberstam (2005) suggests that this and other photographs of Beatie's pregnant body became a matter of public voyeurism. They allowed audiences

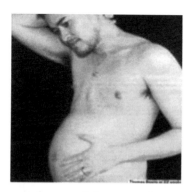

FIGURE 8.4 *Advocate* **photograph of Thomas Beatie, "The Pregnant Man"**
Source: 20/20, **2008, American Broadcasting Company.**

to stare unabashedly at the queer pregnant body and ask questions about female-to-male bodily transitions. And, ask they did. Beatie was subjected to questions about surgeries he had undergone, hormone replacement regimens, the implantation process, etc. However, what remained front and center, even after his daughter's birth, were the pregnancy photographs. In the set-up to her hour-long interview with Beatie, Barbara Walters played a short media montage that featured 12 different photographs of Beatie's pregnant body (2008). In seven of the photographs, Beatie is shirtless or is raising his shirt to expose his pregnant belly. Walters' narration frames the images: "Some see him as a freak of nature. . . Someone to be found in a carnival." As evidence of this, a phone message left at the Beatie home is played: "You're not even a man. You're an *it*!" If viewers themselves do not read the photographs as problematic, Walters insists upon this frame for making sense of Beatie's queer pregnant body. Referencing *The Advocate* photograph, Walters attempts to make Beatie acknowledge the monstrosity of his body. She insists, "It *is* a disturbing picture, Thomas!"

The case of "the pregnant man" uncovers cultural anxieties about a host of issues, including gender roles, changing family structures, body modification, and reproductive technologies. However, it was the visual discontinuity of Beatie's body that caused the strongest responses. Singer (2011) suggests that such deep-seated visceral revulsion to Beatie's pregnant body is a risk when people encounter bodies that so fundamentally disrupt binary understandings of sex and gender upon which their own identities are built. Singer writes,

> In this way, the boundary between self and other is rendered solid through the negative defensive affect of disgust. And the sight and the idea of a

pregnant (trans) man seems to necessitate a strong disidentification that simultaneously de-genders and dehumanizes Beatie as a freak. . . . And this affect-driven dynamic functions to clearly defend the boundary separating the "me" from the "not me."

(p. 155)

In this disidentification process, cisgender viewers are able to reinforce for themselves the "normalcy" of their own sex-gender identities by defining Beatie as "abnormal," with a clear line of demarcation between the two. While media depictions of bodies that disrupt cultural assumptions about heteronormalcy often pathologize them in ways that uphold dominant understandings of gender, sex, and sexuality, we also can imagine how such representations may pose a challenge to heteronormativity.

▶ BODIES OF DISRUPTION AND TRANSFORMATION

This chapter has explored the ways that media work to contain bodies whose desires and gender identity do not conform to our dominant norms of gender and sexuality. A key device of containment has been deploying the gaze as a source of power that turns non-normative bodies into spectacles for display. From displays of same-sex intimacy between women for the pleasure of men, the attempt to *not* see intimacy between men, to the objectification of the transgender body as either a medical mystery to be solved or a monstrous creature to be gawked at, mediated images of bodies often run counter to the discourses of identity-based rights for GLBT people. Gay desire and non-normative bodies have tremendous power to disrupt norms of gender and sexuality. As we introduced earlier, when thinking about bodies, we also need to consider the bodies of spectators. Images, especially ones manipulated into spectacles, can produce intense emotional responses in viewers. By disrupting our normative ideas of sexual desires and gender identity, GLBTQ bodies have the power to emotionally impact us and, through those impacts, transform our own relationship to dominant norms.

Disrupting Desire

Anxieties over representations of same-sex intimacies often are based on the possibility of stimulating same-sex desires in audiences. Anxiety that women might desire same-sex intimacies is based on the fear that they might withdraw from the patriarchal system. Anxieties over male same-sex desire is based on the challenges that desire poses to hegemonic masculinities. However, despite attempts to control images of same-sex intimacy, audiences still react in unexpected ways. For example, the attempt to de-eroticize relationships between lesbians on the screen does not mean that women will not identify with love and affection between women. As Susan Driver (2007) demonstrated, teenage girl viewers of *Buffy the Vampire Slayer* (1997–2003) found extreme pleasure in the tender, rather than erotic, on-screen relationship between lesbian characters Willow (Alyson Hannigan) and Tara (Amber Benson). While scholars took issue with the ways the relationship between the couple was stripped of any hint of erotic connection, including using witchcraft as a metaphor for sex, queer-identified girls took pleasure in what they saw as the genuine emotional connection between the characters that spoke to their desires to find love. In another case, scholars and activists found great fault with the film *Basic Instinct* (1992) for portraying the stereotype of a cunning, manipulative, murderous bisexual. However, a number of studies demonstrated that women, no matter their stated sexual identity, were drawn to the female protagonist's powerful personal autonomy. Research suggested that, more than wanting to be like her, they actually sexually desired her (San Filippo, 2013).

Media producers also can work to specifically resist the gaze and present images of same-sex intimacy that resist the objectification of spectacle and focus on the pleasures of same-sex desires for audiences. For example, M. Catherine Jonet and Laura Anh Williams (2008) argue that the popular Showtime series *The L Word* (2004–2009), although often criticized for objectifying lesbians for male pleasure, actually worked consistently throughout the series to *disrupt* the male gaze. For example, for the young Jenny, witnessing lesbian sex as a voyeur encourages her to explore her own sexual needs, which lead her to leave her heterosexual relationship for a lesbian one. In a season-long story arc, two of the lesbian characters become roommates with a straight man, who secretly begins filming them. When the two women find out, he ends up thrown out of the apartment and left crushed by his betrayal of their friendship.

The genre with the greatest ability to disrupt and transform desire may be pornography. Attwood (2007) writes that not only does pornography offer a space where there are far more representations of gay men than any other form of media, but, also, the desires of gay men are openly explored and validated. Lesbian porn, unlike the porn aimed at straight men, "gains part of its appeal from its evocation of strong images of lesbian community and politics, while queer pornographies often work to subvert and challenge power dynamics, opening up a world of play where 'everything is possible'" (p. 461). The Internet also has expanded the possibilities for displaying many different kinds of desires and intimacies between many different kinds of bodies. The expanding repertoire of the desiring bodies we see on screens may transform our own bodily experiences of desire.

Disrupting Gender

The transgender body, as explored in this chapter, has been turned into a spectacle in the media. The dominant way of framing our understanding of transgender identities is through a focus on the body. While mainstream media objectify transgender bodies as a way of controlling their potential threat to our notions of gender, queer theorists see the spectacle of transgender bodies as potentially liberatory in the way that they disrupt the clear alignment between gender-sex-sexuality and understandings of these categories in naturalized binary terms. The potential for liberation was explored in Judith Butler's (1990) consideration of the ways that drag queens highlight the performative quality of gender. If men can adorn themselves in the ostensibly natural trappings of femininity, then essentialist notions of gender located in the body become destabilized and ideally disrupted. While she later responded to criticisms that her work was overly utopic (see Butler, 1993), she nonetheless was significant for pointing to gender *as* performative rather than *as* natural (see Textbox 8.4).

BOX 8.4   Half Drag

A 36-portrait series by photographer Leland Bobbé intentionally plays on the visual spectacle of drag queens to challenge socially constructed ideas of gender (and sexuality). A slideshow of many of the photographs, titled "Half Drag," went viral in August 2012 after an article in the *Huffington Post* drew attention to the project (Burra). The photographs also have been featured on ABC News, MSN, Sundance Channel, and in *Vogue Italia*. The images are close-up photographs of New York City drag queens, with only half of their faces made up in drag. Although the images look as if they must be two faces Photoshopped together, they are not. Bobbé captured each person literally in "half drag." The visual differences in the two halves of each face are remarkable. The feminine personas have flawless skin, heavy makeup, exaggeratedly long, decorated fingernails, and elaborate jewelry. By comparison, the masculine personas are seemingly "natural," with no adornments, excepting facial stubble and a few simple earrings.

Bobbé describes his photographs as exploring the fluidity of gender:

> With these images my intention is to capture both the male and the alter ego female side of these subjects in one image in order to explore the cross over between males

FIGURE 8.5 Leland Bobbé's photograph of model Azraea in his "Half Drag" series
Source: **Reprinted by permission of photographer.**

and females and to break down the physical barriers that separate them. This in turn questions the normative ideas about gender and gender fluidity.

(Cade, 2013).

These descriptions of "Half Drag" herald it as achieving gender theorist Judith Butler's hopeful potential of drag, described in this chapter. Bobbé's portrait series provides an opportunity to explore both the liberatory and constraining potential of the spectacle of "Half Drag." If you have not already done so, view Bobbé's photographs online and consider the following questions:

1. How do the photographs present masculinity as "natural," and femininity as "constructed?" How might you reverse this assumption and look for the "naturalness" of the feminine and "constructedness" of the masculine?

2. Bobbé emphasizes that images were captured in the camera without post-production splicing together of images. Would you think about the

(Continued)

images differently if he had taken two pictures (one in drag, one not) and then edited them together?

3. Read comment sections on articles about Bobbé's photographs. What do they indicate about the way viewers of these photographs understand gender?

4. How do reactions to Bobbé's photographs compare to reactions of photographs of pregnant transgender man Thomas Beatie?

5. Compare the portraits with Bobbé's nude photographs of drag queen Dr. Flux in his half-woman, half-man persona, taken earlier as part of a photo series of neo-burlesque performers. Does the inclusion of the rest of the body [including the presumption of genitals] make the photographs more or less transgressive?

Transgender bodies can be read as disrupting naturalized binaries and bodily alignments in a way very similar to drag. Whereas drag plays with the gap between the gendered body and its gender display, transgender identities question the very concept of a uniformly gendered body. The bodies of transgender individuals "can confound conventional expectations . . . [they] have unexpected configurations in their particular *geographies*—for example, breasts with penises for some, male chests with vaginas in others—that produces a dissonance" (Currah, 2008, quoted in Norwood, 2013, p. 68, emphasis in original). Viewers might find their security in the link between their bodies and genders less obvious and begin to question the very idea of a gender binary and, ultimately, other heteronormative logics.

▶ CONCLUSION

Bodies might seem like a strange category through which to examine the relationship between sexual identities and the media. Yet, as stressed throughout this chapter, our focus on *identities* often overlooks questions of desire and gendered embodiment. Bodies cut to the very heart of heteronormativity, by acknowledging that what we think of as identity groups are still tied to strong cultural and social reactions against sexual and gender nonconformity. At the same time, media are all about bodies, from the bodies we see on the screens to the impact our viewing practices have on our bodies. Many of us do not passively engage with media, but we *feel* things in response to what we see on our screens. In this chapter, we paid primary attention to mostly visual aspects of the media, with a special focus on the gaze as a mode of looking informed by power, and spectacle, as a mode of representation based on the excessive manipulation of image in order to create intense bodily reactions by viewers. What we stressed throughout is that both the way images are presented on the screen and our reactions to them are strongly shaped by heteronormativity.

We argued that same-sex intimacy looked quite different in the media depending on whether the intimacy was between men or women. Intimacy between women was framed through the male gaze, the same lens that filters representations of women in general. Women's same-sex intimacy was presented as for the pleasure of men, and if it was not, it was simply treated as incapable of providing sexual pleasure at all. Representing intimacy between men is more problematic as the strong link between hegemonic masculinity and the rejection of same-sex desire creates a great deal of cultural anxiety about seeing intimacy between men. From camera angles, to the relative chasteness of representations of sexual encounters between men in main-stream media, to the strong denial of male actors that playing gay roles threatened their own normative desires, intimacy between men is still strongly constrained by heteronormativity.

We further considered the ways that transgender identity, unlike sexual identity, con-tinues to be strongly linked to the body. On the one hand, we examined the ways that a medical gaze is used to ascertain the truth of an individual's gender identity through the body. We further considered the ways that the image of the pregnant man proved so disruptive to our normative ideas of gender that he could only be presented as mon-strous. The potential disruption of transgender bodies was contained through these media texts. But we ended the chapter with a consideration of how these same bodies disrupt and transform normative ideas of sexual and gender identities. By disrupting the visual field, provoking embodied emotional reactions, and asserting the right to express one's sexual and gender identity, bodies also possess the power to transform how we understand and experience them.

▶ REFERENCES

Adkins, T. (2008). A label like Gucci, Versace, or Birkenstock: *Sex and the City* and queer identity. In R. Beirne (Ed.), *Televising queer women: A reader* (pp. 109–120). New York, NY: Palgrave Macmillan.

Attwood, F. (2007). No money shot?: Commerce, pornography and new sex taste cultures. *Sexualities, 10*(4), 441–456.

Banet-Weiser, S. (2012). *Authentic™: The politics of ambivalence in a brand culture.* New York, NY: New York University Press.

Beatie, T. (2008, March 14). Labor of love: Is society ready for this pregnant husband? advocate.com. Retrieved from http://www.advocate.com/news/2008/03/14/labor-love?page=full.

Beirne, R. (2008). Mapping lesbian sexuality on *Queer as Folk*. In *Televising queer women: A reader* (pp. 99–108). New York, NY: Palgrave Macmillan.

Boran, M. (Writer), & Wass, T. (Director). (2010, September 28). Dancing with the stars of Toledo [Television series episode]. In B. Young & D. Kendall (Producers), *Melissa & Joey*. Hollywood, CA: Heartbreak Films.

Burra, K. (2012, August 7). LOOK: Mesmerizing photos simultaneously two sides of drag queens. *Hufftington Post*. Retrieved from http://www.huffingtonpost.com/2012/08/07/leland-bobbes-half-drag-makeup-photos_n_1749018.html.

Butler, J. (1990). *Gender trouble: Feminism and the subversion of identity*. New York, NY: Routledge.

Butler, J. (1993). *Bodies that matter: On the discursive limits of sex*. New York, NY: Psychology Press.

Cade, D.L. (2013, October 13). Half-drag portraits show the before & after transformations of NYC drag queens. *PetaPixel*. Retrieved from http://petapixel.com/2013/10/12/half-drag-photos-show-transformations-nyc-drag-queens.

Chang, J. (2013, May 26). CANNES: 'Blue Is the Warmest Color' wins Palme d'Or. *Variety.com*. Retrieved from http://variety.com/2013/film/news/cannes-blue-is-the-warmest-color-wins-palme-d-or-1200488202.

Coward, R. (1984). Men's bodies. In R. Coward (Ed.), *Female desire: Women's sexuality today* (pp. 226–231). London: Paladin.

Dargis, M. (2013, October 5). Seeing you see me: The trouble with "Blue is the warmest color." *New York Times*. Retrieved from http://www.nytimes.com/2013/10/27/movies/the-trouble-with-blue-is-the-warmest-color.html?pagewanted=all.

Driver, S. (2007). *Queer girls and popular culture: Reading, resisting and creating media*. New York, NY: Peter Lang.

Dyer, R. (1993). *The matter of images: Essays on representation*. New York, NY: Routledge.

Entertainment Weekly Staff. (2013, March 6). This week's cover: Matt Damon and Michael Douglas "Behind the Candelabra" in HBO's Liberace biopic. *Entertainment Weekly*. Retrieved from http://popwatch.ew.com/2013/03/06/this-weeks-cover-matt-damon-michael-douglas-liberace.

Freud, S. (1947/1905). *Three essays on the theory of sexuality*. New York, NY: Basic Books.

Gill, R. (2007). *Gender and the media*. Cambridge, UK: Polity.

Halberstam, J.J. (2005). *In a queer time and place: Transgender bodies subcultural lives*. New York, NY: New York University Press.

Halperin, D.M. (2012). *How to be gay*. Cambridge, MA: Belknap Press.

Handley, W.R. (2011). *The Brokeback book: From story to cultural phenomenon*. Lincoln, NE: University of Nebraska Press.

Hedahl, B. & Besel, R.D. (2013). The rhetoric of sexual experimentation: A critical examination of Katy Perry's "I Kissed a Girl." In T. Carilli & J. Campbell (Eds.), *Queer media images: LGBT perspectives* (pp. 77–87). Lanham, MD: Lexington Books.

Hidalgo, M. (2008). Going native on wonder woman's island: The exoticization of lesbian sexuality in *Sex and the City*. In R. Beirne (Ed.), *Televising queer women: A reader* (pp. 121–134). New York, NY: Palgrave Macmillan.

Jagernauth, K. (2013, May 28). "Blue is the warmest color" author Julie Maroh not pleased with graphic sex in film, calls it porn. *Indiewire*. Retrieved from http://blogs.indiewire.com/the-playlist/blue-is-the-warmest-color-author-julie-maroh-not-pleased-with-graphic-sex-in-film-20130528.

Jonet, M.C. & Williams, L.A. (2008). Reconfigurations of *The L Word*. In R. Beirne (Ed.), *Televising queer women: A reader* (pp. 105–118). New York, NY: Palgrave Macmillan.

Kellner, D. (2003). *Media spectacle*. New York, NY: Psychology Press.

Kessler, K. (2011). Temporarily kissing Jessica Stein: Negotiating (and negating) lesbian sexuality in popular film. In H. Radner & R. Stringer (Eds.), *Feminism at the movies* (pp. 215–226). New York, NY: Routledge.

Krzywinska, T. (2005). Real sex in contemporary art cinema. In G. King (Ed.), *The spectacle of the real: From Hollywood to "reality" TV and beyond* (pp. 223–232). Bristol, UK: Intellect Books.

Lacan, J. (1978/1973). *The four fundamental concepts of psychoanalysis*. Paris, France: Editions du Seuil.

Manders, H. (2013, July 22). Yahoo censors Tumblr's gay and lesbian tags—#why? *Refinery29*. Retrieved from http://www.refinery29.com/2013/07/50340/tumblr-yahoo-blocking-lgbt-tags.

Maroh, J. (2013). *Blue is the warmest color*. Vancouver, BC: Arsenal Pulp Press; MTI Edition.

Martin Jr., A.L. (2014). It's (not) in his kiss: Gay kisses and camera angles in contemporary US network television comedy. *Popular Communication, 12*, 153–165.

Morris, C.E. & Sloop, J.M. (2006). What lips these lips have kissed: Refiguring the politics of queer public kissing. *Communication and Critical/Cultural Studies, 3*(1), 1–26.

Mulvey, L. (1975). Visual pleasure and narrative cinema. *Screen, 16*(3), 6–18.

Norwood, K. (2013). A pregnant pause, a transgender look: Thomas Beatie in the maternity pose. In J. Campbell & T. Carilli (Eds.), *Queer media images* (pp. 65–75). Lanham, MD: Lexington Books.

Plummer, K. (2003). The sexual spectacle: Making a public culture of sexual problems. In G. Ritzer (Ed.), *The book of international social problems* (pp. 521–541). New York, NY: Sage.

Rich, R.B. (2007). Brokering Brokeback: Jokes, backlashes, and other anxieties. *Film Quarterly, 60*(3), 44–48.

Rubin, G. (1984). Thinking sex: Notes for a radical theory of the politics of sexuality. In C.A. Vance (Ed.), *Pleasure and danger: Exploring female sexuality* (pp. 267–293). New York, NY: Routledge & K. Paul.

San Filippo, M. (2013). *The b word: Bisexuality in contemporary film and television*. Bloomington, IN: Indiana University Press.

Savitz, J. (2014, May 2). These are the lesbian photos that got me banned from Facebook: Dear Mark Zuckerberg, why the double standard? *Xojane*. Retrieved from http://www.xojane.com/issues/jodi-savitz-girl-on-girl-facebook-lesbian-censorship.

Singer, T.B. (2006). From the medical gaze to sublime mutations: The ethics of (re)viewing non-normative body images. In S. Stryker & S. Whittle (Eds.), *The transgender studies reader* (pp. 601–620). New York, NY: Routledge.

Singer, T.B. (2011). *Towards a transgender sublime: The politics of excess in trans-specific cultural production*. Unpublished doctoral dissertation, Rutgers, New Brunswick, NJ.

Stern, M. (2013, September 1). The stars of "Blue is the warmest color" on the riveting lesbian love story. *The Daily Beast*. Retrieved from http://www.thedailybeast.com/articles/2013/09/01/the-stars-of-blue-is-the-warmest-color-on-the-riveting-lesbian-love-story-and-graphic-sex-scenes.html.

Sullivan, N. & Stryker, S. (2009). Kings member, queen's body: Transsexual surgery, self-demand amputation, and the somatechnics of sovereign power. In S. Murray & M. Sullivan (Eds.), *Somatechnics: Queering technologisation of bodies* (pp. 49–64). Farnham, UK: Ashgate Publishing Ltd.

Vikki. (2013, August 8). The fosters episode 110 recap: The one with the lesbian wedding. *Autostraddle*. Retrieved from http://www.autostraddle.com/the-fosters-episode-110- recap-the-one-with-the-lesbian-wedding-188750.

Walters, B. (2008, November 18). Journey of a pregnant man. *20/20 Exclusive*. Retrieved from http://abcnews.go.com/2020/video?id=6259840.

Williams, L. (1991). Film bodies: Gender, genre and excess. *Film quarterly, 44*(4), 2–13.

Williams, L. (2008). *Screening sex*. Durham, NC: Duke University Press.

Conclusion

At the end of Chapter 1, we posed a series of questions to guide your thinking:

1. What central assumptions about sexual identity are made available and/or advanced by/through a particular set of media practices?

2. What role might these media practices play in our understandings of our own and others' sexualities?

3. What theoretical perspectives and central assumptions about media and sexual identities are informing the writings of the academics and popular press writers that you read?

As you reach the end of this book, these questions probably make a great deal more sense. They point us away from settling for easy answers by asking us to consider that the relationship between sexual identities and the media cannot easily be explained. From the beginning we have stressed that neither sexual identities nor media are stable objects of study. The makeup of human sexuality is complex, fluid, and historically variable. The idea that our identities are linked to our sex lives is a fairly recent belief in human history. It is a mistake to think of them as "progressing" toward a fixed end point of liberated equality.

Media are, likewise, complex. The encoded meanings and the work of readers to decode messages are socially and culturally situated practices that belie the idea that you can find *the* meaning of any single practice or text. Contemporary media are so diffuse, varied, and spread across different mediums, that even getting a handle on the variety of practices and texts grows increasingly difficult. To make matters even more confusing, there are a number of methodological and theoretical approaches to studying the relationship between media and identity, including the social scientific and critical cultural approaches. One further complexity revolves around the reasons people evaluate media at all. We have considered the tensions between the assimilationist and queer theoretical approaches that greatly shape the conclusions people come to regarding the goals of visibility. In addition, we can consider the ways that people *use* media to negotiate, make sense of, and construct their sexual identities.

After introducing you to these complexities in Chapters 1 through 3, we considered how they played out in five different ways: the relationship between consumer culture and GLBTQ identity; GLBTQ production and reading practices that have resisted the social stigma pervasive in media for many years; the closet as a central and enduring narrative frame for making sense of GLBTQ experience; comedy as a central frame for making sense of GLBTQ media images, but also for understanding the ways that forms of humor developed in the face of homophobia have become mainstream; and finally, the ways that the body, as both the site of desires and gender identity remains a space in which fundamental cultural attitudes are often laid bare. As you finish this book, we encourage you to use the set of questions we introduced from the start and the material in this book to make sense of four emerging questions regarding the relationship between sexual identities and the media.

▶ EMERGING QUESTIONS

We end this book with a discussion of four intertwined emerging questions in the study of sexual identities and the media. These questions emerge out of the changes of the past two decades, as both GLBTQ political rights issues and media visibility become increasingly ubiquitous. The first is the assertion that we have reached a post-gay moment, a corollary to the ideas that we are a post-feminist and post-racist society. The second involves the very recent spike in transgender visibility and whether trans rights represent the next frontier in the GLBTQ rights movement. The third asks whether labels are necessary at all. Finally, more recently scholars have begun to ask questions about the relationship between *heterosexuality* identities and the media.

Post-Gay

In April of 2014 MTV premiered a show with a premise that would have been impossible perhaps even five years previously, *Faking It*. High-school students Karma and Amy decide to fake being lesbians in order to gain social capital at their ultra liberal Austin, Texas, high school. A show about two girls *pretending* to be gay to become more *popular*? Almost 20 years ago, Ellen DeGeneres's real life and fictional coming out came with a flurry of media attention and eventual cancellation of her sitcom. Are we are in an era when gayness becomes a tactic to gain attention in the series, and to gain media attention *for* the series? Is this the sign that we have finally entered a post-gay world, one where gayness simply does not matter anymore or is no longer a central part of people's identities?

The emerging post-gay rights discourse is based on the idea that gay rights have been achieved, rendering the need for a politics of recognition and inclusion unnecessary. Because of this, GLBTQ individuals' sexuality need no longer be the defining factor in their own senses of self. For example, many movies and television shows today focus on gay and lesbian characters whose sexuality is never an issue, thus reinforcing the idea that parity exists and supporting those who argue that the fight for civil rights is a fight for special rights. The use of the term "post-gay" draws from the concepts of post-feminism and post-racism, introduced in Chapter 7. Post-feminist discourses in popular culture are ones in which feminism is acknowledged, but also considered unnecessary because women have achieved equal rights. This allows for the representation of sexist ideas under the guise of irony. Similar to "hipster racism," those in a position of privilege feel that because they understand the discourses about racism, sexism, or homophobia, they are free to make jokes, claiming that they were not serious.

After reading this book, you might consider exactly how successful the gay and lesbian rights movement has been in securing equality. After all, this book has pointed out that there are a few clear patterns in the range of representations of GLBTQ life available in the mainstream media. First, white gay men are at the forefront of gains in visibility. As desired consumers, and as those most likely to find employment at the center of media production, they are the group most likely to find images of themselves. Second, lesbians are less visible than their male counterparts. Bisexuals and transgender men and women are still hardly visible at all, never mind anyone who does not in some way conform to normative ideas about gender and sexuality. Third, by and large the faces of GLBTQ images remain largely white. If we assert that we have reached the post-gay moment, we no longer pay heed to the very narrow view of gay and lesbian identity that has taken hold in public discourse. Across the chapters, from web series, documenting bear life, modes of representing same-sex intimacy, to the objectification of the transgender body, we have asked you to question just how limited media visibility is.

BOX 9.1   Post-Closet Hollywood?

FIGURE 9.1 Dustin Lance Black on the cover of *The Advocate* (June/July 2009)

In late 2013, we had the opportunity to interview Academy Award-winning screen writer, Dustin Lance Black (personal communication, December 5, 2013). Black won the award for his 2008 film *Milk*, which told the story of San Francisco city councilman Harvey Milk, one of the first openly gay elected public officials, assassinated in 1978. Discussing his experience making the film, Black notes that he had a difficult time getting any funding for the project and did the research and script-writing with his own money. It was only after he got Gus Van Sant to sign on as director that Hollywood became interested in the project. The box office success of *Milk* and other films about gay life, such as *Brokeback Mountain*, have led to a significant shift in Hollywood's attitudes. Black reports that in 2013 he was actually *approached* by ABC about writing for a miniseries documenting the rise of the gay and lesbian movement in the United States:

> so that's a huge shift to me from having to write an LGBT themed film on spec [with his own funds] and sort of taking a chance on the credit card and really begging and pleading to having the networks actually come to me and say, "Hey, it's become clear there is a market for this. There is incredible, an incredible amount of interest around this subject and we want you to provide content that fulfills that desired need." So, it's a huge shift.

Despite this progress, Black is quick to point out that Hollywood still has a way to go. A particularly important stumbling block in his experience has actually been talent agents. Everyone involved with *Milk* wanted to hire GLBTQ-identified actors, but when they went to talent agents asking for a list of their gay and lesbian actors they were met with silence. Black considers that agents invest a lot into young actors, wanting to turn them into stars:

> They don't want to stack the deck against themselves, so already they're likely filtering out what they consider a liability, which is a gay and lesbian actor, so they're already doing a filtering process. . . . If a client, an actor, does say that he or she wants to come out, the resistance to doing that is coming from the manager or agent. They have invested their time, and energy and money and they don't want to see anything potentially get in the way of recuperating that. . . . Ideally what they want is an A-list star who can green light a picture, meaning by attaching their name alone the studio will green light the film, and they don't want to let anything get in the way of that because that's where the big bucks are. . . . I have found that it's these guys, these managers and agents who are keeping the closet door shut in Hollywood.

As Black points out, currently there are not *openly* gay or lesbian stars who can green-light a film.

There can be no doubt that mainstream media produce more images of gays and lesbians, and even bisexuals and transgender individuals than in the past, but the process is still uneven. While Black sees that younger stars want to be open about their sexuality, they find themselves negotiating a system in which the logic of the closet continues to reign.

Transgender "Tipping Point"?

Transgender activist and actress Laverne Cox made waves in the early summer of 2014. She appeared on the cover of *Time* accompanied by the text, "The Transgender Tipping Point" (Steinmetz & Gray, 2014), and gained increasing public attention for her work in the popular Netflix series about a women's prison, *Orange is the New Black* (2013–). As one of the first transgender characters played by a transgender actress, Cox gained critical attention for the program's honest and sympathetic struggles faced by her character, Sophia Burset. One episode explored Burset's life before transitioning into a woman by using Cox's twin brother to portray the early years of her process. Cox's success in the

FIGURE 9.2 Laverne Cox on the cover of *Time* (June 9, 2014)

role was awarded in June 2014 with an Emmy nomination as Best Supporting Actress in a Comedy Series.

Clearly related to post-gay discourses, a more recent discourse is that the time has arrived for the fight for transgender visibility and rights. Drawing on the growing public belief that gays and lesbians have achieved equal participation in social institutions, many argue that the time has come for the organizations that have fought for such inclusion and media visibility to turn their attention to transgender rights. In this way, transgender rights are linked to a progress narrative. As Cox tells *Time*:

> We are in a place now where more and more trans people want to come
> forward and say, "This is who I am." And more trans people are willing to
> tell their stories. More of us are living visible, so people can say, "Oh yea,
> I know someone who is trans." When people have points of reference that are
> humanizing, that demystifies difference.
>
> (Steinmetz & Gray, 2014, p. 40)

You might recognize this as very similar to early calls for gay and lesbian social and media visibility. However, after reading this book, you might also now be aware of the potential pitfalls of visibility. As much as visibility can bring progress, it also just as easily can narrow our definitions of what it means to be trans. If middle-class, white gay men, committed to the values of hetero- and homonormativity, have become the dominant face of gay and lesbian visibility, who will emerge as the face of transgender visibility? In what ways will transgender visibility intersect with cultural discourses surrounding race, class, and even gender? In what ways might media visibility obscure, as well as make visible, the experiences of transgender individuals and communities?

Labels

In early 2014, after facing criticism for providing only two labels for gender identity, male or female, Facebook announced that it now would offer 56 setting options for gender identity, including: gender fluid, female to male, genderqueer, pangender, transgender man, transgender, male, and even two spirit. If those settings were not adequate, Facebook added a further option for customization (Weber, 2014). In June of 2014, Pride Toronto, a Canadian GLBTQ advocacy group, hosted the one-day International Sexuality Conference, explaining,

> with a growing community over the last 10–15 years, discussions of asexuality have provided fertile ground for developing new concepts and language related to sexual and gender diversity, many of which overlap and intersect with discussions taking place in the wider LGBTTIQQ2SA community.

Even the long list here indicates the growing number of labels that fit under the larger umbrella of sexual identity. The 2014 USA series *Sirens*, in addition to featuring one of the few African-American gay characters on television, also featured a supporting character, a woman, who identified as asexual.

The proliferation of labels seems to beg a number of questions. At what point does this system of labeling get overloaded? At what points do such labels begin to lose any sense of coherence? Do these labels clarify or further confuse people's sense of their own sexual and gendered identities? Does the proliferation of labels expand or close down ways of imaging ourselves—i.e., does it reinforce that we need labels at all? How can we use categories like visibility to make sense of the relationship between these sexual and gender identities and the media? At what point might advocacy for visibility for ever more finely defined groups end up overwhelming even the most well intentioned media producers? Will the collapse of labels come because we have reached equality and the expansion of existing social institutions to include new sexual and gender identities? Or will the collapse come only after existing social institutions have changed, and rather than asking different groups to adapt to the values of heteronormativity, more expansive understandings of identity will emerge?

Heterosexuality

Disney's *Frozen* (2013), in addition to frustrating the parent of every young child in the United States determined to sing "Let It Go" over and over again, was heralded as a new kind of Disney story. Rather than retelling the typical girl yearning for her prince story, it ultimately focused on the love between two sisters, one forced into isolation for fear of her "power" to turn everything into ice. In Chapter 6, we discussed how the film has been read as telling a story of gay acceptance, as the story of Elsa and her secret certainly mirrors the coming-out narrative. Yet, the movie does more than this. It decenters the heterosexual love plot so central to Disney films. In this film it is not the romantic love between a man and woman that saves the day, but the love between sisters Elsa and Anna.

Just as the feminist and civil rights movements influenced the way we think about gender and race, it is impossible to think that the GLBTQ rights movements would not have an effect on our understanding of heterosexuality. As scholars and students focus attention on representations of dominant groups in the media through whiteness and masculinity studies, they also study the construction of heterosexuality in the media. The intertwined relationship of homo- and heterosexuality, where each category requires the other to make any sense at all, necessitates that change in one will bring change in the other. We see these changes emerge in both popular culture and in the growing scholarly interest in heterosexuality not as a given, but as a historically constructed identity. Indeed, when we talk about sexual identity, our first instinct is to talk about GLBTQ identities. We rarely think of heterosexuality *as* an identity. In this way, the category of heterosexuality has become ideologically naturalized to the extent that the powerful social forces that contribute to its definition have become all but invisible to most people (see Textbox 9.2).

BOX 9.2   Heterosexual Identities and the Media

One only has to look across the media landscape to think of the incredible number of narratives aimed at reinforcing heterosexuality. In *The Bachelor* (2002–) and *Bachelorette* (2003–), to *Millionaire Matchmaker* (2008–), wedding-oriented programs, romantic comedies, and sitcom stories about heterosexual coupling abound in the media. In fact, the very same questions we asked about GLBTQ identities and the media can be asked about media and heterosexuality. While the "Hetero-sexual Questionnaire" introduced in Chapter 1 focused on questions of individual sexual identity, the questions below are aimed at thinking about the relationship between media and heterosexuality, where heterosexuality is not taken as a given, somehow existing outside of media, but as a historically variable, culturally defined sexual identity.

1. What role do advertisers play in shaping our views of heterosexuality?
2. What role do the media industries at the center and periphery play in telling different stories of heterosexuality?
3. What heterosexual practices are more likely to be found in the center or margins?
4. What role does comedy play in either challenging or reinforcing a particular definition of heterosexuality?
5. What kinds of heterosexual behaviors are considered deviant and must be "hidden" in a closet?
6. How is heterosexual intimacy represented in the media?
7. What are the differences between the ways that male and female cisgender heterosexuals are represented in the media?
8. How does race, class, gender, and ethnicity shape the way we see hetero-sexuality?
9. How are the bodies of cisgender individuals represented in the media?
10. What forms of resistance have some heterosexuals developed against domi-nant ideas about heterosexuality?

There is, of course, the ideal face of heterosexuality. White, middle-class, monoga-mously coupled, cohabiting with a romantic partner (preferably married, but no longer necessary), and either raising or planning to raise children. This is reiterated as the norm across a range of media, from reality shows and Disney films to romantic com-edies, even though recent census data indicate an increasingly smaller group of people organize their lives this way. As we look across the media, we can see that, as much as homosexuality as a category used to be considered non-normative, today it is clear that, as discussed throughout, gays and lesbians who mirror the dominant view of het-erosexuality are, in Rubin's terms, allowed into the "charmed circle." We also see that a number of practices related to sexual identities of *anyone*, including heterosexuals, can be seen as non-normative. Thinking of heterosexuality as one among many sexual iden-tities allows us to no longer take heterosexuality as a given, but requires us to examine the ways that media work to reinforce and challenge its logics.

▶ MEDIA MATTERS

As you reach the end of this book, we ask you to reflect on what you have learned about the relationship between sexual identities and the media. No doubt you and your fellow students came to this book with very different ideas about sexual identities and about the media. Some of you probably were hoping for easy answers as to what is right and wrong in representation, and some of you might have been worried that media you enjoyed would be called into question. Others might have wondered why media mattered at all. Hopefully, you have learned new ways to think about both sexual identities and media. One thing we have stressed continually throughout this book is that there is no single way to evaluate a relationship as complex as that between sexual identities and the media. How you see the relationship depends a great deal on what you see as the goals of visibility.

On the one hand, we have explored the assimilationist approach that advocates for the inclusion of GLBTQ individuals into mainstream social institutions such as marriage and the military. Based on the notion of equality, it is an approach that works to expand social acceptance to different groups into dominant norms and ideas. Media images that emphasize equality by representing GLBTQ individuals and communities as equal to heterosexual ones are largely met with approval for being positive. On the other hand is a queer theoretical approach that calls into question the ways that assimilationists seek to reinforce heteronormativity and homonormativity. Media images and practices are evaluated to the extent that they challenge, rather than reinforce, dominant norms of sexual and gender identities. Two individuals, each holding one of these perspectives, or even both, might very well look at the same piece of the media and disagree on its meanings for sexual minorities.

After reading this book, you probably have a clear sense of which of these perspectives is closest to your own. You might even find yourself somewhere in the middle or holding both simultaneously. Wherever you find yourself, we encourage you to remember the approach we introduced in Chapter 3: "yes, but." "Yes, but" encourages us to recognize the gains that sexual and gender minorities have made over the past 20 years; indeed the past 5 years! In terms of political and social recognition and media visibility, things have improved. Yet, as we have further explored, there are still many constraints on political and media visibility. Based on whether your own personal views are closer to an assimilationist or queer perspective, what you see as a "yes," and what you see as "but" likely will vary.

At the very least, as you continue as a consumer and/or producer of media, we hope that you will be reflective of your own practices. At the end of the day, improving the lives of sexual and gender minorities is not in their hands alone, but in all of our hands. As media scholars, we most hope that you will remain a reflective, vigilant viewer, not afraid to point out through the various channels that allow us to speak back to media today when you see something that fits in either the "yes" or "but" category. As a potential producer of content, we further urge you to reflect on the ways that your own practices can contribute to a world where sexual and gender minorities are acknowledged for their full humanity.

▶ REFERENCES

Pride Toronto. (2014). *The International Asexuality Conference.* Retrieved from: http://www.world-pridetoronto.com/festival/events-calendar/2014/the-international-asexuality-conference-.

Steinmetz, K. & Gray, E. (June 9, 2014). America's transition. *Time, 183*(22), 38–46.

Weber, P. (February 21, 2014). Confused by all the new Facebook genders? Here's what they mean. *Slate.com.* Retrieved from http://www.slate.com/blogs/lexicon_valley/2014/02/21/gender_facebook_now_has_56_categories_to_choose_from_including_cisgender.html.

Index